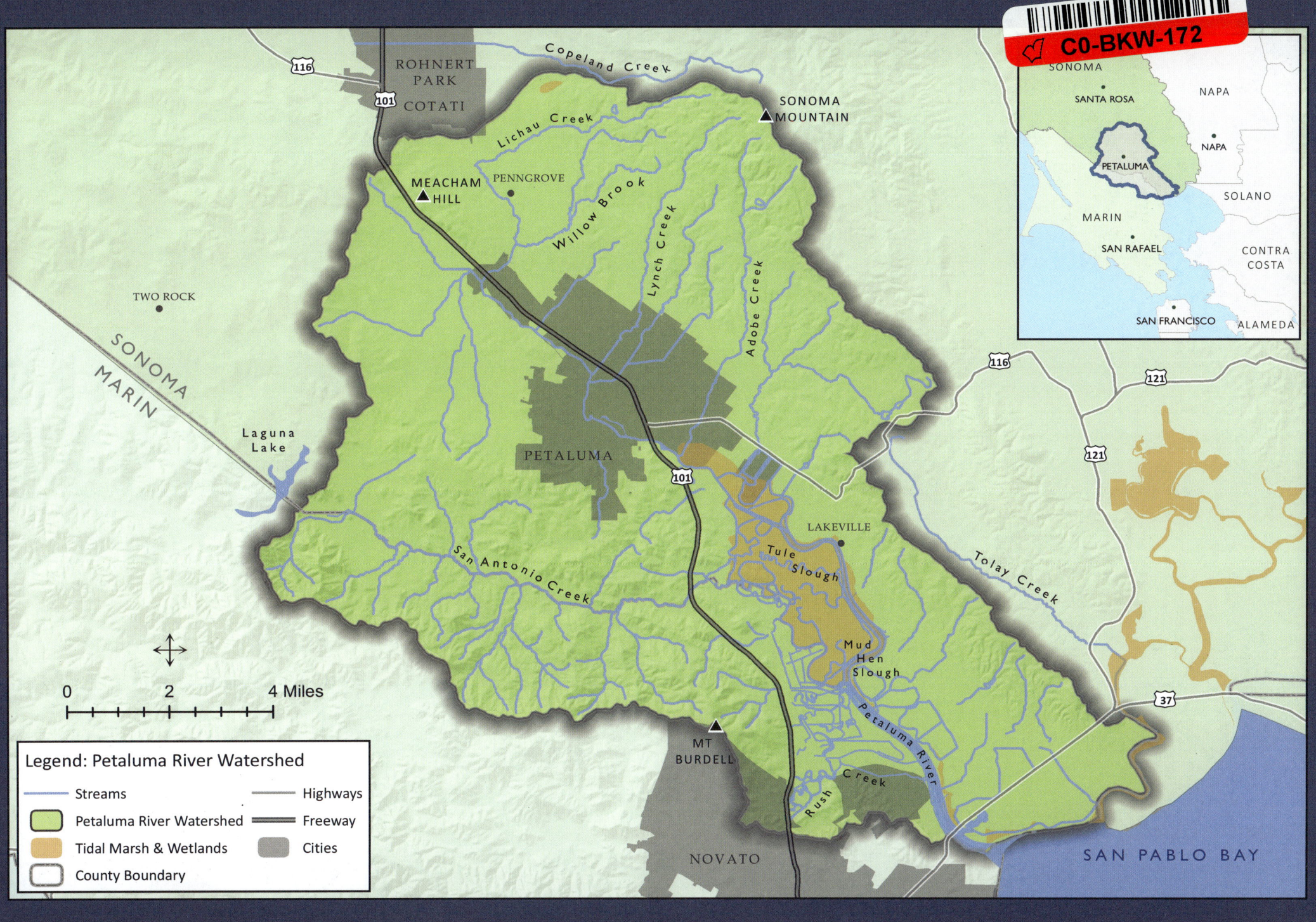

On a River Winding Home

On a River Winding Home
Stories and Visions of the Petaluma River Watershed

Scott Hess, *photographer*

John Sheehy, *storyteller*

ENSATINA PRESS | PENNGROVE, CALIFORNIA

Contents

PROLOGUE
    The Early Ones 2
    The Working Landscape 4
    The River Town 6

INTRODUCTION
    Preface 10
    A Special Place 12
    The Photographer 16
    The Storyteller 18

PART ONE: *The Early Ones* 22
    Lekituit 24
    Olompali 26
    Tolay Lake 28

PART TWO: *The Working Landscape* 32
    Petaluma Adobe 34
    Rancho Olompali 40
    Two Rock 44
    Saltwater Highway 48
    Haystack Landing 52
    Lakeville 54
    Sonoma Mountain (Oona-pa'is) 60
    The Oak Groves 66
    Chinese Rock Walls 70
    Cattle Ranches 72
    The Battle of the Washoe House 78
    Penngrove Rock Ranches 80
    Eucalyptus Stands 82
    Cow Heaven 86
    Boss Chicken Town 90
    Horse Ranches 96
    Sheep Ranches 100
    The Petaluma Gap 106

PART THREE: *The River Town* 114
    Main Street 116
    Cedar Grove 118
    The McNear Buildings 120
    The Train Depot 126
    Hatcheries 132
    Towers of Grain 136
    The Silk Mill 140
    The Creamery 144
    The Railroad Trestle 146
    Plazas 152
    Places Called Home 158
    St. Vincent's Church 162
    The King of Hardware Stores 166
    The Last Tugboat Company 168
    The Speakeasy 170
    Brothels 174
    Theaters 180
    Hotel Petaluma 186
    B'nai Israel Synagogue 190
    Bars & Taverns 194
    The Turning Basin 198

EPILOGUE 204

Notes & Sources 206
Index 215
Biographies, Acknowledgments & Colophon 222

ii-iii *Petaluma River Watershed from Sonoma Mountain*

iv *City of Petaluma from headwaters of Thompson Creek*

vi *Chileno Valley, winter*

Prologue

The aboriginal village, the Mexican ranch, the American small town—each was here, each changing the landscape and changed by it, each considering itself the stable, secure end of historical development, and each in turn swept away, all finally historical spindrift. 'One generation passeth away and another generation cometh: but the earth abideth forever.'

ARTHUR QUINN

Chileno Valley, summer

The Early Ones

There wasn't anything on this earth a long time ago. Everything was empty, no trees or grass, no hills either. The earth was covered with water. The only thing that showed above the water was the very top of Oona-pa'is (Sonoma Mountain).

O-ye the Coyote-man was just like a god. He made everything; he destroyed everything. That's how he ran the world. In the beginning he came across the ocean from the west on a long and narrow raft of tules and split sticks. He landed on the top of Oona-pa'is and threw his raft-mat out over the water—the long way to the north and south, the narrow way to the east and west. The middle of the raft rested on the rock on top of the Oona-pa'is peak. This was the beginning of the world, and the world is still long and narrow like a mat—the long way north and south, the narrow way east and west.

When O-ye was sitting alone on top of Oona-pa'is and all the rest of the world was covered with water, he saw a feather floating toward him blown by the wind from the west, the direction from which he himself had come.

He asked the feather, "Who are you?" The feather made no reply.

He then told the feather about his family and all his relatives. When he mentioned Wek-wek, his grandson, the feather leaped up out of the water and said, "I am Wek-wek, your grandson." O-ye the Coyote-man was glad, and they talked together.

O-ye noticed that Ko-to-lah, the frog-woman, was sitting near him. Every time he saw her he reached out his hand and tried to catch her, but she always jumped into the water and escaped. After four days the water began to go down, leaving more land on top of the mountain, so that Ko-to-lah had to make several leaps to reach the water. This gave O-ye the advantage, and he ran after her and caught her. When he caught her he was surprised to find that she was his own wife from across the ocean. Of this he was glad.

When all the water went down and the land was dry, O-ye planted the buckeye, elderberry, and oak trees, as well as all the other kinds of trees, and also bushes and grasses. But there were no people and he and Ko-to-lah wanted people. So O-ye took a quantity of feathers of different kinds and packed them up to the top of Oona-pa'is, where he threw them into the air. The wind carried them off, scattering them over all the country, where they turned into people. The next day there were people all over the land.

Coast Miwok Creation Myth
from story told to C. Hart Merriam by
Hookooeko woman at Tomales Bay in 1902

Looking northwest from the top of Sonoma Mountain Road

The Working Landscape

The visitor from the East, even from the more southern portions of the United States, looks with ever increasing wonder and admiration upon the exposition of our grain and fruits. Their stock may be as fine and perhaps more celebrated, but in the products of the earth, its cereals, fruits, and flowers, no state in all the broad realms of the United States can vie with ours. Fruits and flowers grown under glass in the East and sparingly exhibited at their fairs, here, from outdoor growth, load our tables with such marvels of beauty and size, as no other country in the world can show.

The glory of this land cannot be overestimated. What mountains! rugged and grand, or melting into the tinted lying far distant in the clear atmosphere. What hills! rounded into soft outlines gaily decked with vernal beauty, or crowned with golden harvests. What valleys! sleeping in quiet repose amid mountains solitudes, or vocal with lowing herds and the busy hum of life. What streams! laughingly issuing from the dense shadows of mighty forests to rush wildly down the rocky bed of some mountain ravine, or leap madly from the brow of some lofty cliff, until beaten into creamy foam by the resisting air, they fall white and shimmering like a bridal veil. Turn whichever way we will, the sublime or beautiful meet us at every step to awe or ravish the soul. It is the duty of man placed in this "goodly heritage" not to wait, but by his genius and labor to adorn and beautify it still farther by filling it with the cheerful and cultured homes of a free, intelligent people.

The past age of California has been an age of extravagance. Like all youths she has been intent upon sowing her wild oats, unheeding the warning lessons of wisdom. It has been an age of exhaustion. We have had no thought of the morrow. The placer mines have been exhausted. The time has forever passed when multitudes from every rank and profession in life can rush to rich mining regions in the state and without capital or skill speedily secure, even by severe toll and exposure, an independent fortune.

There has been rapid exhaustion also in the soil of the state during the last 20 years. When first these valleys were settled the wild oats grew in such luxuriance that horses roaming over the plains would be lost to sight amid the grain, and the traveler riding across those valleys could tie the heads of the grain over his saddle bow! Such growth is now unknown in all the valleys. These fields too, when first cultivated, used to produce crops of wheat, oats, and barley seen to us as almost fabulous. The amount of each such crop has steadily diminished each year showing conclusively that we are exhausting our soil by our methods of culture.

We are impelled to extensive farming rather than skillful farming. Our present interest is best served by exhaustive culture of large farms. There has been as yet very little systematic rotation of crops which is found to be beneficial in other countries. With our old mining habits we sought to farm, and where a few won, many toiled. There was no thought about the future, no care indeed. "Let us make our 'pile' and go home," said they.

Edward S. Lippitt
1870 keynote address to Sonoma-Marin District Fair

Dolcini Ranch, 6970 Red Hill Road, Hicks Valley

The River Town

As all the San Francisco world knows, or ought to know, we have two swift and safe steamers plying between your city and Petaluma, the *Ellen Craig* and the *E. Corning,* making daily alternate trips from Pacific Street wharf. These steamers perform the trip between the two ports in about five hours, and often in less time, and this without racing, or in any way endangering the lives of the passengers.

The distance from the mouth of the Petaluma River to the town is about 18 miles, and the stream winding through one of the most delightful flower-carpeted regions imaginable; birds singing in all directions, green trees waving on every hand, beautiful stretches of level and slightly undulating country, forming landscapes which, terminating in verdure-clad mountains, would be fit subjects for the pencil of the artist.

The town, nestling in a broad valley at the foot of a fine, picturesque range of hills, seems to invite the city traveler to pass a few days or weeks ruralizing among the cottages, or wandering through the many shady groves which surround the neat country residences of the inhabitants. Here all is quiet and seclusion. But do not imagine from this remark that no business is done here. Any dealer in produce will attest to the fact that Petaluma and its vicinity is exceeded by few in the amount of produce shipped annually to the San Francisco market. But these are facts too well known to need comment.

The crops in this section of the country promise gloriously; wheat, barley, and potatoes are flourishing, and the recent rains have imparted a freshness to the rich green of the fields, decidedly grateful to the eye unused to such rural beauties.

Out of three or four nicely furnished hotels, fortune directed my steps on my arrival here to the well known and hospitable house of Mr. Bassett, known as the Petaluma Hotel, where all the luxuries of country fare, cooked in the most approved style, can be found to solace the complaining citizen who may labor under the apprehension that no scientific cooking is to be found outside of San Francisco.

In a word, all the comforts of home may be found here. Pretty cottages and neat gardens may be met with in all directions, their number and the general good taste displayed in their building and arrangement attesting to the refined society congregated in this vicinity.

Letter from "The Traveller,"
Daily Alta California, April 16, 1855

Petaluma Turning Basin

Introduction

Our place is part of what we are.

GARY SNYDER

Chileno Valley looking north to Mount St. Helena

Preface

"If you don't know where you are, you don't know who you are."

Wendell Berry

Our relationship with the place we live is one of our closest bonds. The sights and sounds, smells and textures, climate and terrain that we experience in our daily surroundings shape our lives. They influence our social experience—how we feel and act, the ways we communicate, the quality of the work we do, the connections we form with others, our general sense of being-in-the-world. Consciously or not, we become products of our place, and that place in turns provides us with an anchor in the daily jumble of our lives.

All of us who have settled in the Petaluma River Watershed have arrived from elsewhere, whether by our own choice or a choice made by our parents or ancestors. In either case, the watershed has made its mark upon our lives through the accumulation of time and experience. For the newcomer, that process began with simply learning to navigate the landscape. For those long-settled, the challenge often becomes renewing one's appreciation for a landscape that has become overfamiliar.

In either case, photography helps by literally providing us with a fresh lens on our surroundings, offering insights and viewpoints we may have overlooked or long taken for granted. Good photography doesn't reproduce what we see so much as it helps to make us see. Likewise, photography's ability to capture a moment in time reminds us of the inherent duality that comes with settling in a place. There is the place that existed before us and that will continue to exist after we have gone. In between lies the place that happens to us.

The built and natural landscape we experience every day is itself a palimpsest, holding layers of history under its surface, many passed down to us in the form of myth and lore. Our tendency to "keep the past"—restoring historic houses and buildings, protecting ranchland, conserving natural settings—serves to place us at the very borders of such history. Through remembrance of the past we form a sense of continuity across time, not only with those who have gone before us, but with those who will follow.

Communities that lose their collective memory often lose their sense of meaning and identity. That's especially true in a society geared more toward looking forward than looking back, to promoting mobility as opposed to settling down. Over time, distinct local landmarks give way to generic spaces like homogenous housing developments, suburban business parks, and chain stores that, by seeking to lessen the displacement of those in transit everywhere, reduce the places they occupy to essentially nowhere. Many of these spaces are built for short-term obsolescence, foreshadowing a future where we mourn the passing of things we never came to really know. For those long-settled in a place undergoing such growth and change, there is often a pervasive sense of having been uprooted while still being physically present.

The intention of this book is not to promote a nostalgic yearning for the past nor to lament that which has gone by the wayside. Its purpose is to bring alive the Petaluma River Watershed in all of its complexity, past and present, for the sake of place-loving people, specifically those already rooted, becoming rooted, or even rerooted in the area.

By pairing contemporary images of the Petaluma River Watershed with stories of its past, we hope to increase awareness of the delicate balance that changes to the watershed must strike in evolving the watershed forward while protecting its unique natural, social, and historic built environments.

Communities are made by nesters—those who settle, and in settling come to deeply know, love, and care for the place they have settled into. This book seeks to foster and deepen that fundamental commitment.

Masonic Building and town clock

A Special Place

"A river is not a place: it is a maker of places."
Eavan Boland

Without the river there would be no Petaluma. No native village, no Spanish ranchero, no Gold Rush trading post, no booming river town, no Egg Basket of the World, no bedroom community. The Petaluma River Watershed's many incarnations over time have all been witnessed, absorbed, and reflected back to it by the river that flows through it. Yet, in truth, it is not a river at all.

Petaluma River is a fictitious name given by the federal government in 1959 to what is actually an estuary creek. The government's pragmatic purpose was to make the waterway eligible for dredging by the U.S. Army Corps of Engineers. Hence, the stories reflected in the Petaluma River's surface and held in the silt of its shallow depths do not "roll on" like a normal river. They ebb and flow with the ocean tides in repeated rhythms of reinvention and collapse, boom and bust, exploitation and resiliency, with each incarnation leaving its imprint. To reside in the Petaluma River Watershed is to inhabit a living palimpsest marked by old wharves, iron-front buildings, dilapidated chicken houses, repurposed hatcheries, abandoned railroad tracks, and an adobe fort scattered about the modern landscape.

Bringing that palimpsest to life in photos and stories is the purpose of this book. It begins with geology.

The Petaluma River Watershed encompasses a pear-shaped basin of 146 square miles, offering rolling hills, spring-fed streams, estuaries, golden fields, majestic oaks, and open valleys. Nestled between Sonoma Mountain to the east and an expanse of gentle hills to the west, the watershed stretches from Penngrove in the north, to southwest Sonoma County and northeastern Marin County in the south, ending at the San Pablo Bay. Through the Estero Gap at its northwest corner, banks of fog funnel in from the coast, furnishing the watershed with its Mediterranean climate.

The headwaters and tributaries of the watershed begin on the steep western slopes of Sonoma Mountain and the eastern slopes of Mount Burdell to the south. They flow into the Petaluma River as it cuts a meandering path through the central valley floor, extending from San Pablo Bay to the city of Petaluma. Roughly 56 percent of the watershed is mountainous and hilly, 33 percent valley, and the remaining 11 percent salt marsh.

Throughout its long history, the Petaluma River Watershed has been submerged, folded, faulted, eroded, and withstood volcanic attack. In cross-section, the land resembles a layer cake that tilts slightly south toward San Pablo Bay. At the base is a floor of rocks known as the Franciscan group—quartz, sandstone, and serpentine—that accumulated during the Jurassic period more than 100 million years ago. Then comes a layer of Tolay volcanics (named for a local lake), atop which lies a stratum of clay, sandstone, and shale called the Petaluma formation, covered by a band of loose stone known as Merced sandstone, and finally the Sonoma volcanics, made up of basalt, buff andesite, and tuff, laid down about three to four million years ago. The valley floor is then frosted with a thin surface of gravels, sands, and clays washed down from the higher areas, as well as silt left by the seas that once covered the valley. The layers of this rocky cake are all visible at various parts of the watershed.

Extending across the watershed is a vast human hive whose history is as extraordinary as the landscape in which it resides. A microcosm of much of California as a whole, the Petaluma River Watershed has been a stage for the passing exploits of land stewards and pillagers, community builders and adventurers, boosters and steely-eyed entrepreneurs, immigrants and suburban commuters. In making a living space of the watershed, their efforts extend from the inspiring to the dispiriting, the noble to the disgraceful, the sublime to the ridiculous. They are in other words, human.

Among their ranks are the Native Americans who for millennia hunted in the hills and fished in the estuaries; the Spanish explorers and padres who arrived on a Sacred Expedition to convert the watershed and its inhabitants; the lost boys of the Gold Rush who set about enriching themselves; the river town entrepreneurs who filled the fields with wheat, crammed the river with scows and steamers, and packed the rail lines with flatbeds and boxcars; the successive waves of cattle, dairy, and chicken ranchers who unfurled their domesticated creatures across the landscape; the merchants of tanneries, granaries, hatcheries, and mills who strove to feed a burgeoning San Francisco; the developers of suburban housing tracts who accompanied the advent of the freeway; the city politicians who successfully imposed the first national limits on planned community growth; the activists who fought to preserve the open spaces that remained; the preservationists who revitalized the historic downtown and revived the river for recreational use;

Looking east from Wilson Hill Grade

the boom and bust of the telecom industrialists who left behind a legacy of sprawling business parks; the proliferation of wine growers and equestrians who dotted the landscape with vineyards and horse ranches; the champions of sustainable local agriculture who ushered in the farm-to-table movement; the commuters who welcomed the return of passenger trains as a means of bypassing the clogged highways.

Over time, the watershed has been carved up into a crazy quilt of borders, ranging from tribal areas to Mexican rancherias, county lines, city limits, property lines, and community separators. All of the watershed's resources have been subjected to years of extraction or exploitation, leaving behind some good along with much harm.

Through it all—the greed, slaughter, clear-cutting, uprooting, fouling, paving, and erecting of edifices— the beauty of the watershed's natural landscape has remained its most enduring quality. More than two centuries after the Europeans first sailed up the river, setting off a development bonanza, there has begun in recent years changes in farming and ranching practices, business enterprises, land use laws, and aesthetic perceptions that recognize the natural landscape as our most valuable resource.

This book seeks to provide an intimate portrait of the Petaluma River Watershed, both as a memento for those currently inhabiting it and an introduction for those who will follow. The particular locations featured in the book have been selected with the aim of collectively expressing the watershed's unique beauty, in both its natural and built landscapes, as well as the strong sense of place the watershed has provided.

Preference has been given to locations that either have historical significance, or in the case of local establishments, have demonstrated staying power over time. A few liberties have been taken to feature sites that reside in bordering watersheds, such as Two Rock and Cotati. Ultimately, this is an idiosyncratic gallery of photos and stories that, largely for lack of space, excludes many other well-founded locations. We apologize for the worthy places we've left out.

The book is organized around three broad areas— the aboriginals, the working landscape, and the city. It is based on a combination of recorded facts, newspaper accounts, and the memories and writings of others. While the book offers no new discoveries—old newspaper accounts provide an archive of open, if often forgotten, secrets—untangling fact from fiction in past accounts can be challenging, as much of the early history of the Petaluma River Watershed has been shrouded in lore, mythology, ethnocentric views, or simply omission. Where possible, we try to set the record straight.

The overall intent of the book is more impressionistic and spatial than historically comprehensive—there are plenty of books already written for that explicit purpose. Instead of following a strict chronological order, the book is rendered more in the creative drift of a walking tour, with the photographs imparting a visceral experience and the stories providing historical background.

We hope that like any good walking tour, this book leaves the reader with a stronger sense of community, optimism, and shared memory of our collective home in the Petaluma River Watershed.

Downtown Petaluma looking south

The Photographer

"The camera is an instrument that teaches people how to see without a camera."

DOROTHEA LANGE

OVER THE YEARS I have made thousands of photos of the Petaluma River Watershed in its many moods and many seasons. I grew up in upstate New York on Lake Ontario, and our family had a great respect and love for the gifts of the natural environment. I was originally drawn to the Bay Area because of the open, creative, adventurous, and activist culture, and because of the bounty and beauty of the Pacific edge. I wanted to sink into the natural rhythms of this chosen place and explore what it could reveal.

As I've moved through the Petaluma River Watershed, I've kept my field of vision tuned, like a hunter's, to its subtle movements. When something catches my eye—a sparkling of aesthetic magic that touches my heart—I try to capture its spirit and essence in a photograph. I have found myself repeatedly drawn to the building blocks people have used over the ages to orient themselves here—Sonoma Mountain, the Petaluma estuary, the historic downtown that rings the tidal basin. Their prevailing presence through the changing seasons expands my own sense of time and being.

Before moving to Petaluma in 1986, I spent 12 years living in a spiritual community focused on meditation, service, and detachment from material concerns. Like a number of young people coming of age in the 1960s, I wanted to heighten my consciousness and become more aware of the spiritual nature of this world.

Upon leaving the community, I took up photography. At first, my photographs tended toward the abstract. But as I began working professionally as a cityscape photographer in New York and Miami, I learned how to dial my camera into the visual reality of everyday life, inviting people to see commonplace things in a different way.

Upon arriving in the Petaluma River Watershed, I immediately felt like I had come home. With its vintage architecture, agricultural heritage, warm community life, and connection to the cosmopolitan cultures of the Bay Area cities, the valley had strong echoes of my childhood home. I married and raised two boys here, Evan and Lukas. As the years passed, my awareness practice became simply to explore, observe, reflect on, and respond to what was going on immediately around me. I wandered about the hills, creeks, groves, coast, and city streets, mapping the territory as I went, trying to form a sense of the watershed as a whole and its spirit of place.

Each of us is connected in our very transience here, often in ways that go beyond our full understanding. To explore that mystery, I have set out to document through a steady flow of imagery what the Petaluma River Watershed looks like from one passing lifetime.

Clouds arise from the ocean and break on the mountaintops. Rains wash down over rocks and minerals. The waters run, nourishing the soil, gathering in universal branching patterns, flowing back to the sea in one grand cycle. Microbes, fish, birds, mammals, and human beings follow in these patterns, residing together in this circle of life. What a miracle and a pleasure to reflect on all of this. What a fascinating, dynamic place we live in.

SCOTT HESS

Photographer Scott Hess at Olompali State Historic Park

The Storyteller

"History isn't about dates and places and wars. It's about the people who fill the spaces between them."
      Jodi Picoult

Being a fourth-generation native like me means being a placed person, whether you wish to be or not. The sense of local history you carry with you is like a river coursing through your veins. Oft-told tales shared around the family dinner table or among close friends are distilled and amplified over the years until they are worn smooth into apocryphal folklore. In the spirit of "no good story is quite true," fictional details or those slightly embellished are as good as facts, since what actually happened may not be as important as the mythical meaning a story conveys in its retelling.

My story is that I was born and reared in Petaluma. (My grandmother, who was raised on a local ranch, insisted that only livestock were "born and raised".) One of my paternal great-grandfathers came to Petaluma in 1863 from County Kerry, Ireland, five years after the city was formally incorporated. He and his brother homesteaded a wheat farm in Lakeville, which, along with Sonoma Mountain was where Irish immigrants largely settled at the time. My other Irish great-grandfather arrived in Petaluma in the 1870s via Australia, where he had been temporarily exiled by the British as a member of the revolutionary Irish Republican Brotherhood. He opened a painting and paperhanger shop on Kentucky Street (site of the present-day Hideaway Bar) that he later passed along to his two sons, who operated it as Sheehy Brothers until 1930.

My mother's family were newcomers to the area, having arrived during World War II after being evacuated from the Aleutian Islands in Alaska, where my mother descended from an Aleut princess and Russian sea captain on the island of Unga.

Growing up in Petaluma during the 1960s and early 1970s, I was shaped most perhaps by the town's self-sufficiency—I don't recall ever having to travel out of the city limits for anything—and by the openness of the surrounding fields and rolling hills. As I grew older and started to experience the freedom that came from riding the back roads on my motorcycle, I increasingly felt the weight of local history I had inherited. After three generations of settling, I still had some of the wanderlust of my great-grandfathers in me.

The local Carnegie library at 4th and B streets, designed in 1906 by famed Petaluma architect Brainerd Jones, became my refuge. There I was able to lose myself in stories of lands and people far away from my small-town existence. After graduating from high school, I used my hard-earned savings to purchase a one-way ticket abroad—my first time aboard an airplane—and quickly lit out of town, desirous for the fresh perspective that comes with distance.

Over the next 25 years I lived in a dozen different locales, hungry for adventure, expansion, and the freedom to create my own story. But I never felt completely at home in any of them. Being in perpetual motion robbed me of belonging to anything outside a society of fellow roadside transients, each of us lacking a stomping ground to call our own.

Homesickness can be a great teacher. It taught me that I came from a Mediterranean climate of grassy, oak-studded hills that had two seasons—golden brown in summer and fall, green in winter and spring—where the fog rolled in most summer evenings, burning off by midmorning, and the sun rose over a gentle, set-back mountain to the east, setting each evening into the hills to the west in hues of red, purple, and orange. I learned that I missed the sight of hay bales stacked neatly in summer fields, the stench of the tidal slough we called a river at low tide, the song of the redwing blackbird in spring, and the bright lights outside the Mystic Theater, where I watched scores of Disney movies as a child and, later, as a teenager, sheepishly changed the weekly marquee during its brief incarnation as a porn theater.

Having a place to call your own means becoming deeply rooted in and shaped by a place's stories, be they history, yarns, or legends. Some come to such places by birth, others arrive there later in life, and some learn the hard way, as I did, that the place they left behind is the one they had been searching for all along.

Memories ride on whirlpools down a river, and for me that river runs home to a place called Petaluma.

      John Sheehy

Storyteller John Sheehy outside Petaluma Historical Library and Museum, built 1906

Part 1: The Early Ones

The landscape was our bible, our sacred text. Features of the landscape were stories, mnemonic pegs on which stories were held, and how we knew ourselves. When we were moved from the land and when the land itself was radically altered, it was comparable to having that sacred text burned.

Greg Sarris

The Early Ones

The explorers, missionaries, settlers, and gold prospectors who set foot in the Petaluma River Watershed in the 19th century were not able to see the place for what it was. The lands they had come from in Europe and back East had been ecologically degraded, deforested, mined, and overgrazed. They arrived in California looking for a "New World" or a "frontier" where they could begin anew.

For them, the Petaluma River Watershed was a blank slate upon which to project their dreams, fears, aspirations, and greed. Through that distorted lens they saw only what they wanted to see, be it an uncivilized wilderness, a place to do God's work, a bounty of untapped wealth, or a place of untouched beauty. They willingly chose to ignore that the place they had arrived in was no wild, uninhabited Eden, but in fact a sophisticated habitat, carefully managed for millennia by the indigenous people they largely viewed as wild and inferior beings.

In the eyes of the native people, the Coast Miwok, the valley was not a wilderness, nor a place of untouched nature, but a tended garden. Unlike the new agrarian settlers, they did not distinguish between managed land and wild land, nor between humankind and nature. Their livelihoods depended upon an intimate knowledge of the watershed, fostering a deep and reverent relationship with the land, plants, and animals that was as much spiritual as cultural.

At the time of the first European contact, there were approximately 20,000 to 30,000 Coast Miwoks and Southern Pomos living in the area now known as Sonoma and Marin counties. Through centuries of keen observation and experimentation they had determined how to judiciously harvest and cultivate the plant kingdom in a manner that served their needs without destroying the kingdom's diversity. They converted roots, berries, shoots, bones, shells, and feathers into medicines, meals, bowls, and baskets of great artistry. They managed the valley as a controlled habitat, tilling, pruning, watering, fertilizing, trimming, planting, and most importantly, burning. Through the use of gentle, controlled burns they eliminated the understory and pests that threatened the groves of oak trees they depended on for acorns, a main staple of their diet. Regular burning also minimized the danger of catastrophic fires, encouraged vegetation diversity, and created a better habitat for game.

The grasslands teemed with herds of deer and tule elk. The tidal marshes abounded with waterfowl so abundant that when the birds took off, the sky went dark. The creeks and streams ran so thick with salmon and trout that fish could be caught by hand.

Through environmental land management, the natives created a way of life in which all human needs were provided for—housing, food, clothing—with the expenditure of only two to four hours of labor a day. The rest of the day was free, leaving ample time to simply experience nature and being.

The watershed was a place where people had lived for a thousand years in harmony with their habitat, their knowledge of how it worked and how to steward it passed down by generations of elders. They didn't advocate for leaving nature alone, but instead identified with it, and in doing so assumed a sense of responsibility for it at the deepest level of their being, grounded in both practical application and spiritual practice, allowing the living and supernatural realms to co-exist in harmony.

Rich legends and oral traditions defined their surroundings. The boundaries of their territory were marked by creeks, boulders, ridges, and springs. Every plant and place was named, with the understanding that nothing could be acknowledged let alone possessed without a name. Accustomed as they were to a sense of harmony that did not exist in unfamiliar places, a person rarely traveled outside a radius of five to 10 miles from their birthplace, except perhaps to trade. Being at home meant that generation after generation of people were born, lived, and died in the same familiar surroundings. The greatest calamity that could befall a person was to be removed from the place where his or her father and mother lived and were buried. It was best to die and be buried in the same place you were born, where the ground knew you, and was waiting to receive you home.

Today, people of Coast Miwok ancestry are included with the Pomo in the Federated Indians of Graton Rancheria, a federally recognized tribal organization of fewer than 1,400 people, all of whom trace their ancestry to one of 14 survivors of the original tribes.

Temple Rock, Spring Hill Road

Lekituit

The territory of the Coast Miwok encompassed present-day Marin and southern Sonoma counties, covering large stretches of coastline and bay shores, and including extensive lagoons, sloughs, marshes, valleys, and foothills. The territory was organized into two subdivisions, or moieties, Land and Water. Within each moiety were several small nations consisting of one or more large villages and several small ones. A web of informal trade networks linked village with village, nation with nation, and the nearby territories of the Pomo to the north and the Wappo and Patwin to the east. Clamshell beads—circular, flat disks with holes drilled in them—were used as currency to trade among the villages for such things as medicinal plants, obsidian for making arrowheads, and salt from the ocean.

Lekituit was the name of both a Coast Miwok nation and what is believed to have been one of the nation's larger villages. The village was located at the upper head of navigation on the Petaluma River in the present-day city of Petaluma (just north of the Lakeville Bridge in an area now called Cedar Grove). The other large village in the Lekituit nation, Petaluma, is believed to have been located about three and a half miles northeast of the city that today bears its name.

The river location of the village of Lekituit provided it with access to a supply of fish, shellfish, and waterfowl that was used for exchange on the trading route that passed through the territory. The valley plain also provided access to an abundant supply of acorns, an important part of the Coast Miwok diet. Harvested in the fall from groves of valley oaks, tanbark oaks, and black oaks, the acorns could be stored for long periods of time in granaries until needed. Used for making flour, the acorns were first cracked, their outer shells husked off, and the kernels ground into a powder, which was then leached of acidic tannin to make it edible. Families often adopted specific oak groves to care for and harvest, tending to the same trees for successive generations. Oaks in the hills were shared by the village as a whole.

The Lekituit had year-round access to large herds of deer and elk, which were hunted with bows and arrows made with obsidian tips acquired from Lake County. The hides and furs of the deer and elk were used for making clothing, bedding, and containers. Their bones and antlers were fashioned into a variety of tools, as well as into ornamental and ceremonial items, such as ear spools and whistles. Jackrabbits, cottontails, and quail were trapped for food in baskets traps set in brush fences or nets. Migrating geese and ducks were hunted in winter with bone-headed bolas. Salmon were caught on seasonal runs in dip nets, basketry wraps, or else speared, while sturgeon were trapped in nets stretched between two tule balsas. Eel were netted, and soft-shelled crabs were gathered by hand.

Various forms of gardening were intricately woven into the changing seasons. A form of fire-stick farming was used to clear areas of old growth and encourage new growth of edible plants, both for human consumption as well as to attract wild game.

In late spring, fresh new greens of Indian lettuce (also known as miner's lettuce), wild onion, clover, and brodiaea were gathered. The women used fire-hardened digging sticks to reach deep-set soaproots and other bulbs, which were then roasted in earthen ovens.

During the summer, much of the Lekituit population would disperse among smaller villages and camps, occupying them for a few days or many weeks while resources were collected and processed. The summer sun ripened the grasses and flowers, whose seeds were gathered by hitting the seed pods with a beater basket and letting them fall directly into a collecting basket. Blackberries, strawberries, thimbleberries, gooseberries, and elderberries were also gathered in great quantities.

Fall was the season for collecting acorns and other nuts, including buckeye, hazel, and bay. Pepperwood nuts were made into soft cakes after parching and pounding. Honey was gathered from hives of ground-dwelling bees. Tule was cut and dried for making houses, boats, skirts, and mats. The onset of winter and early spring often brought times of food shortage when stored acorns and seeds became sources of nourishment.

The village of Lekituit was abandoned sometime around 1817 when Spanish missionaries drove the Coast Miwok to their new mission established in San Rafael. The Lekituit nation was subsequently divvied up into large ranches granted to Californios (California-born people of Spanish and Mexican descent) after the missions were secularized in 1834. A smallpox epidemic introduced by a Mexican soldier in 1838 took the lives of many of the natives in the area. In 1850, Yankee meat hunters, looking to feed Gold Rush miners in San Francisco, established a trading post on the former site of the Lekituit village, which, within eight years, grew into the incorporated city of Petaluma.

Village of Lekituit on Petaluma River (now Cedar Grove)

Olompali

The Olompali nation comprised 25 square miles of territory, bounded on the north by a low ridge above San Antonio Creek, on the south by a ridgeline of hills south of the San Marin Valley, and on the east by the ridgeline separating Petaluma Valley from Sonoma Valley.

The name Olompali was derived from the words *olum*, meaning "south," and *bolli*, meaning wells, referring to the underground springs that distinguished the area. The Coast Miwoks who lived there named the mountain in their territory Olompais, which translates as south mountain. The name was changed to Mount Burdell by Galen Burdell, an American settler, in the 1860s.

Olompali was also the name of the nation's main village. Its tribelet had as many as 400 inhabitants, and was located at the base of Mount Olompais near the tidal marshes of the Petaluma River. Smaller villages were primarily clustered along San Antonio Creek.

Village houses were of two types: earth-covered and tule thatch. The earth-covered variety functioned as either dance houses or sweat houses. Residential structures accommodated six to 10 people, and were rarely occupied by more than one biological family. Special menstrual huts were provided for the women. Major settlements also had a dance house that served as a ceremonial center for "secret societies," comprising either both sexes or a single sex.

Village women customarily wore a deerskin wraparound skirt, hair side out with one leg exposed. Men were usually naked. Women wore tattoos on their face with patterns of diagonal or zig-zag lines originating at the edges of the mouth and terminating at the edge of the chin. Men wore tattoos on their arms. The ears of men and women were pierced for a bone earplug. Clamshell disc beads were worn on a string as decoration and also used as a medium of currency.

The Coast Miwok culture was egalitarian. Village members were not ranked except in terms of ceremonial occupations and as craftsmen or craftswomen of accomplishment. At village dances and ceremonies participants wore feather headbands decorated with abalone pendants, feather aprons, topknots of upstanding crow or condor feathers, feather boas, and feather belts of woodpecker scalps. The dance houses featured clowns, firemen, magicians, and fire-eaters. Two women of importance were usually placed in charge of organizing various ceremonies, sending out invitation sticks for the dances and selecting the performers, as well as directing the construction of the dance houses.

Every large village like Olompali had a male chief known as the *hoipu*. The hoipu's duties were primarily caring for people, offering advice, and addressing the tribelet daily. Succession of leadership from the hoipu was not hereditary—whoever chosen was picked for his suitability rather than his lineage. Anyone could nominate a young man for the position, but a committee of four older women chose the candidate and were also responsible for training him in the art of leadership. When the successor was ready, the incumbent was replaced.

Each tribelet also had a number of women leaders called *máiens*. Not necessarily married to the hoipu, the maiens were highly respected and very powerful. Some were chosen because they showed signs of being clairvoyant, others because they were the wife of the village shaman known as the *wál·ipoh*. Following the dance for his investiture, a new wál·ipoh would chose a young woman from among the female dancers, after which she would accompany him to the hills for two days and two nights, during which time she was thought to die and return to life, as the wál·ipoh himself already had done. In addition to holding a position of leadership in a village, it appears that the maiens may have composed a broader secret female society among the tribes that served to initiate and train young people.

The powers of the hoipu and the maiens were limited and never authoritarian. They controlled asocial behavior through suggestions and influence rather than through coercion and dominance.

Much of the Olompali nation was included in the land grant given by the Mexican government in 1843 to a Coast Miwok leader named Hueñux, who had been baptized by the missionaries as Camilo Ynitia. In 1852, as new settlers began flowing into the area, Hueñux/Ynitia sold the land to Marin County's first appointed assessor, a Scottish settler named James Black. In 1981, the site of the original Olompali village was included in the establishment of the 700-acre Olompali State Historic Park.

Olompais Mountain (now Mount Burdell)

Tolay Lake

TOLAY LAKE was the southernmost freshwater lake in a chain of small lakes spread across Sonoma County, each with a specific ceremonial purpose for the Coast Miwok. Tolay's purpose was healing and renewal.

The lake drew people seeking the best treatment from medicine men and women who traveled there from miles around to engage in sacred ceremonies and confer with peers on doctoring techniques. The lake also served as a spiritual setting for prayer and reflection. Its western ridge offered a world-at-your-feet perch from which to view the San Pablo Bay, the Petaluma River basin, and the mountaintops of Mount Diablo, Mount Tamalpais, Mount Burdell, Mount St. Helena, and Sonoma Mountain, all believed to possess supernatural powers.

No more than 20 feet in depth, Tolay Lake encompassed 300 acres. An earthen barrier at its southern tip prevented water from rapidly draining into nearby San Pablo Bay. The lake sat in the territory of the Alaguali, a tribelet of the Coast Miwok, whose principal village, Cholequibit, was located southeast of the lakebed on San Pablo Bay. In addition to providing freshwater for drinking, bathing, and cooking, the lake was full of sedge beds, the roots of which the Alaguali used for basketmaking. Migrating birds were also drawn to the lake, providing the Alaguali with easy access to fowl. According to the journal of Franciscan missionary José Altimira, who stopped by the lake in 1823 while traveling from San Francisco to present-day Sonoma, where he established Mission San Francisco Solano, the lake was named after Tola, "the chief of the Indians."

Tolay Lake was also a depository for charmstones. The Coast Miwok fashioned charmstones out of stones such as green schist and granite into a number of designs. Most of the stones were about two to three inches long, and varied in shape from oblong to round and squat. A number were perforated or grooved, suggesting they may have been fastened as weights to nets that were used in catching fish and birds. Some stones were phallic-shaped, and may have been used in fertility rites. Among the thousand charmstones discovered at Tolay Lake, archaeologists have determined that many originated from places as far away as Mexico and Washington State. A number are estimated to be more than 4,000 years old.

In addition to their utilitarian uses, the natives believed that the charmstones carried mystical power. After being used by medicine people to extract illness from the sick and injured, the charmstones would be drowned in the lake to fully eradicate the illness. Afflicted charmstones not drowned could be used as a source of secret power to protect a person against their enemies.

The belief in such powers, sometimes nurtured with the assistance of secret songs and spirit guides, meant that physical violence was relatively rare among the Coast Miwok. If someone did resort to a physical assault, it revealed their lack of any secret power, meaning they could be counterattacked without worry of supernatural retribution. Through this spiritual deterrent of violence, the Coast Miwok were able to maintained balanced relationships with one another and other nearby tribes. If a group of Miwok wished to travel into Pomo territory, they would send a runner ahead to present pieces of cordage to Pomo tribelet leaders on their path. The string would be tied with as many knots as there would be days before the Coast Miwok people would arrive.

The Coast Miwok believed that spirit beings controlled the changing seasons and all of the living things inhabiting the earth. In the complex network of interactions between humans and the spirit beings, they relied upon rituals and the use of myth, legend, and storytelling to meld the experience of their everyday existence with the world of the supernatural. In their oral tradition, prominent parts of the landscape, such as Tolay Lake and the mountaintops surrounding it, served as mnemonic pegs used to perpetuate a sense of continuity for the Coast Miwok over the centuries.

Their longstanding culture came to an abrupt end in the early 19th century with the arrival of the Spanish, Mexican, and American colonists, who drove the natives into servitude, first in missions and then on their large ranches. In 1859, Tolay Lake was purchased by a German immigrant named William Bihler, who subsequently dynamited the lake's natural dam on its southern end, allowing the lake to completely drain out into the San Pablo Bay. In the dry lakebed, Bihler planted a potato and beet patch. The lakebed remained part of working farms throughout the 20th century. Between the 1970s and 1990s, the county of Sonoma entertained plans to convert it into a wastewater treatment center. In 2005, the lakebed was purchased as part of the 3,434-acre Tolay Lake Regional County Park.

Tolay Lake, with Sonoma Mountain in the background

PART II: The Working Landscape

Providence, you see, and manifest destiny were understood in those days to be on our side.

JOSIAH ROYCE

McEvoy Ranch, 5935 Red Hill Road

The Working Landscape

The settlers entering the Petaluma River Watershed in the early 1850s were gamblers, speculators, and adventurers. Restless and ambitious, they saw themselves as pioneers with little interest in looking back at history or their own sometimes questionable actions. A small number of them had struck it rich in the gold fields, either from mining ore or "mining the miners" through selling them food and goods, but most had come away from the Gold Rush empty handed. The bulk of them were middle-class men looking to escape the drudgery of over-civilized life in the mills or storefronts back east or abroad, and still itching with gold fever.

The watershed appeared to them a beautiful, uninhabited wilderness, its marshes and creeks thick with waterfowl and fish, its prairie tall with wild oats, its woodlands abounding with elk, quail, grizzly bears, deer, and antelope. The indigenous natives had been decimated by a smallpox epidemic in 1838. The herds of longhorn cattle and sheep, introduced by Mexican missionaries, had been rounded up during the Gold Rush and fed to miners. The new settlers, possessed with gold mining habits, quickly set out to extract and exploit whatever natural resources they could find, with little thought of the future. They wouldn't be disappointed. Everyone with even a modest stake of capital soon realized that gold was the smallest part of California's abundant storehouse.

Within two years of the discovery of gold in 1848, California's nonindigenous population exploded from 10,000 to 200,000. San Francisco, the new state's main port of entry, became an instant pop-up city and one of the busiest commercial centers in America. Feeding the city's burgeoning masses became paramount. The Petaluma River, a saltwater tidal slough meandering north from San Pablo Bay, found itself transformed into one of the city's main supply channels.

The profusion of wild game and fowl in the watershed was the first to go. Meat hunters established a trading post at the abandoned Coast Miwok village of Lekituit along the river that became the genesis of the city of Petaluma. Next, woodsmen clear-cut the valley's prolific oak groves to provide charcoal for fueling San Francisco's stoves and steam engines. The new settlers then set about reordering the watershed by laying out roads, rechanneling creeks, reclaiming wetlands, and planting extensive crop systems of imported vegetables, fruit, and grain. They brought in new herds of cattle and sheep, turning them loose on the meadows and hills where they devoured the native perennial grasses, allowing settlers to reseed the entire watershed with Mediterranean annual grasses better suited to heavy grazing. The rest of the watershed's indigenous life, including what remained of its native people, were decimated or displaced, surviving, if at all, on the fringes of the new settlements.

By the mid-1850s, the Petaluma River was filled with scow schooners, sloops, and steamers transporting cargo and passengers to and from San Francisco. Easy access to the city's international ports set off a wave of volatile boom-and-bust cycles in Petaluma, beginning with a potato boom in the 1850s, during which fortunes were rapidly made and lost due to overproduction. The monocrop phenomenon continued with California's wheat boom in the 1860s and 1870s, which turned Petaluma into a bustling river town. The town's pioneer days came to an end in 1870 with the introduction of the San Francisco & North Pacific Railroad, which bypassed Petaluma in favor of a new river terminus near Lakeville, putting an end to the town's shipping monopoly and making Santa Rosa the county's new agricultural hub. As a result, Petaluma's economy began to stagnate. In the 1880s, a declining wheat market, undermined by international competition and soil depletion, forced farmers to convert their land to cattle, sheep, and dairy ranches.

Beginning in the 1890s, Petaluma embraced an egg boom spawned by the local invention of an efficient egg incubator. Along with the local dairy industry, the boom elevated Petaluma to unprecedented heights of prosperity during the 1910s and 1920s. The Great Depression of the 1930s, followed by a shift to large factory farms in the Central Valley after World War II, dealt a lethal blow to local chicken and dairy ranches.

Petaluma's symbiotic relationship to San Francisco was renewed in 1956 following the introduction of Highway 101, which set off a new boom in suburban tract housing for commuters. During the 1970s, equestrian ranches and Sonoma County's new monocrop, grape vineyards, began replacing dairy ranches. In 1998, voters imposed a 20-year urban growth boundary around the city to protect the surrounding ranchland. To survive, ranchers began diversifying with niche products that commanded premium prices in the market, including organic milk, artisan cheeses, organic vegetables, and pasture-raised beef and lamb.

Open Field Farm, 2245 Spring Hill Road

Petaluma Adobe

In 1835, a year after Mexico secularized its missions in Alta California, Governor José Figueroa ordered Lieutenant Mariano Vallejo to provide the native converts, or neophytes, of the Sonoma and San Rafael missions with their choice of mission lands in the North Bay. By decree of the Mexican Congress, they were entitled to one-half of the land, goods, and livestock that they had helped the missions accumulate, with the other half reserved for Mexican colonists. The neophytes chose 80,000 acres of a large inland valley called Nicasio, after which the governor instructed Vallejo, his commandant general of Alta California's northern frontier, to ensure they would not be disturbed. He apparently didn't realize that he was asking a fox to guard the henhouse.

The 27-year-old Vallejo was part of a new generation of Californios (people of Spanish and Mexican descent born and bred in Alta California). The son of a Spanish military sergeant, he was barely in his teens when Mexico broke away from the Spanish crown in 1821, declaring itself a republic based on the American model. A student of the classics, Vallejo became an admirer of the Romans' hard, pragmatic reason and of their empire building, seeing Roman echoes in the Spanish-Mexican conquest of California's native "barbarians" by a small group of "civilized men." It was a view he shared with his childhood companion and nephew Juan Alvarado, who, only a year younger than Vallejo, was raised in the Vallejo household after his father died.

Persistent and well-connected, Vallejo rose quickly through the ranks of the Mexican army, distinguishing himself in the Indian wars, before being appointed military commandant of the North Bay by Governor Figueroa. Known for his steadiness, fair-mindedness, and good humor, Vallejo could also at times be egotistical, autocratic, and Machiavellian, all qualities that would serve him well in the shifting political winds of Alta California. The most significant shift occurred in the early 1800s with the discovery of Northern California's abundant sea otter population. Yankee fur traders had found that they could sail their ships to Alaska, where the Russians had established an extensive sea otter hunting operation, and, in exchange for goods and a percentage of the take, procure crews of Aleutian hunters with their nimble two-man kayaks for hunting otter along California's northern coastline. In 1811, a Yankee ship named the *Albatross* returned from Drakes Bay with a cargo of 73,402 pelts. The next year the Russians decided to establish an outpost on the coast at Fort Ross from which to hunt sea otter as well as supply their Alaska settlements with California-grown wheat and fruits. The Spanish, who had not ventured north of San Francisco in their colonizing, moved to curb the Russians' advance by establishing two new Franciscan missions in San Rafael and Sonoma.

The zealous Franciscans were attracted to danger, hardship, and martyrdom. They had first set foot in California on Father Junipero Serra's Sacred Expedition in 1768. Looking to expand Spain's influence north of Mexico, the expedition began erecting a chain of missions in 1776 from which to convert, educate, and transform California's indigenous people into Spanish citizens. Once that had been accomplished, their plan was to distribute the mission wealth and lands among the civilized natives, and turn the mission churches over to an order of less zealous parish priests.

The reality was quite different. While technically free by Spanish law, the natives could always be acquired by soldiers, missionaries, and later Mexican rancheros through force, if necessary. As a result, they would remain either in servitude or debt. After baptizing their neophytes at the missions, the Franciscans set about orienting them to the steady labor of farming and ranching, introducing them to European fruits, vegetables, wheat, cattle, sheep, and horses. Put to work as plowmen, shepherds, cattle herders, blacksmiths, and carpenters, the neophytes were also taught to tan hides, make candles, and weave wool.

One emerging challenge the Franciscans faced at their labor camps was the spread of deadly diseases introduced by the Spaniards. By the early 1800s, the mission in San Francisco was losing 30 to 40 percent of its neophytes to diseases, a majority of them to syphilis (Spanish soldiers tended to regard sexual exploitation of native women as a right of conquest). To recruit replacements, the military began resorting to the use of force, especially among the North Bay tribes, leading to general unrest among the natives. As a result, attacks on missions becoming frequent and widespread.

After Mexico declared its independence from Spain in 1821, a longstanding schism began to widen between the missions and government authorities. The Franciscans viewed the indigenous people as fully human, regardless of how primitive they appeared to be, and made it clear that their quest was to save their souls,

Petaluma Old Adobe, built 1836

not to educate them in becoming obedient subjects of Mexico. The authorities, who had initially viewed the Franciscans as an effective means to an end, increasingly saw the them as impediments to further conquest and colonization. Soldiers and settlers, many of them sent by force to California by the Mexican government, began themselves looking upon the missions with their well-tilled fields, orchards, gardens, herds of livestock, and thousands of neophytes laborers, as fonts of wealth, there for the taking.

In 1834, the Mexican government moved to secularize the missions, dividing their land holdings into grants for Californio settlers, many of them former soldiers. Government authorities, seeking to divide the neophytes from the missionaries, promised the neophytes greater personal freedom and a share of the missions' land and wealth. The land grants averaged about 10,000 acres each. In the North Bay, the newly appointed commandant general, Lieutenant Mariano Vallejo, was given his own land grant of 44,000 acres to eventually distribute among settlers. Within a year, he expanded it to 66,000 acres. The grant, which Vallejo called Rancho Petaluma, stretched from the banks of the Sonoma Creek west to the Petaluma slough, north to Cotati, and south to the San Pablo Bay.

Faced with the encroaching Russians at Fort Ross and the threat of hostile natives to the north, Vallejo brought with him a unit of cavalrymen from the Presidio in San Francisco. Making relatively small distributions of cattle, seed, and food to the neophytes, he wasted no time stripping the Sonoma and San Rafael missions of everything he wanted for Rancho Petaluma—cattle, sheep, horses, orchards, a carpenter's shop, a tannery, a granary, and a vineyard. With the use of native labor, he built a fort in the Petaluma Valley he called the Petaluma Adobe. In addition to serving as a military outpost, the fort generated the wealth Vallejo needed to feed and clothe his soldiers, as well as fund his political and diplomatic efforts on the northern frontier.

Between 600 and 1,000 natives labored at Rancho Petaluma, the majority of them from the Coast Miwok tribe, along with members of the Southern Patwin, Southern Pomo, and Wappo tribes. Many of them were neophytes who had turned over their livestock to Vallejo to manage in exchange for their labor. Others had been kidnapped or taken prisoner in military raids. Together, they plowed the fields for planting wheat (much of it surreptitiously exported to the Russians at Fort Ross), tended the herds of cattle and sheep as vaqueros on horseback, worked as tanners making leather bridles, reins, lariats, boots, and shoes, or spun wool for making apparel and blankets.

The Petaluma Adobe's main revenue came from selling tallow and hides. About a quarter of Vallejo's herd of 12,000 to 15,000 Mexican longhorns was slaughtered each year, their tallow and hides transported down Casa Grande Road in lumbering oxcarts to the Petaluma slough and loaded onto river boats that carried them to ships in San Francisco bound for Europe and New England. There, they were used in making leather goods, candles, soaps, and lubricants. The annual roundup of longhorns was marked by a large rodeo and week-long festival of feasts, singing, fandango dancing, and the popular blood sport of bear and bull fights. The events served to showcase Vallejo's position as the most powerful and influential land baron in the North Bay.

To maintain control of his position, Vallejo strategically placed himself between the Mexican governor in Monterey and the local natives. In any dispute with the governor, Vallejo had his own battle-seasoned troops at hand, paid for out of his own pocket. In his dealings with the natives he was known for being relatively fair, but not above engaging in the Roman tactic of divide and conquer. Unlike the Franciscans, who had endeavored to end traditional hostilities between tribes, Vallejo played them up. Where hostilities did not exist, he created them, giving one tribe the autonomy to fight another, but only until the other tribe was vanquished. For maximum enforcement, he deployed his callous brother, Salvador, and his most prized ally among the natives, the six-foot, seven-inch warrior Chief Solano, on murderous military campaigns against hostile tribes to the north. Long term, Vallejo's strategy was to create a new social order of Californio rancheros in the North Bay, one that left the indigenous people free to live as serfs on the new ranches or at their fringes as seasonal laborers.

Until he could attract enough experienced rancheros—ideally men of reason who professed a loyalty both to him and the governor in Monterey—Vallejo's approach was to buy time from the natives with promises. Among them was the promise he had made to the mission neophytes in 1835 for the 80,000-acre Nicasio

Texas Longhorns, Twisted Horn Ranch,
11399 Valley Ford Road

land grant (legal paperwork for which was never found). Soon after, Governor Figueroa, who was part native, and had secured Vallejo's assurance that the natives would not be disturbed at Nicasio, died in office. He was replaced in 1837 by Juan Alvarado, Vallejo's nephew and childhood companion. With Alvarado in place, Vallejo repossessed the Nicasio grant, along with the cattle and horses the neophytes had been given, claiming they were not making good use of the property. He promised them that Nicasio would be returned "when circumstances should be more favorable."

When those circumstances failed to materialize by 1839, three of the neophyte chiefs appealed directly to Governor Alvarado, who assured them that they could always rely upon his uncle for protection. Convinced that they had been taken in, the Nicasio natives surrounded the pueblo of San Rafael, threatening to lay siege to it. Vallejo, once again looking to buy time, provided them with a written conveyance to 7,600 acres of the original grant, despite the fact that he had no legal authority to do so, and doled out to each neophyte three cattle and one horse.

Meanwhile, the political landscape around Vallejo was rapidly changing. In the winter of 1838, one of Vallejo's soldiers, Ignacio Miramontes, visited the Russian colony on the coast and contracted smallpox. Upon his return to Sonoma, the disease slowly spread through Northern California, killing an estimated 60,000 to 70,000 natives. While smallpox vaccinations were available during the epidemic, only a small number of indigenous people received them, suggesting Californios cared little for their survival despite relying upon them for labor. Politically, the epidemic eliminated the threat of hostile Indians to the north, but it also diminished Vallejo's workforce. In 1841, the threat from the Russians on the northern frontier ended when, after continual crop failure and severe depletion of the seal and sea otter populations, the Russians sold their holdings at Fort Ross to John Sutter, a Mexican citizen of Swiss origin. The new foreign threat facing Alta California came from the Americans, whose merchant fleets increasingly controlled trade. As more Americans immigrated into California, often marrying Californio women to assume legal land ownership, Vallejo foresaw an inevitable American takeover, and began making plans to obtain more land as a means of securing his position.

In 1842, after Vallejo's nephew Juan Alvarado was replaced as governor in Monterey by Manuel Micheltorena, Vallejo resigned his position as commandant general of the northern frontier. A few months later, Alvarado and Vallejo decided to formally obtain the Nicasio land grant for themselves. First, they set out to establish legal ownership in the name of the neophytes—something Vallejo previously had been careful not to do—presenting the chiefs with title to the full 80,000 acres, after which they had the chiefs sign the title over to Alvarado in exchange for the promise, but not the delivery, of $1,000 from Vallejo. Alvarado then wrote to Governor Micheltorena, asking that the governor acknowledge him as the legal owner of the land grant. Unknown to Alvarado and Vallejo, the governor had already assigned the land grant six months earlier to two Californio petitioners. Although Alvarado fought the legality of the governor's assignment for years, in the end the courts ruled against him.

On June 14, 1846, the day Vallejo had long anticipated came, but not as he had envisioned. A band of Yankees known as "Bear Flaggers" invaded Vallejo's home in Sonoma and took him prisoner. War between Mexico and America was declared a month later. Vallejo, released from prison after two months, returned home to find his Rancho Petaluma stripped bare by the Americans, and most of his native labor force gone. In 1849, a year after Mexico conceded control of California to the Americans, Vallejo, having accepted American citizenship, was elected to the new California state senate. During the senate's first legislative session, he helped lawmakers draft the Act for the Government and Protection of Indians that legalized slavery of the natives. (It would not be fully repealed until 1937.)

A period of personal and financial problems followed for Vallejo, during which he sold most of his land holdings. He remained active in politics for many years, including serving twice as the elected mayor of Sonoma, where he continued to live until his death in 1890.

Vallejo's vision of a new agrarian social order founded by men of reason had lasted merely a decade between the secularization of the missions and the American takeover, but it was, arguably, the most colorful period in the colonist history of Alta California, and Vallejo, the last of the Mexican Dons, lived it to the hilt.

Estero de San Antonio, Valley Ford-Franklin School Road

Rancho Olompali

By the time of his marriage in 1843, James Black had seen a bit of the world. After leaving his native Scotland as a teenager, he voyaged throughout the Mediterranean as a seaman and then worked ships along the entire west coast of South America before making his way to California in 1832 at the age of 21. There, he made a living hunting sea otters for their pelts. In 1835, the Mexican Commandant of Northern California, Mariano Vallejo, asked Black to settle along the north Sonoma coast and serve as a peaceful deterrent to potential Russian expansion from Fort Ross. As a reward, Vallejo presented him with the Cañada de la Jonive, a large land grant near present-day Freestone and Occidental.

In 1845, at the age of 34, Black chose as his bride 15-year-old Maria Augustina Saez, a third-generation Californio (California-born people of Spanish and Mexican descent). Her grandfather, Justo Saez, had been a member of an elite Spanish military unit known as *soldado de cuero*, or leather-jacketed soldiers (their jackets protected them from Indian arrows), and was among the original nine settlers of San Jose in 1775. In 1848, Black sold his land grant to Jasper O'Farrell, an Irishman who had made his money surveying the original grid of San Francisco and other parts of California. O'Farrell in turn sold Black his share in the 56,000-acre Rancho Nicasio, which totaled 9,478 acres.

After establishing a cattle ranch on the east side of Black Mountain near present-day Nicasio Reservoir, Black drove the herd of 2,000 longhorns to the gold fields in the Sierra foothills, where he sold them for as much as $500 a head (more than $14,000 in early-21st-century currency). Returning home a wealthy man, Black became the first Marin County assessor in 1852. He used his riches to acquire more of Rancho Nicasio along with the 8,878-acre tract known as Rancho Olompali. By the 1850s, Black owned 30,000 acres of land stretching from the Petaluma River to Tomales Bay. To generate income, he rented out much of the land to farmers and dairy ranchers.

Black's marriage to Maria Augustina produced one surviving child, a daughter named Mary. In 1863, at the age of 17, Mary fell in love with a San Francisco dentist twice her age, Galen Burdell. Trained in New York, Burdell had been lured to California in 1849 by the Gold Rush, but had made his fortune inventing a popular powder for cleaning teeth. Despite his misgivings about the match, Black made his daughter a gift of the 8,878-acre Rancho Olompali on her wedding day in October of 1863.

Rancho Olompali was centered on the Coast Miwok village of Olompali at the foot of Mount Olompais (now Mount Burdell). The village had served as trade crossroads for centuries, one well-beaten route running south along the Petaluma estuary to the shore of San Pablo Bay, another extending west along San Antonio Creek to the coast. Olompali included the oldest house erected north of San Francisco, an adobe structure built in 1776 by Chief Olompali following the Coast Miwoks' first encounter with Spanish explorers.

In 1817, after Spanish missionaries began driving the Coast Miwoks into Mission San Rafael, Olompali remained an agricultural outpost of the mission. Following the secularization of the missions in 1834, Mariano Vallejo, Mexican Commandant of Northern California, promised the Coast Miwok 80,000 acres in land grants, asking them to choose the acreage, since their original lands had been taken away by the missions. The 80,000 acres were granted to the Coast Miwoks in 1835 by Mexican Governor José Figueroa, but eventually the tribes were swindled by the Mexican government and left with only the 8,900 acres known as Rancho Olompali, which was granted to the Olompali village leader Hueñux, baptized as Camilo Ynitia, in 1843.

Camilo Ynitia maintained a small tribe on the ranch, running cattle and sheep, and raising grapes, fruit trees, and wheat. He built himself an adobe house, in part with bricks from the one his father, Chief Olompali, had erected in 1776.

When the Americans assumed control of California in 1848, they left Camilo Ynitia's land grant intact. In 1852, after the United States Land Commission began to call all Mexican land grants into question, Camilo sold most of the ranch to James Black for $5,200 ($145,000 in early 21st-century-currency), reserving 1,400 acres for himself, where he died in 1856.

In 1864, Olompali's new owners, Mary and Galen Burdell, returned from their honeymoon abroad. Shortly after their return, Mary's mother went to her new son-in-law, Galen Burdell, to have a tooth extracted. After being administered chloroform to deaden the pain, Maria Augustina died in the dentist chair. Burdell was absolved of blame, but James Black was furious and never forgave him. Two years later, Black married Maria Loreto Pacheco, a longtime acquaintance and the widow

The former Burdell Ranch at Olompali State Historic Park

of a wealthy Marin landholder named Ygnacio Pacheco, without informing his daughter, Mary. Soon after, he made extensive changes to his will, disinheriting Mary without her knowledge.

Black's remarriage was not a happy one. A straightforward man who could read but not write, he was not his new bride's social equal. Lonely and disgruntled, he resorted to drinking. In late 1869, he fell from his horse one evening while riding with his vaqueros to a rodeo on his ranch, sustaining a brain injury. He died soon after. The holder of an estimated 35,000 acres of land between San Pablo Bay and Tomales Bay at the time of his death, Black left everything to his widow. At the reading of the will, Black's daughter, Mary Burdell, asked to see the document. Once given it, she bit off the portion with her father's signature and tore it into small pieces. Although a certified copy of the will existed, Mary's stepmother had her arrested for destroying the will.

After legally contesting the will for years, arguing that her father had been under the influence of alcohol and of Mrs. Pacheco when he drew it up, Mary Burdell was finally granted a jury trial. Three trials in Marin ended in hung juries, but a fourth jury in San Francisco ruled in her favor, after which Mary and her stepmother agreed to divide the estate.

Galen Burdell promptly retired from his dental practice and made his home with Mary at Olompali Ranch, where he implemented a soil reclamation project along the Petaluma River and planted orchards of fruit trees, wine grapes, and even bananas. Mary, designing a Victorian garden with palm trees and exotic plantings from her travels to the Far East, turned Olompali into a showplace. The Burdells built a two-story house around Camilo Ynitia's original adobe, which they used as a living room. Although Mary retained sole ownership of the ranchlands, she deeded her husband 950 acres at the south end of Tomales Bay. Once the North Pacific Coast Railroad passed through the property in 1875, Galen Burdell turned his holdings into the railroad town of Point Reyes Station, erecting a hotel there.

The Burdells had two children, James and Mabel. In 1895, James and two friends from Petaluma, William Fairbanks and Fred Follis, opened the Mira Monte Gun Club, a resort surrounded by a wild game preserve for hunting on an eight-acre mound called Burdell Island in the marsh between the Olompali Ranch and the Petaluma River. At the junction of San Antonio Creek and the Petaluma River, the resort's hunting preserve consisted of 1,200 acres filled with ducks, doves, quail, pheasant, deer, rabbit, fox, raccoon, and mountain lions. Guests could arrive by boat, or take a special train to nearby Burdell Station. During Prohibition, the resort was reputed to have been used by bootleggers.

Mary Burdell became an investor in Petaluma's factory district in 1897, constructing the Burdell Building on Lakeville Avenue and East D Street that housed the city's first cold storage plant, the Western Refrigerating Company, along with the Burdell Creamery and the Electric Light & Power Company of Petaluma. She held 100 percent of the capital stock in all three enterprises.

In 1900, Mary Burdell died while being operated on for gallstones. Before the operation she made out a will dividing her holdings among her husband and two children. After Galen Burdell passed away in 1906, James Burdell and his wife, Josephine, transformed Olompali into a palatial country estate, including a 26-room mansion built, like his parents' house, around Camilo Ynitia's adobe home. In 1925, James' sister, Mabel, sued him for robbing their mother's estate. James died in 1933, and 10 years later his widow sold the Olompali ranch.

After passing through a number of hands, the ranch became a hippie commune in the 1960s, attracting various celebrities (the Grateful Dead were tenants in 1966). Founders of a commune called "The Chosen Family" bought the ranch in 1967 and lived there until an electrical fire gutted the old Victorian mansion in 1969. The fire also exposed a part of Camilo Ynitia's adobe home that had been protected by the walls of the mansion. Developers proposed turning Olompali into condominiums, but residents in the area opposed that plan and helped to preserve the ranch's remaining 700 acres in a state park in 1981. James Burdell's former resort on Burdell Island was purchased by the Sonoma-Marin Area Rail Transit in 2013, and its remaining 56 acres were restored to tidal wetlands and wildlife habitat.

Laguna Lake, Chileno Valley

Two Rock

ON AN EARLY SPRING DAY in 1955, five ranchers gathered at Two Rock's Iowa School on Purvine Road. Trustees of the Two Rock School District, the men—Francis Collings, Claude Martin, Bill Bianchini, Americo Albini, and George Mickelsen—were there to shutter the 100-year-old school, along with two other schoolhouses in the area, Walker School and Two Rock School. Students from all three schools were being sent to the new Two Rock Union School on Spring Hill Road.

Solemnly sorting through the property of the one-room school—flagpole, teacher's desk, slate blackboard, clock, pictures of U.S. presidents, piano—the men began to reminisce about their school days. Some had ridden to school each day by horse. Others had traveled aboard the first school bus, a black Model T that looked like a hearse moving through the countryside. All of them had commuted into Petaluma for junior high and high school aboard the Petaluma and Santa Rosa Railroad's electric train known as "the juice line."

Back in the 1910s and 1920s, Sonoma County had 115 one-room schoolhouses. Iowa School was among the oldest, having been established in 1853 by a group of squatters who had traveled on a wagon train of 50 families across the plains. They were led by Charles Purvine, who had been west before during the Gold Rush of 1849. This time Purvine returned with his brother-in-law Silas Martin and their families to homestead in Two Rock.

Named for two prominent rock formations set close together on a hill, Two Rock had originally served as a landmark along the trail to Bodega Bay for Coast Miwok Indians. After the Spanish conquest of the area, Two Rock, or "Dos Piedras," became the site of a military outpost intended to thwart the Russians settled at Fort Ross from making any southern incursions. Following the secularization of the Spanish missions in 1834, Mariano Vallejo, Mexican Commandant of Northern California, was instructed to grant and settle open lands in the area as an additional barrier to Russian expansion. He chose Dos Piedras as the intersection of four large Mexican land grants: Roblar de la Miseria, Balsa de Tomales, Blucher, and Laguna de San Antonio.

The Rancho Laguna de San Antonio comprised 25,000 acres, extending from the Two Rock Valley south to Chileno Valley. Vallejo, who prized loyalty above all else, granted the rancho to one of his subordinates, a portly, middle-aged soldier named Don Bartolomeo Bojorques. (His step-daughter married a Chilean, hence the name Chileno Valley.) Following Mexico's surrender in the Mexican-American War of 1848, the Bojorques land grant was subjected, like all Mexican grants, to American legal review under the Land Act of 1851. The laborious process lasted 20 years. In the meantime, Borjorques extended an undivided equal interest in the rancho to each of his seven children.

Charles Purvine and Silas Martin, attracted to Two Rock's rich, sandy loam and its access to water, purchased large parcels of land from the Bojorques family in 1852. As review of the Bojorques land grant made its way through the courts, Purvine and Martin began planting potatoes, wheat, barley, and oats. Purvine built a two-story house along Purvine Road, while Martin, inspired by a popular book of the times called *The Octagon House: A Home for All, or a New, Cheap, Convenient, and Superior Mode of Building*, constructed an octagon-shaped house on Spring Hill Road with the help of Chinese laborers.

In 1853, Purvine and Martin, realizing they needed a school for their children, built one, naming it Iowa School after their home state. It soon became known as the "roving school," moving three times along Purvine Road due to flooding in the winter, until it was ensconced atop a hill on Purvine's property.

The Purvines and Martins weren't the only farmers struggling with the needs of schooling. With the distance to Petaluma too far to travel by horseback or carriage, rural ranchers and farmers were left to build their own schoolhouses and recruit their own teachers. Unlike the city of Petaluma, which in the mid-19th century had as many private schools as public schools, country schools tended to be largely egalitarian, with the children of ranch owners and ranch hands treated equally.

According to historian Ables Bray Dickinson, a descendant of Silas Martin born in Tomales in the 19th century, the early rural schools were usually built of rough lumber, the outside walls boarded up vertically with the cracks battened. Two or three small windows were placed on each side for natural light, as well as a door (or two, in the case of schools with separate entries for girls and boys). Inside, the children sat at rough tables with benches. They each carried their own books and a personal slate in a wooden frame for scribbling and figuring to and from school.

The schoolmaster—in the mid-19th century they were usually men—sat behind a table at the front of the classroom on a platform raised half a foot off the floor so

Landmark rocks at Two Rock

the teacher could keep an eye on the class. Early teachers were often chosen more for their ability to maintain discipline than for their academic skills. While students did their schoolwork, the teacher patrolled the aisles, wielding a cat-o'-nine-tails or black-snake whip at the sign of any loafing or monkey business.

Students continued in school so long as parents were willing to spare them from chores at home. Many got tired and dropped out early. Others attended only between the seasons of plowing and harvesting. School began at 9 a.m. with the teacher ringing a bell for pupils to assemble from the yard. Boys and girls each formed single-file lines outside the entrance. As the teacher beat time with the bell, students entered the classroom, dropping out of line as they reached their seats. They remained at attention until the teacher gave the command to be seated. Before taking up lessons, a few minutes were often spent singing. If a piano or organ was in the room, the teacher or a musically talented girl played accompaniment. If a boy bellowed out instead of singing, he was made to stand beside the teacher's table all day with a conical dunce cap made of paper on his head.

When members of the class were called upon to recite, they trooped up to a long bench before the teacher and took a seat. When asked to answer a question, each student stood up before doing so. The teacher meanwhile kept an eye on the rest of the students, making sure they kept their noses in their books. Rotating class recitation continued all day, broken up by intervals of written work, such as arithmetic and penmanship. Grades were not given. Instead, students were advanced based upon proficiency with different reading levels.

Classes let out for a 20-minute recess at 10:30 a.m. and again at 2:30 p.m. to whoops of joy. Boys and girls were seldom allowed to play together. Popular games included hide-and-seek, hopscotch, Mother May I, Red Rover, and tag games like Dare-Base and Anti-I-Over. Marbles, spinning tops, and kite flying were also popular, assuming the season was right. The boys played town ball—a forerunner of modern baseball—or lap-jack, a game where two boys stood facing each other, each slapping the other's legs with willow switches until one gave ground. When rivalries got out of hand, the teachers would yank the combatants inside by the ear or the nape of the neck and worked them over with the cat-o'-nine-tails or black-snake.

Lunches were carried to school in tin buckets. On rainy days, everybody gathered around the big wood stove in the classroom during the noon hour to eat. School let out at 4 p.m. Unless they were fortunate to have come by horse, students large and small usually walked several miles over the hills and fields to get home in time for chores.

The original Iowa Schoolhouse stood until 1859, when the members of the newly formed Iowa School District voted to raise $475 through a property tax to build a new school. In 1906, after that schoolhouse burned down, a new school, designed by Petaluma architect Brainerd Jones, was erected in its place. Petaluma grain merchant G.P. McNear donated a bell to the school. Originally brought around Cape Horn by ship in the mid-19th century, the bell had served in firehouses in both San Francisco and Petaluma before ending up in McNear's warehouse.

In the late 19th century industrialization created new economic opportunities that led many men away from teaching and into professions with better pay. Women filled the vacant positions, drawn in part by the independence and sense of purpose they provided. By the turn of the 20th century they composed nearly 75 percent of America's teachers. Iowa School was no exception. In 1910, Ella Purvine, the daughter-in-law of Charles Purvine, was appointed the school's new teacher, a position she faithfully served in for the next 20 years. She later became principal of the Two Rock School District, which by that time included Walker School and Two Rock School.

By the 1950s, road improvements and larger school buses made it easier for students to travel long distances to school, spelling an end to many one-room, rural schoolhouses. In 1955, the five trustees of the Two Rock School District—all former students of Ella Purvine—sold off the district's three one-room schools. Iowa School was purchased by one them, Francis Collings, with the intention of turning it into a social hall. After discovering that the insurance was too high to maintain the building, he sold it to a neighbor who tore it down, and used the lumber to build his own house.

Francis Collings managed to salvage the bell that had hung in the school tower since it was presented by G.P. McNear. He and Claude Martin hung it in a bell tower outside the new Two Rock Union School on Spring Hill Road, where it still calls children to class.

Octagon House, 3925 Spring Hill Road

Saltwater Highway

In 1944, Jerry MacMullen described a ride up the Petaluma River aboard the steamer Petaluma *in his book* Paddle-Wheel Days in California:

ALONGSIDE PIER 3 of the San Francisco Embarcadero lies a little stern-wheeler, the last of the commercial steamboats in the state. She has a box-like superstructure and an odd-looking elevator, capable of accommodating a sizable lift truck, located just forward of her pilothouse. Unlike other inland steamers, her small, thin stack is located far aft, like that of the single-end, coastwise steam schooners of the early days. She could do with a bit of paint, but she probably can do her work just as well without it. She is the Petaluma and Santa Rosa Railroad's steamer *Petaluma,* third to bear the name.

At about 5:30 in the afternoon the last of her cargo is aboard—an assortment of plunder and poultryfeed consigned to the merchants of Petaluma or, by transshipment on trains of the Northwestern Pacific, to Santa Rosa or Sebastopol or Healdsburg, or perhaps even as far as Eureka. Her lines are let go; a resonant "Bong! Bong!" comes from her engine-room gong—she is innocent of such modern refinements as the engine telegraph—and her big wheel begins to turn. A prolonged, quavering blast comes from her whistle, and she backs out into the Bay.

Bravely, albeit slowly, she plods along past Angel Island into San Pablo Bay, where she swings off to port as the pilot lays his course through the narrow dredged channel across that shallow sheet of water, toward Black Point, at the mouth of Petaluma Creek. One by one the channel marks are checked off in the logbook, for even on the clearest night she is navigated by the compass course steered and the number of minutes and seconds on each heading. The pilot admits that this may look a bit odd, but maintains it would be bad practice to do it any other way.

"Suppose it's foggy tomorrow night?" he says. There is the answer: He must keep an accurate record of each night's work, so that if on the following night nothing is visible but a wall of gray, he will know how to reach his destination.

Now the red lights on the drawbridges across the entrance to the creek are close at hand, and again the *Petaluma* sounds a long blast. There is an answering signal from ashore, and the string of lights begins to move; the span is opening. Now the lights turn to green—the channel is clear, and the little steamboat paddles through. The bridge swings shut behind her, and she heads on, up the winding slough.

From the creek's mouth to the head of navigation she will alter her course approximately 50 times, and the pilot will be a busy man; he must remember all of those courses by points and quarter-points, and how long he has to remain on each heading. Over the steering-compass is mounted a watch with an oversize second-hand; with the aid of these two the pilot goes on. Some courses will be as long as seven minutes; the shortest one is 30 seconds.

Twin House, The Haystacks, Cloudy Bend—he checks them off in his log, and the *Petaluma* plods on, through a channel so narrow that at times you can all but touch each bank with an oar. Motionless and silent in the night, cows peer at the maritime intruder in the midst of their pastures.

Now the lights of Petaluma loom up ahead, and the crew, most of whom have been sleeping below, begin to appear. The steamer deftly executes a 90-degree turn in the tiny basin at the head of the creek, and swings in alongside the pier. At the spring stages, the tide at Petaluma has a range of 13 feet—greater than that of any other California city. If the tide is out, there will be lots of work for the elevator in the forward part of the vessel as she unloads. The crew, now fully aroused, are busying themselves with the job of trundling cargo out on the wharf or directly into waiting railway cars. It is about midnight, the run of some 36 miles up from San Francisco taking anywhere from six to eight hours, depending on the stage of the tide.

With startling rapidity, the *Petaluma* is cleared of cargo. And now the job of loading begins. Eggs—eggs—more eggs. It is an agricultural community, and the chicken farms of Petaluma are famous for their output; not for nothing is the city known as "The Egg Basket of the World."

Meanwhile Petaluma sleeps, secure in the knowledge that there will be grain on hand for feeding the poultry and that today's eggs will promptly reach the markets of San Francisco and beyond.

Cloudy Bend on the Petaluma River

LEFT: *Aerial view of marshlands at Cloudy Bend*

RIGHT: *Alman Marsh at Shollenberger Park*

LEFT: *Railroad drawbridge at Haystack Landing on Petaluma River, built 1903 (replaced 2015)*

RIGHT: *Turning Basin with D Street drawbridge, built 1933*

Haystack Landing

John McNear stepped onto the platform of the Petaluma & Haystack Railroad depot at 1st and B streets on the morning of August 27, 1866, bound for San Francisco. Since settling in Petaluma nine years earlier, McNear and his brother, George, both New England sea captains, had become wildly successful grain merchants, operating California's largest grain warehouse and a fleet of shipping schooners that plied the Petaluma River around the clock. In 1866, the McNear brothers were in negotiations with San Francisco export merchants to begin sending their grain to Europe.

As McNear boarded the train, Joe Levitt fired up the steam locomotive. A tugboat operator, Levitt was temporarily filling in while the rail line searched for a new train engineer. Levitt was still getting used to the locomotive, which was powered by steam generated from a large boiler with copper tubes heated by a firebox. As the wood fire stoked the water in the boiler, steam filled the copper tubes, which, when released, moved the pistons that turned the train wheels. With metallurgy not that far advanced, train engineers had to guess how much pressure a boiler could withstand. Human error made explosions of steam-powered trains and boats a common occurrence.

Levitt blew the whistle one last time, signaling the train's imminent departure.

The ride on the Petaluma & Haystack line was relatively short, as the track extended only two-and-a-half miles south of downtown to Haystack Landing, a spot on the river originally named for stacked hay awaiting shipment to San Francisco. At the landing, passengers would board a steamboat to take them down the Petaluma River, which traversed 16 miles of 88 twists and turns before reaching San Pablo Bay.

In 1851, when Petaluma was first being established, small boats like schooners and packets were common on the river. Steamboat captains, though, would not venture north of Lakeville, six miles south of Petaluma, for fear of running aground on low tide. From Lakeville, passengers were transferred to a stagecoach line that ran north to Petaluma or east to Sonoma.

In 1852, two enterprising Petalumans, Henry Hintzelman and M.G. Lewis, began constructing a pop-up city nicknamed Newtown at the end of Casa Grande Road just north of Haystack Landing (present-day Rocky Dog Park). Looking to supplant Petaluma's river port, Hintzelman and Lewis persuaded the captain of the *Red Jacket* steamboat to successfully navigate its way to Newtown. A month later, Petalumans convinced the *Red Jacket's* captain to paddle up to "Old Town" Petaluma. He got as far as Haystack Landing without scraping bottom, after which Newtown was shut down.

Following the *Red Jacket's* successful run, Charles Minturn, a man known as the "Ferryboat King," purchased the steamer and rechristened it the *Kate Hayes* after a popular singer of the day. Minturn had originally rounded Cape Horn in 1849 aboard a side-wheel steamer called the *Senator* that he purchased back East. One of many boats steaming to California to cash in on the Gold Rush, the *Senator* made Minturn a quick fortune transporting miners and goods up and down the Sacramento River from San Francisco, often grossing $50,000 per trip, or roughly $1.8 million in early 21st century currency. As the Gold Rush wound down, Minturn invested his earnings in monopolizing ferryboat traffic between San Francisco and the East Bay. By 1852, he was ready to seize control of shipping on the Petaluma River.

Purchasing two additional steamers for the Petaluma River run, by 1854 Minturn dominated passenger and freight shipping from Petaluma to San Francisco. To solidify his transportation monopoly, he set out in 1864 to build a train line from Petaluma to Black Point east of San Rafael. The third rail line built in California, the Petaluma & Haystack Railroad got only as far as Haystack Landing before Minturn gave up.

The rail line had been in operation for two years when John McNear boarded it on the morning of August 27, 1866. Having just taken his seat in the passenger car, McNear was leaning over to tie his shoelace when an explosion suddenly ripped through the car, sending a piece of timber soaring within inches of his head. The steam boiler had exploded. Engineer Joe Levitt was dead, along with four people on the platform waiting to board the train. Passengers inside the train, including McNear, suffered only superficial wounds.

After the accident, Minturn promised to acquire a new steam locomotive, but instead installed a "hayburner," a train car drawn down the tracks by horses and mules. After Minturn died in 1873, railroad baron Peter Donahue incorporated the Petaluma & Haystack into his new San Francisco & North Pacific Railroad, and extended the line to San Rafael.

Boats at Haystack Landing

Lakeville

Julia Moriarty was 10 years old when her mother died in childbirth in their native County Kerry, Ireland. Her father left her in the care of relatives while he made his way to San Francisco, sending for Julia four years later, in 1868. After sailing around Cape Horn, Julia arrived in San Francisco at the age of 14 and immediately went to work as a domestic in the home of a wealthy family named Whitney. At the age of 18, she left the Whitneys to marry John Casey, a fellow County Kerry immigrant, who, along with his brother, Jeremiah, had established a wheat farm in Lakeville.

The Casey brothers had arrived in Lakeville in 1863, as part of the Irish diaspora that constituted the first large wave of immigrants to the Petaluma area in the 1850s and 1860s. They were joined by two sisters, Mary and Catherine, both of whom were soon wed to Lakeville ranchers—Mary to George Eades, and Catherine to John Gregory. In marrying into the Casey clan, Julia Moriarty found herself in the middle of a familiar Irish community in Lakeville, which was sometimes referred to as "Little Ireland." Like most of the Irish, the Caseys were drawn to the Petaluma River Watershed by wheat mania, which the *San Francisco Bulletin* compared to the Gold Rush:

> At the beginning of the last rainy season the excitement in the favor of wheat growing had only been exceeded by some of the more memorable mining excitement of former days. There was a rush and a furor for wheat lands. Nearly every novice about to try his hand at agriculture, bought or rented lands for wheat culture.

Among a handful of crops that could be raised without irrigation, wheat was particularly well suited to the watershed's mediterranean climate. Instead of planting in the spring, farmers waited for the November rainy season to soften the sun-baked soil for plowing and seeding. The seeds germinated during the valley's mild winters, beginning their growing cycle in mid-February. If the watershed received several inches of rain in early spring, the crops matured well; if not, they were stunted.

Wheat farming required little expertise or capital, and unlike fruit trees or grapevines that took years to mature, it returned a good profit the first year, earning a reputation among the Irish as a "poor man's crop." The farming itself was highly mechanized and not particularly labor intensive, allowing large acreages to be easily planted, harvested, sacked, and shipped. By the late 1880s, the steam plow had been refined to the point where it could turn 160 acres in 24 hours. Harvesting was done with 12-foot headers that clipped the wheat stalks and pitched them into a wagon on the side for stacking with forks. Drawn by teams of horses or mules, each machine was able to cut 15 to 25 acres a day. By the 1890s, wheat headers were replaced by large combines.

The Lakeville region, seven miles south of Petaluma along the river, was prime wheat growing country for aspiring farmers like the Casey brothers. A number of the farms in Lakeville were made up of reclaimed marshlands along the east side of the Petaluma River that the state of California began selling off in 1860, on the condition that the land be diked, drained, and reclaimed for farming or grazing in order to generate tax revenues.

The little village of Lakeville itself was originally a boat landing settled in 1853 by a squatter named A.M. Bradley. As farms and ranches became established in the area, the village began to grow. In 1860, San Francisco Bay's "Ferryboat King," Charles Minturn, began running a steamboat from San Francisco to the Lakeville landing, where passengers transferred to stages bound for Petaluma and Sonoma. By the time the Caseys arrived in 1863, Lakeville contained a post office, a blacksmith shop, hotels, a saloon, a dance hall, a racetrack, and a bear and bull pit where the two animals were set against each other for sporting entertainment.

The Casey brothers purchased 120 acres in the hills directly east of the boat landing. The top quarter of their property was encompassed by Tolay Lake, from which Lakeville took its name. The largest body of freshwater in the Petaluma Valley, Tolay Lake covered 300 acres. Located on an active fault, the lake was actually a sag pond, fed by springs brought to the surface by tectonic activity. In 1859, a German immigrant named William Bihler acquired Tolay Lake as part of an 8,000-acre tract of land extending from the Petaluma River east to the outskirts of Sonoma. In the 1860s, Bihler dynamited the lake's natural dam on its southern end, allowing the water to drain out into the San Pablo Bay, where it created its own estuary. In the dry lakebed Bihler planted a potato and beet patch, and later grapes.

The majority of wheat grown in the Petaluma River Watershed was exported to foreign markets. Prior to the

Gilardi's Lakeville Marina, 5684 Lakeville Highway

overleaf: *Lakeville area looking west to Mount Burdell*

introduction of the refrigerated railroad car in the late 1880s, wheat was the only major crop durable enough to withstand long periods of storage without spoiling. At the beginning of the wheat boom in the 1850s, more than 50 percent of California wheat and flour exports went to Australia and New Zealand. In early 1860s, after grain exports from the Midwest became disrupted by the Civil War, the state's export market expanded to Europe. By 1867, 80 percent of California's wheat and flour exports were being shipped around Cape Horn to Great Britain.

As wheat became Petaluma's primary growth engine during the 1860s and 1870s, grain and flour mills sprung up along the riverbanks of the downtown. The local export market was dominated by the McNear brothers, John and George, who dissolved their partnership in 1874 when George decided to strike out on his own in San Francisco, where his business prowess soon earned him a reputation as the state's "Wheat King." Beginning in the 1890s, rising competition from the Midwest and Russia, along with soil exhaustion and the introduction of new varieties of superior grain, sent California's wheat market into a steady decline. Many small farmers in Lakeville like the Caseys transitioned to hay and dairy farming. By the early 1900s, local wheat farms had all but disappeared.

Lakeville's prominence as a steamboat landing and stage transit station was usurped in 1870 by railroad baron Peter Donahue, who purchased a knoll of land a mile downriver to serve as the southern terminus of his San Francisco & North Pacific Railroad. Donahue originally planned to make Petaluma his terminus, but city leaders rejected his request to use Main Street as a right-of-way for the line. Instead, he decided to build a town of his own, reportedly chiding Petalumans that he would someday take pleasure in seeing grass growing in their streets.

Donahue erected his town—which he modestly named Donahue—nearly overnight, furnishing it with a roundhouse and turnstile for his locomotives, a saloon, two blacksmith shops, a dance hall, a school, warehouses, and a stable. Primarily a company town for his railroad workmen—all of whom were Irish, as Donahue refused to hire Chinese laborers—the Donahue township grew to a population of about 200 before being shuttered in 1884, when Peter Donahue moved his railhead to Tiburon. He took most of the town's buildings with him, leaving behind only a stable and dance hall.

In 1887, Julia Casey's husband, John, contracted the measles and died. Within a decade, both her brother-in-law Jeremiah and his wife Catherine had passed away. Julia, now a widow with seven children to raise, sold the Casey farm, and moved into Petaluma, buying a handful of houses on Bassett Street, which she initially converted to boarding houses before eventually selling them off to members of her extended Irish family.

The town of Lakeville began to decline once the rail terminus at nearby Donahue was moved to Tiburon in 1884. In the 1920s, the town's original landing was converted to a popular striped bass fishing resort by James Gilardi. Known as Gilardi's Lakeville Marina, it became the lone commercial fishing and boating facility on the Petaluma River.

Lakeville hay fields

Sonoma Mountain (Oona-pa'is)

When Frank Burton first settled his ranch along Roberts Road in Penngrove, he claimed that the trout in nearby Copeland Creek ran so thick that he could reach in and catch them by hand. For Burton and other early settlers in the 1850s, the creek's abundance of fish and year-round freshwater made it a valuable resource. But they soon learned that Copeland Creek had a darker side. During heavy winter rainstorms, the creek jumped from its usual streambed in the Russian River Watershed into the adjacent Petaluma River Watershed, filling the river with silt and debris that impeded riverboat navigation and contributed to flooding in downtown Petaluma.

Calls in Petaluma for finding a remedy to this "evil in the hills"—as the *Petaluma Argus* called it—began in the early 1860s. They were consistently met with concerns over private property rights, government regulations, and questions about where the funding would come from to dam the creek.

Meanwhile, the city of Petaluma had other designs on Copeland Creek. Situated on a saltwater slough, the city had relied for its water supply on wells and a couple of springs in town. But as the town's population began to grow in the late 1850s, the hilly terrain made deep well drilling impractical, leaving residents reliant upon water cart deliveries. In 1860, a group of private investors formed the Petaluma Mountain Water Company and set out to deliver water downtown via pipes from natural year-round springs on Sonoma Mountain.

At first glance, Sonoma Mountain doesn't look like much of a mountain. With a peak elevation of 2,464 feet, the mountain ascends gradually from the valley floor in undulating hillsides that were pushed up from the Pacific Ocean seabed 10 million years ago thanks to a combination of tectonic movement and magma under the earth's surface. The Coast Miwok called the range *Oona-pa'is*. In one Coast Miwok origin myth, its summit was said to have been an island in the primordial ocean at the beginning of time. While winter rainstorms drop an average 23 inches of rain on the Petaluma Valley, the top of Sonoma Mountain captures an average of 50 inches, its crest literally scraping water from low-hanging clouds.

The key to the mountain's water sources is the variability of its geology. Once a raindrop hits the mountains it is either taken up by soil or rock and eventually spilled out in a time-release fashion via artesian wells and springs, or it is sent down the mountain via stream canyons. The mountain's eastern slope facing the Sonoma Valley is heavily forested, while the western slope facing the Petaluma Valley receives afternoon heat, making it warmer and drier, and yielding more of an oak savanna sprinkled with woodlands of oak, fir, bay, madrone, and redwood, the stands largely determined by the flow of water down the mountainsides.

Copeland Creek originates from Elphic Spring near the summit of Sonoma Mountain, naturally flowing onto the Santa Rosa Plain at the southern edge of the Russian River Watershed. Prior to the 1870s, rainwater flowed down Copeland Creek and fanned out into a large seasonal lake across parts of present-day Cotati and Rohnert Park, providing a habitat for egrets, herons, ducks, amphibians, and trout. The annual floods distributed nitrogen-rich silt and debris in alluvial fans that made for productive riparian corridors. They also recharged the groundwater and cleared the valley floor of dead and dying trees and shrubs, spurring the growth of new vegetation.

The increasing development of wheat farms by settlers like Frank Burton led to the reclamation of Copeland Creek's seasonal wetlands. In the 1870s, a nine-mile channel was constructed to connect the creek with the main stem of the Laguna de Santa Rosa, ultimately feeding the creek into the Russian River. But the collection of sediment and storm debris that built up during winter storms tended to hinder the channel's flood control function, contributing to Copeland Creek's inclination to jump into the nearby Petaluma watershed. The channeling also appears to have brought about a steep decline of trout in the creek.

In the 1860s, the Petaluma Mountain Water Company proposed diverting water from Copeland Creek into Petaluma's waterworks as a means of flood control. Undercapitalized, the company sold out in 1868 to the newly formed Petaluma Water Company, which created a 12-acre reservoir on Lawler Ranch adjacent to Adobe Creek on Sonoma Mountain to supply water to Petaluma. After building the reservoir, the company struggled to get enough money to pipe the water into town.

In 1872, a third group of investors led by three large Sonoma Mountain landowners—banker William Hill, real estate developer Thomas Hopper, and cattleman

Sonoma Mountain from the Petaluma River

OVERLEAF: *Looking south toward San Pablo Bay from Sonoma Mountain*

Henry Hardin—announced the formation of the Sonoma County Water Company, capitalized with $150,000, or roughly $3 million in early-21st-century currency.

Securing perpetual water rights to Copeland Creek and Lynch Creek, the company hired Chinese laborers to build a diversionary dam midway up Copeland Creek, piping half of the creek's streamflow to Lynch Creek. From there, the water from both creeks was piped to a reservoir dug out at the back end of the Oak Hill Cemetery in town, later part of Oak Hill Park. They secured access for their pipes across private ranches in exchange for water rights and stock in the company.

In 1877, the Sonoma County Water Company bought out the struggling Petaluma Water Company and assumed its rights to the water of Adobe Creek, expanding the Lawler Reservoir along the creek to a capacity of 60 million gallons of water. By 1880, the water company had installed 20 miles of cast-iron pipes through Petaluma with 13 high-pressure hydrants. They had also constructed a third reservoir west of Cypress Hill Cemetery that held 45 million gallons of water.

The diversionary dam on Copeland Creek was only used in the summer, as the force of the rising waters in winter proved too rough for the feed pipes. That meant the annual winter flooding of Copeland Creek remained a threat to Petaluma. State engineer reports in 1896 and 1902 called for remedies in shoring up the creek's banks, but ranch owners responded with threats of trespassing lawsuits. In 1914, the U.S. Army Corps of Engineers, custodians of the state's rivers and harbors, recommended constructing a retaining wall along the creek. In 1918, local congressman Clarence Lea secured an appropriation of $91,000 from Congress to build such a wall, as well as to widen and dredge the Petaluma River and construct a turning basin at the foot of B and C streets in town. The Cotati Land Company, a large landholder, sued the city of Petaluma, arguing that the retaining wall would result in flooding of their Cotati farmlands. While the Petaluma River was dredged and the turning basin constructed, it doesn't appear that the retaining wall was ever built.

Heavy rainfalls in the late 1920s brought repeated flooding due to the overflow of Copeland Creek to hundreds of chicken ranches then surrounding Petaluma and Penngrove. Citizen petitions for flood control were met with a deaf ear by the Petaluma City Council.

By 1940, 69 percent of Petaluma's water supply was coming from Copeland Creek and Adobe Creek. In 1959, Petalumans approved a revenue bond that purchased the rights and assets of the privately owned water company, then called California Water Service Company. Those assets included the 270-acre Lafferty Ranch that held the headwaters of Adobe Creek, but they excluded the water rights to Copeland Creek.

With local poultry and dairy industries in decline in the 1950s, the city of Petaluma began developing suburban tract homes for San Francisco commuters on the valley floor east of the city, and industrial business parks at the north and south ends of town. Water was once again a limiting factor. In 1961, Petaluma agreed to build an underground aqueduct diverting water to town from the Russian River via the newly constructed Coyote Dam on Lake Mendocino. Subsequent water capacity was added in 1982 with the completion of the Warm Springs Dam—delayed for years by environmentalists and slow-growth advocates—along the Russian River west of Geyserville.

After the state declared that Lawler Reservoir was vulnerable to earthquakes in 1992, the city of Petaluma shut down its Sonoma Mountain waterworks. Lafferty Ranch was subsequently designated by the city council to be converted to a city-owned park, but a controversial legal battle over property rights with the ranch's neighbors ensued for decades, delaying its opening.

The "evil in the hills" returned in the Valentine's Day Storm of 1986, followed by major rainstorms in 2006 and 2017, each causing Copeland Creek to jump its banks and flood into Petaluma. Calls for damming the creek were met with the usual hurdles of private property rights, state and federal regulations, and funding sources. New on the list of concerns was the creek's protected habitat for steelhead trout. Not so long ago, they ran so thick as to be caught by hand.

Copeland Creek on Sonoma Mountain

The Oak Groves

"The valley is covered with majestic oaks placed as no human hand could arrange them for beauty. I almost have to cry for joy."

Luther Burbank

IT WASN'T UNTIL 1869 that the early Yankee settlers in the Petaluma River Watershed experienced the full fury of nature's wrath, when one early October morning a small straw fire in nearby Rincon Valley erupted into a firestorm that raged for days. Stoked by the Diablo winds—literally a devil's brew of high temperatures, low humidity, and northeast gales that blow in from the Great Basin each fall—the blazes filled Petaluma with such a thick veil of smoke that residents believed they were surrounded by fire on all sides. Flames consumed forests north of Santa Rosa as well as wheat and hay fields both east and west of Petaluma. Fortunately, a late change in wind conditions spared the town itself.

Prior to the settlers' arrival, catastrophic fires occasionally swept through the mountains and coastal prairie of what came to be called Sonoma County. As a preventive measure, Coast Miwok natives deliberately set seasonal fires in order to reduce fuel on the ground. They also applied selective burning as a means of pruning and weeding the watershed. In doing so, they modified the grasslands, shrub lands, riparian zones, forested areas, and even wetlands. The burns decreased plant competition and controlled insects and diseases that threatened their food sources, most critically the oak trees, whose acorns provided a key staple of their diet. In addition to regularly burning the underbrush around the oak trees, they pruned branches and fertilized the soil with ground seashells.

As a result, the Petaluma River Watershed was a cornucopia of oak trees. In the deep soil lining the creek beds majestic valley oaks grew to heights of 150 feet with trunks eight to 12 feet in diameter. Beneath their understory a variety of unique plants and fungi thrived, while in their massive canopies flocks of egrets, geese, and other waterfowl nested. Stands of black oaks lined the shady canyons of the hills, their large leaves sharply tipped. On the hillsides, Oregon oaks rimmed the meadows with their bright-green, lobed leaves. The ubiquitous coastal live oaks grew as high as 70 feet with canopies that extended up to 60 feet wide.

The Spanish padres and soldiers who first entered the valley in 1820 were so taken by the oak woodlands that they called them "roblars," or highly cultivated park groves. Regardless, to justify their colonialist and crusading intentions they convinced themselves that they were setting foot in a wilderness, a dangerous and wild place that had to be conquered and cultivated by "civilized" people. In fact, thanks to the effective farming techniques employed for centuries by the Coast Miwoks, they were entering a carefully tended garden.

Native families often adopted specific oak groves in the valley to care for and harvest, tending to the same trees for successive generations. Such family sites contained the best trees, ones that bore larger and less bitter acorns. Oaks in the hills were owned and shared by the village as a whole. The Coast Miwok's long tradition of stewardship came to an end when Lieutenant Mariano Vallejo, Mexican comandante of the Petaluma Adobe, banned their deliberate burns in the first formal treaty negotiated between the Mexican government and native tribes in 1836, in order to expand his large herds of cattle and sheep on the prairie. (He also banned the Coast Miwok ritual of daily bathing in the creeks, over concerns about nudity.)

With the arrival of Yankee settlers in the 1850s, the old-growth oaks faced another fate. Coal was a critical source of heat in homes and businesses, as well as for powering steam engines in the new city of San Francisco. Before the transcontinental railroad began transporting coal from the Rocky Mountains in the 1870s, the city relied on shipments from the Pacific Northwest, British Isles, and Australia. To supplement these often limited and expensive coal supplies, loggers turned to the oak groves. After leveling the easy-to-reach woodlands around the San Francisco Bay, they took their axes to Sonoma County, wasting no time clearing many of the old-growth oaks from the valley before descending on Sonoma Mountain, which they completely denuded.

In many cases the oaks were cut into four-foot lengths and piled into charcoal mounds as large as 25 feet in diameter and 15 feet in height. The mounds were then covered in dirt, and the wood inside set on fire to burn slowly for as long as a month. The charcoal produced by this slow burn was than loaded into sacks and shipped by rail and boat to the steam-powered mills in San Francisco and Oakland. With the arrival of the railroad to Petaluma River Watershed during the early 1870s, old-growth oaks were milled for use as railroad ties or used as firewood in the boilers of steam-generated

Valley oak at rock outcrop, D Street Extension

locomotives. By the late 19th century, the deforested Petaluma River Watershed had largely been converted to wheat and hay fields and grazing land. Then came the fires.

Following the wildfires of 1869, the next major firestorm arrived on the morning of September 19, 1900. This time, abundant underbrush and dry, imported pasture grasses provided ready tinder. A fire that started in the woods near Cazadero divided into three branches, with one branch burning toward Sebastopol, a second toward the coast, and the third bearing down on Valley Ford. Together, they burned 100 square miles. Fires also raged between St. Helena and Healdsburg, in Kenwood, and south of Petaluma on Mount Burdell, where a fire that started from a charcoal pit burned 18,000 acres of oak trees before heading west toward Nicasio, where it torched herds of grazing livestock.

Wildfires returned to Petaluma 23 years later on September 17, 1923. Strong Diablo winds first blew over dozens of small poultry houses that by that time dotted the hills, before igniting a fire near Nicasio. The inferno spread across Mount Burdell and down to the Petaluma River. Fire also burned through the redwood groves and cottages along the Russian River, through the forest outside Cloverdale, and down the Sonoma Valley to Boyes Hot Springs.

Forty-one years later, on September 19, 1964, the Hanly Fire started in two spots—from a blown transformer east of Glen Ellen and from a hunter's cigarette on the southwest slope of Mount St. Helena. Spread by hot winds of up to 80 miles per hour, the fires quickly spread toward Calistoga, Sonoma Valley, and northern Santa Rosa along U.S. Highway 101, torching 60,000 acres and 151 homes. One year later, almost to the day, Petaluma was surrounded by a ring of 10 fires fed by strong winds reportedly blowing up to 100 miles per hour. The largest fires burned through Crane Canyon north of town and out west between Eastman Lane and the D Street Extension. Jack Kessler, head of the state's forest firefighting effort at the time, pointed out that the problem was bound to get worse as long as people insisted on building homes in highly combustible areas.

Sadly, Kessler's prophecy came to tragic fruition on the night of October 8, 2017, when the Diablo winds brought the fiery dual inferno of the Tubbs Fire and the Nuns Fire that burned across Sonoma County for 23 days, charring more than 114,000 acres, destroying 5,300 homes, and killing at least 23 people. In a reminder of the past, the Tubbs Fire in the northern part of the county burned through essentially the same area as the Hanly Fire 53 years earlier. The difference was that the county population had grown from 140,000 to 500,000 during that time period, with new housing developments placed in parts of the historical fire zone.

The lessons of living with fire were something the Coast Miwoks became intimate with over centuries in the Petaluma River Watershed. They used those lessons to maintain the health of their habitat and to cultivate the oaks that were so important to their existence. Not so the settlers who came after them.

Oak trees at Lafferty Ranch

Chinese Rock Walls

Like most Chinese who immigrated to California in the 19th century, Ang Tai Duck was a sojourner. In the late 1870s he came to "Golden Mountain," as California was known in the Far East, seeking fortune and the chance to return home a wealthy man. Instead, he found himself at the center of one of Sonoma County's most notorious crimes.

The majority of Chinese immigrants like Ang Tai Duck were single men from Guangdong Province in South China, a region wracked by civil unrest, Opium Wars, floods, famines, and drought. The first wave of arrivals fled the chaos in 1848 to the goldfields of California. As few Chinese women were able to immigrate due to Chinese custom and U.S. law, the majority of Chinese men lingered in bachelor limbo, prevented from gaining citizenship—a privilege reserved only for white foreigners—or from owning land and filing mining claims. They resorted to either laboring for white miners or reworking old, abandoned claims.

As the newcomers' numbers grew, the newly established California legislature passed the Foreign Miner's Tax Law in 1850, officially taxing all immigrant workers but meted out only to Chinese and Mexicans. Subsequent taxes were imposed on Chinese males 18 years or older and on new Chinese arrivals, along with measures that were adopted to restrict the Chinese to jobs as apprentices and exclude them from testifying against any white person in court. None of these efforts, however, succeeded in stemming the tide. By 1870, the number of Chinese in California had grown to 50,000.

In Sonoma County, pioneer Hungarian winemaker Agoston Haraszthy began employing Chinese for clearing, planting, and harvesting the vineyards of his groundbreaking Buena Vista Winery. By 1872, there were more than 7,000 acres of grapes planted in the county, many of them using Chinese labor. Petaluma's preeminent business leader John McNear put Chinese laborers to work in his brick manufacturing plant and shrimp boating operation at McNear Point 20 miles south of Petaluma, and also employed them in straightening parts of the Petaluma River for shipping access. A hard-driving businessman, McNear defended the Chinese against local prejudice, stating they were tolerable as long as they performed labor that Americans would not do, and at lower wages than Americans would accept.

Among the Chinese were skilled stonemasons who were employed to erect dry-stacked rock walls as cattle fencing prior to arrival of barbed wire in the county.

In Petaluma, roughly 500 Chinese set up laundries, restaurants, and shanties, penned into "Chinese colonies," the most prominent of which was on Petaluma Boulevard between Western Avenue and B Street. Many, like Ang Tai Duck, worked as cooks for wealthy households. His employer, Captain Jesse C. Wickersham, a Petaluman who had relocated to a secluded sheep ranch west of Cloverdale, was the nephew of Isaac Wickersham, a prominent Petaluma banker and the wealthiest man in Sonoma County at the time. The captain's wife, Sarah, was the younger sister of Isaac Wickersham's wife.

During a widespread economic downturn in the 1870s, a growing number of white laborers, many of them Irish immigrants, came to view the Chinese as threats to their precarious livelihoods. In 1882, Congress passed the Chinese Exclusion Act, prohibiting Chinese from entering the country for 10 years. The act was strengthened and extended for another decade in 1892 thanks to an effort led by Sonoma County Congressman Thomas Geary. Anti-Chinese Leagues and "anti-coolie" associations sprang up across California, imposing boycotts on Chinese labor and businesses, and vowing to "rid themselves of the Chinese evil." Following newspaper accounts that portrayed the Chinese as a troublesome, often criminal, underclass, a suspicious rash of fires began breaking out in houses and shops in Petaluma's Chinatown area.

In the midst of this xenophobia came the grisly murder in January 1886 of Jesse and Sarah Wickersham. The couple was found shotgunned to death in their Cloverdale farmhouse. Despite questionable evidence, blame for the murder was quickly pinned on their missing cook, Ang Tai Duck. Having caught the "down-train" out of Cloverdale, Ang Tai Duck allegedly managed to board a steamer in San Francisco bound for Hong Kong. A man supposedly matching his description was arrested when the ship docked in Yokohama, Japan, although the evidence is sketchy. Facing extradition, that man committed suicide by hanging himself in his jail cell.

The murders set off an organized campaign to rid Sonoma County of all Chinese. In Petaluma, 2,000 people turned out to press for a universal boycott. Most of the Chinese fled town, abandoning their colony on Petaluma Boulevard. Following their departure, John McNear constructed the McNear Building on the site of their former colony.

A rock wall built on Sonoma Mountain, circa 1870s

Cattle Ranches

A GROUP OF COWBOYS gathered in the small cabin office of Caulfield Stockyards in the fall of 1948, drinking coffee and chewing the fat before saddling up for what would be the last cattle drive across East Petaluma. Burned into the cabin's front door were the brands of herds that had passed through the stockyards for more than half a century. Trucks with trailers were now hauling cattle to market instead of cowboys herding them there on horseback. Along the dusty trail from the Caulfield Stockyards to their slaughterhouse on McDowell Road at Lindberg Lane, the first tract homes were going up for returning World War II veterans and their young families. Within a decade, the valley floor would be cut in half by a new freeway, paved over with new roads, and beginning to fill up with housing subdivisions built by John Novak and Blackwell Builders.

The morning of the cattle drive, the cowboys mustered around the cabin's potbelly stove by the glow of kerosene lamps, listening to Will and Tom Caulfield, both renowned Irish storytellers, recount tales of past roundups. The Caulfield brothers had inherited the stockyards from their father, Thomas Caulfield Sr., a feisty Irishman who immigrated to Petaluma in the late 1870s. At the time, Sonoma County, along with West Marin, encompassed the largest coastal prairie in Northern California. Prior to the arrival of Franciscan missionaries in 1823, the prairie consisted of perennial green grasses that supported large grazing herds of deer and tule elk. That changed with the missionaries' introduction of longhorn cattle.

Mission San Francisco de Solano, founded in 1823 in Sonoma, had 2,500 head of branded cattle. After Mexico's secularization of the missions in 1834, the Petaluma River Watershed was carved into large rancheros granted primarily to former soldiers of the Mexican government. The watershed became essentially one vast cattle ranch as the longhorns took favorably to the climate and pastures of the coastal prairie. The largest and most populated of the rancheros was the 66,000-acre Rancho Petaluma, belonging to Mexican commandant Mariano Vallejo, across which roamed a herd of 12,000 to 15,000 longhorns.

The value of the cattle lay solely in their hides and tallow, which drew good prices in Europe and later New England for the making of leather goods, candles, soaps, and lubricants. Native Americans provided much of the labor on Vallejo's ranch, a number of them either prisoners captured in military campaigns, laborers provided through Vallejo's alliance with Chief Solano, a leader of the nearby Suisun tribe, or ex-mission neophytes who, upon the secularization of the missions, had been given cattle by the Mexican government which they then had placed into Vallejo's care, having little interest in owning the livestock themselves.

From February to May, Coast Miwok and Mexican vaqueros would periodically round up the steers for branding, marking the event with a large rodeo and festival of hearty feasts and singing and dancing. They would also conduct an annual slaughter of as many as a quarter of the ranchero's steers, processing the hides and tallow for Yankee skippers. The *calaveras,* or "place of skulls" as the slaughtering grounds were called, were usually set up in a wooded area beside a stream. Two days were allowed for skinning, stretching the hides, rendering the tallow, and packing it into bags made of bladders and entrails. Some of the meat was dried, but much of it was discarded, making the calaveras big draws for flies, turkey vultures, and grizzly bears.

The bears were often captured for the popular blood sport of bear and bull fights, where the two animals, each with a leg or paw tied behind them, would fight to the death before a cheering gallery of men, women, and children. Over the years, as the more docile of the longhorns were annually rounded up and killed, many in the remaining herd increasingly reverted to being *cimarrones,* or wild cattle, wary of human beings.

The Gold Rush of 1848 transformed the raising of cattle from a pastoral endeavor to a speculative business. With the demand for meat in the mining camps outstripping supply, the price of cattle soared from $4 a head in 1847 to more than $500 a head by 1849, depleting herds across the Petaluma River Watershed and the rest of California, and setting off cattle drives of rangy longhorns from Texas and Mexico. After the Gold Rush played out, prices dropped but the demand for beef continued with the expanding population of San Francisco.

One of the gold miners who had struck it rich, a New Yorker named Harrison Meacham, established a ranch in the Two Rock area in 1853 and stocked it with cattle he obtained from an early Mexican grant owner, Cyrus Alexander, in northern Sonoma County's Alexander Valley. Meanwhile, early ranchers like William Bihler, who owned an 8,000-acre ranch in Lakeville, began importing domesticated stock like Devons, Durhams,

Black Angus cattle, Marshall-Petaluma Road

Herefords, and Angus on cattle drives from Missouri, or else bred from pureblood stock shipped around Cape Horn from the East Coast. For new immigrants to the Petaluma River Watershed in the 1850s, cattle raising was an attractive business, as it required little capital to get started and little labor to tend the stock. Cattle also provided their own transportation.

The resulting cattle boom peaked in 1860, after which overbreeding and increased competition began to drive down beef prices. By that time much of the watershed's perennial grasslands had been chomped down to their roots by the huge herds, whose voracious appetites didn't allow the grass to regenerate. A massive flood in 1861-1862 drowned thousands of cattle. It was immediately followed by a severe two-year drought that killed an estimated 300,000 cattle in California, diminishing the state's herd by nearly 50 percent, and leaving the barren countryside littered with rotting carcasses.

The early Europeans to the area had brought with them seeds of annual grasses from the Mediterranean region. The grasses died in summer but sprouted again each rainy season, and were able to withstand excessive grazing, unlike the native perennials. After the drought of 1863-1864 killed off much of what was left of the perennials, the returning rains accelerated the invasive growth of the foreign annual grasses. From the mid-1860s onward, the watershed's visual appearance changed from year-round green to two contrasting colors—a light gold in summer and fall, and a verdant green in winter and spring.

The California wheat boom that began in the mid-1860s filled the Petaluma River Watershed with wheat farms and established Petaluma as a vibrant and prosperous river port for exporting grain from Sonoma County. But the boom further diminished the local cattle industry. Ranchers increasingly battled with wheat farmers over grazing rights, leading the California legislature in 1874 to pass the "No-Fence" law, making livestock owners responsible for crop damages inflicted by their free-grazing animals, regardless of whether a farmer had erected a fence or "no fence" on their land. The introduction of barbed wire at that time put an end to the watershed's open range once and for all.

After the wheat boom began to wane in the late 1880s—a victim of soil erosion as well as increased competition from Midwest and international growers—many of the farmers in the watershed shifted to raising cattle or dairy cows. They included new immigrants to the area, with a large Italian-speaking Swiss contingent arriving in the 1870s and 1880s, many of them from the Maggia River region in the Canton of Ticino, followed in the 1890s by Portuguese from the archipelagos of the Azores and Madeira, as well as Danes and Germans from the Baltic Isle of Fohr. Young immigrant workers were sometimes sold a small stake in a large dairy that after a number of years accrued equity in the form of cash or livestock they could use to start their own dairies.

It was during the resurgence of the livestock industry in the late 19th century that Thomas Caulfield Sr. established himself as a major cattle dealer in Petaluma. In 1901, he welcomed his two eldest sons, James and Will, into the business. The sons subsequently launched Caulfield Brothers, a meat wagon service that provided home deliveries of meat cut to order. They also opened a meat market at the Caulfield family's headquarters on East Washington and Wilson streets.

It was, however, Caulfield's youngest son, red-headed Tom Jr., who would go on to take his father's place as Petaluma's top cattle baron, as well as one of the town's most illustrious and popular citizens. After briefly enrolling in medical school following high school, Tom Jr. spent some time railroading, performing in traveling theater troupes, and playing semipro baseball before returning to the family business. Even then, during off seasons from cattle buying, he joined traveling minstrel shows to satisfy his artistic proclivities.

Following a performance of Tom Jr.'s troupe one night, the author Jack London invited the cast to dinner. A lifelong teetotaler, Tom Jr. refused London's many offers of whiskey and wine at the meal, prompting London to remark: "Son, you're the first man I've ever met who would stand up for his principles." London's compliment would leave a stamp on Tom Jr.'s reputation, not only in the cattle business but also in his lifelong hobbies as a sought-after rodeo judge and boxing referee. Tom Jr. went on to become one of London's good friends and his personal cattle buyer, as well as the basis of a character in London's 1913 novel, *Valley of the Moon*.

After the death of his older brother James in 1920, Tom Jr. took over Caulfield's Meat Market at 426 East Washington Street, and soon expanded to a second store at the corner of Bodega Avenue and Baker Street. By 1926, he was operating meat markets in Cotati, Mill Valley, Cloverdale, Middletown, Windsor, and Sonoma.

Cattle grazing on Brown Bag Farms, 5901 Red Hill Road

Such neighborhood butcher shops were the face of a robust local livestock industry that included large-animal veterinarians, hay haulers, feed mills, bull services for insemination, frozen meat lockers, meat processing plants, and rendering services, the largest of which was the Royal Tallow and Soap Company, established in 1931 on Lakeville Highway just south of Casa Grande Road. Royal Tallow, which recycled dead livestock and waste from the meat plants into tallow, grease, and bone meal for animal feed, famously waged a battle for more than half a century with the city and its citizens over the strong odors emitting from the plant.

By 1948, when Tom and Will Caulfield set out on their last cattle drive across East Petaluma to their slaughterhouse at McDowell Road and Lindberg Lane, Sonoma County had more than 9,000 head of beef cattle. In the 1950s, cattle ranching in California became largely centralized in factory feed lots in the Central Valley. After the death of his brother Will in 1956, Tom shut down the stockyards and retired. Four years later he passed away. The original Caulfield's Meat Market at East Washington and Wilson streets changed hands before closing down for good in 1966, pushed out like many other neighborhood butcher shops by the arrival of grocery markets with their own in-house butchers. The Caulfield Market site was converted to a gas station in 1970 and then to a small strip mall in 2013.

Meanwhile, Caulfield Stockyards on Lakeville Highway at Caulfield Lane was purchased by Lucky Stores in 1987 and developed into a shopping mall. The same year, Royal Tallow and Soap Company on Lakeville Highway fell to the wrecking ball, and was eventually replaced by an apartment complex. By the early 21st century, the number of beef cattle in Sonoma County had grown to roughly 20,000 head thanks to the ability of local ranchers to serve a niche in pasture-raised beef that commanded premium prices in the market. But the 18 or so auction stockyards and the 30 slaughterhouses that once operated in the North Coast during the Caulfield era were reduced to just Petaluma's Marin Sun Farms slaughterhouse on Petaluma Boulevard North and the Petaluma Livestock Auction Yard on Corona Road adjacent to Highway 101.

Cattle grazing, D Street Extension

The Battle of Washoe House

IN THE DAYS FOLLOWING the tragic assassination of Abraham Lincoln in April 1865, Major James Armstrong ordered the members of Petaluma's Militia, a uniformed unit of California's Irish Brigade known as the Emmett Rifles, to saddle up and ride for the Confederate stronghold of Santa Rosa. Composed mainly of Irish immigrants, the unit (also known as the Hueston Guards) had been formed by two Petalumans—city marshal Lieutenant John Cavanagh and Captain Thomas F. Baylis, an early pioneer. Like most Petalumans, Cavanagh and Baylis were fierce Union loyalists. Santa Rosa and Healdsburg, on the other hand, were occupied largely by Southern sympathizers. Unable to join in the actual fighting—transporting militia from California to the front lines was too costly for the Union Army—the Emmett Rifles focused their partisan passions on their Rebel neighbors to the north.

When the Civil War began, Captain Baylis requested a shipment of modern weapons from the California Militia, reporting that rebellious secessionists had surrounded Petaluma. He wasn't exaggerating. While the Petaluma River Watershed had been settled largely by seamen, merchants, and farmers arriving by boat from the Northeastern states, the Santa Rosa and Russian River valleys had been predominately settled by farmers from Missouri, Tennessee, and Kentucky who had traveled overland by covered wagon. A number had done so at the encouragement of former Missouri Governor Lilburn Boggs, who had immigrated to Sonoma County in 1846. The cultural difference between the bustling river port of Petaluma and the farming plain of Santa Rosa was so vast that Santa Rosa was often referred to as "Little Missouri." Politically, the sympathies of each group remained with their native origins, with a large contingent of Irish immigrants in Petaluma throwing in with the Yankees.

Captain Baylis's fears were realized on September 22, 1862, when California governor Leland Stanford dispatched Baylis and the Emmet Rifles to Healdsburg to squelch a rebellion of Rebel squatters. The squatters were members of the Settlers' League that had been originally formed to challenge the legality of Mexican land grants made before California became a state in 1850. The league insisted that its members had the right to carve out homesteads on any unused land they found, much as American settlers had done in other states on the western frontier. They took their case all the way to the U.S. Supreme Court, which ruled against them in 1856. Disgruntled members then formed secret societies, terrorizing grant holders, resisting legal governmental authority, and eventually aligning themselves with the Secessionists in the South against the federal government.

The first serious confrontation between the squatters and the Emmet Rifles occurred in the town of Bodega in 1859, when the sheriff's effort to evict a group of squatters was thwarted by 90 armed members of the Settlers' League. In July 1862, anticipating a similar showdown, Sheriff J.M. Bowles of Petaluma brought with him a posse comitatus of 300 men to serve eviction notices on squatters in the Healdsburg area. He was met by 50 armed and determined league members, who shot and killed a member of the posse. Two months later, at the governor's order, Sheriff Bowles returned to Healdsburg with Captain Baylis and his Emmet Rifles, who succeeded in peacefully evicting the squatters.

Aside from the land grant battles, the most vitriolic clashes in Sonoma County were waged between the two county newspapers, Santa Rosa's *Sonoma Democrat*, and the *Petaluma Argus*. The *Sonoma Democrat's* editor, 23-year-old Thomas L. Thompson, was a native of Virginia and an advocate for states' rights, as reflected by his paper's motto, "The World Is Governed Too Much." The editor of the *Petaluma Argus*, 30-year-old Samuel Cassiday, hailed from Ohio, and was an adamant Union supporter, attacking his rival newspaper as "a brazen-faced, hypocritical, treason-breeding tool of Jeff Davis."

The vicious tirades reached a fevered pitch during the presidential election of 1864, when Sonoma County was the only county in California to give Lincoln's opponent, General George McClellan, a majority of its votes. Lincoln carried only the towns of Petaluma and Bloomfield, then a booming potato-farming center. In the immediate aftermath of Lincoln's assassination on April 14, 1865, five Secessionist newspapers in San Francisco were sacked and burned, inspiring an angry Major James Armstrong to order the Emmett Rifles to saddle up and ride for Santa Rosa.

According to legend, the Irish militia got as far as the Washoe House, a stagecoach stop with a tavern midway between Petaluma and Santa Rosa, where, overcome by thirst, they stopped for a drink or two. As Penngrove historian Chuck Lucas noted, the only casualties in what became known as the "Battle of the Washoe House," were large quantities of lager.

The Washoe House, 2840 Roblar Road, built 1859

Penngrove Rock Ranches

WHILE GROWING UP in Tuscany, where quarrying was a way of life, Andrew J. Camozzi learned from his father, a stonemason, how to square up the corners of a stone block.

"You took the chisel and the hammer," Camozzi said, "and you turned the block over as many times as you wanted to, to make it square. The average thickness of each paving block was between three and four inches wide, six and seven inches long. You just went along—tap, tap, tap—and once you knew the stone, you knew just where to hit it and just what to do. That was the Italian style."

Camozzi arrived in California in 1910 at age 16. Like a number of young men from the Tuscany region, he dreamed of pursuing a a life different from his father's, but instead was quickly put to work making paving stones in the quarries. Blockmaking was big business in the North Bay from the 1870s to the 1920s, with 35 quarries operating in Sonoma County at the turn of the century. Between 1887 and 1913 alone an estimated 136 million paving blocks were produced from quarries in Sonoma, Marin, Napa, and Solano counties for San Francisco, Oakland, and other new cities around the Bay Area, at a value of $5,712,000 (roughly $140 million in early-21st-century currency). Some local blocks even paved the streets of port cities in Asia, after being used for ballast on return voyages of Chinese clippers. Prior to the influx of skilled stonemasons from Northern Italy in the 1890s, Chinese and European immigrants from Ireland, Scotland, Wales, and Sweden made up most of the early quarry labor force in the region.

The first Bay Area quarry was established south of downtown Petaluma at Hein Quarry. A large rock outcrop just north of Haystack Landing, the quarry was in operation as early as 1857, providing stone for local builders. In 1864, the quarry began sending paving stones to San Francisco. Street paving had been a challenge for the city since the Gold Rush, as the city had scrambled with little civic planning or funding to accommodate an increasing number of people, horses, mules, and drays traversing its rolling hills and sandy waterfront. Planks of Douglas fir from Oregon were the first material used for roadbuilding. A cheap stopgap measure, they proved unreliable for the long term. Then came rounded cobblestones from the American River, which offered durability but were treacherous to horses, especially on hilly streets, and noisy. Finally, in the mid-1870s, San Francisco settled on basalt paving blocks from Sonoma County as its standard paving material. Although still noisy, their uniformity provided a smoother ride than the rounded cobblestones.

Given the weight of hauling stones—each block weighed 20 pounds—early quarries had to be near sources of water or rail transportation. Haystack Landing, the main terminus for river traffic in the mid-19th century, made Hein Quarry a natural choice to supply San Francisco. Paving blocks were transported by wagon to the landing and then by scow schooner or barge to San Francisco. Once the Northwestern Pacific Railroad was completed in 1870, access opened up to an additional half-dozen quarries, or rock ranches, along Sonoma Mountain near the railroad depot in Penngrove. The basaltic andesite from that area, commonly called basalt, was hard, dense, and resistant to abrasion, making it ideal for paving the streets of San Francisco.

The rock ranches in Petaluma River Watershed boomed until the advent of the automobile, when new innovations in the petroleum industry led to the use of asphalt for street paving. A less expensive material than basalt, it provided a smoother and quieter ride for automobile drivers. By the 1920s, the demand for paving stones had plummeted, and with it the need for stonemasons. As Andrew J. Camozzi later put it, "The art was gone."

Camozzi settled on a farm in Penngrove, not far from the scars of rock ranches that can still be seen in the form of small rocks and boulders dotting the hills of Sonoma Mountain between East Railroad Avenue and Roberts Road today.

Meanwhile, the boom-and-bust cycle of Hein Quarry followed a pattern of many extraction industries in the Petaluma River Watershed: first, as a source of local building stone; then, of paving blocks bound for San Francisco; next, of crushed rock for making highways; and finally, in the 21st century, as the name of a housing development built on its remains—Quarry Heights.

Basaltic andesite remains of the former Barnes Rock Ranch, 7750 Petaluma Hill Road

Eucalyptus Stands

The writer Jack London drove his wagon over Sonoma Mountain to Petaluma in the winter of 1911 to place an order for some eucalyptus trees. London had become convinced by some dubious research that the oil in eucalyptus wood made it impervious to pests such as shipworms, which were wreaking havoc on the wharf pilings lining the docks of San Francisco and Oakland. Looking to restore both his financial fortunes and his 1,500-acre Beauty Ranch in Glen Ellen, London decided to make a run at cornering the market for wharf pilings. In Petaluma he placed an initial order of 30,000 trees at the nursery of William Stratton.

Known as California's "Eucalyptus King," Stratton was no stranger to eucalyptus speculation. He had launched his nursery at the start of the first eucalyptus boom in 1870, and successfully ridden the frenzy until the market fizzled in the late 1880s. With eucalyptus mania again on the rise at the turn of the century, Stratton wasted no time promoting himself as the tree's most fervent evangelist, peddling the popular blue gum tree not only as a solution for telephone poles and railroad ties, but as a panacea for everything from bronchitis, asthma, sore throats, itchy scalps, headaches, baldness, and rheumatism to the common cold. By the time London pulled up to his nursery, Stratton was selling more than one million eucalyptus seedlings a year.

A native of Sullivan, New York, William Stratton had sailed around Cape Horn at the age of 17, arriving in San Francisco in 1853 just as the Gold Rush was winding down. After finding work as an apprentice in a city nursery, he joined the San Francisco Committee of Vigilance, a militia of Protestant vigilantes intent on clearing out the Tammany Hall-style political machine of Irish Catholics running the city. Stratton was among the vigilantes who famously hung a handful of Irishmen at Fort Gunnybags near the Embarcadero in 1856.

In 1864, Stratton moved to Petaluma, where seven years later he established the first full-scale nursery within the city limits. Located at 417 Upham Street between Stanley Street and Bodega Avenue, the nursery encompassed an entire city block. Initially, Stratton planned to specialize in roses and flower seeds of his own cultivation, since Petaluma was already served by a handful of tree nurseries on the outskirts of town, most prominently W.H. Pepper's Liberty Nurseries on Pepper Lane. But his interest in exotic species led him to gamble on introducing 500 Tasmanian blue gum eucalyptus seedlings to Sonoma County. Within a decade, the gamble paid off, earning Stratton the moniker of "Gum Tree Wizard."

Eucalyptus seeds first arrived in California from Australia in the 1850s, reportedly imported by William Walker for his Golden Gate Nursery in San Francisco. Initially planted for city ornamentation and beautification, the trees didn't gain popularity until the easy-to-reach tree stands around the San Francisco Bay had been logged out. Old-growth redwoods—advertised as "nature's lumber masterpiece"—were the first to go, lusted after for building everything from furniture and Victorian mansions to railroad ties, sidewalks, and egg incubators. Old-growth oaks faced another fate, either cut down for firewood or burned on-site for charcoal to feed the steam-powered mills in San Francisco and Oakland.

By the 1870s, the clear-cutting of the Bay Area began to raise fears of wood scarcity, especially for firewood, the main source of heat in homes and businesses. Given the slow development of second-growth shoots and seedlings, horticulturists were pressed to find faster-growing alternatives. After testing many species, they selected the eucalyptus tree, which could grow to 125 feet high at a diameter of 20 inches within 10 years. Like the native oaks, the eucalyptus thrived on regular moisture and mild temperatures, making it ideal for the area's fogbelt. Able to weather a feast-or-famine rainfall climate by hoarding water and nourishment in its large storage roots, the tree also scavenged nutrients from poor soil that would starve other plants, and conserved energy by shedding senescent branches and used-up bark.

The exotic eucalyptus was soon being touted in horticultural journals as a jack-of-all-trades, offering a cheap source of fuel, boosting farm productivity, defeating malaria, preserving watersheds, forming sturdy windbreaks, and supplying shade cover for grazing animals. Some simply valued the tree for its statuesque beauty, lining backroads with stands on either side. Local speculators like Harrison Meacham, who owned a 7,000-acre ranch extending from the Washoe House on Stony Point Road to Two Rock, became convinced that eucalyptus was the next big thing. He planted hundreds of groves across his ranch, boasting that one acre could produce 500 cords of firewood. In the midst of the hoopla many conjectured that eucalyptus would become the most valuable tree on the planet.

Eucalyptus stand at Ellis Creek Water Recycling Facility

William Stratton nursed the boom, creating new strains of *E. globulus,* the popular blue gum tree, through ongoing experimentation. He also began introducing new varietals from Australia to the area, including red gum and sugar gum. As eucalyptus mania spread in the early 1880s, Stratton was shipping thousands of seedlings cross-country by train and overseas by ship.

By the late 1880s, disenchantment with the tree began to set in. The tree's expansive root system robbed nearby plants of moisture and nutrients. As windbreaks, the young trees tended to topple over in heavy gusts. When used as telegraph poles, the trees rotted in the ground and were prone to beetle infestation. As firewood, they burned hot but produced a constant symphony of popping and fizzing. The final blow came with the discovery of oil in Southern California and an increase in coal importation, both of which reduced the demand for eucalyptus as firewood.

In 1907, a second eucalyptus frenzy was ignited when the U.S. Forest Service, alarmed by the forest clear-cutting taking place across the country, predicted an impending "hardwood famine" for construction, raising concerns about the nation's economic growth. Speculators rapidly began investing in eucalyptus plantations with an expectation of reaping the rewards of an instant industrial forest within 10 years. Overnight, William Stratton's nursery was once again booming with seedling orders.

What the new speculators didn't realize was that the tree's reputation as a quality source of building lumber was based on samples taken from Australian old-growth trees. Wood from younger trees had to be carefully milled and long-seasoned, otherwise it was prone to warping. Likewise, young eucalyptus trees used for wharf pilings were just as susceptible to shipworms as any other hardwood. In 1913, the U.S. Forest Service issued a study declaring that the eucalyptus mania had been built on fictions, delusions, and fallacies, putting an end to the boom. A few years later, the introduction of concrete and steel construction solved the impending hardwood famine.

Jack London, whose ranch was filled with eucalyptus trees when he died in 1916, went to his grave still dreaming of cornering the market on wharf pilings. William Stratton lived for another decade to the age of 90, the oldest surviving member of the San Francisco Committee of Vigilance. His nursery was purchased after his death in 1926 by local dairy rancher M.F. Tunzi, who developed it into a tract of modest homes bisected by today's Tunzi Parkway.

In the late 20th century, California environmentalists branded the eucalyptus as "America's largest weed," demonizing it as an "invasive alien" that posed a fire danger as well as a threat to ecological biodiversity. An initiative was undertaken to eradicate the tree from Angel Island in the San Francisco Bay. Fans came to the defense of the eucalyptus, pointing to the tree's documented medical benefits and the critical habitat its elaborate crown provided for waterfowl, migrating monarch butterflies, and bees. Calling the tree a "beautiful mistake," they raised the question of how long any species had to live in California before being considered native, a question that found resonance in a state established by immigrants.

Stand of eucalyptus, Lakeville Highway

Cow Heaven

Clara Steele set out for Two Rock from a farm in Ohio with her two children and her in-laws in April 1856. Traveling first by train to New York City, the family boarded a ship bound for Panama. There, they crossed the Isthmus of Panama overland on a calamitous train ride that ended in a crash, killing 200 passengers. Safely reaching the Pacific, the Steeles set sail for San Francisco, arriving in the city on May 20th. As they disembarked at the waterfront, they witnessed two men being hung by the city's band of vigilantes.

Waiting for them on the docks were Clara's husband, Rensselaer, and his cousin, George. The two men had come to California the year before seeking to make their fortunes in the goldfields. Unsuccessful, they made their way to the Petaluma River Watershed, where they returned to the farming life they knew. Renting a small farm in Two Rock, they began cultivating hay and potatoes, the valley's first two cash crops, for export to a burgeoning San Francisco.

Many of the early pioneers trekking overland in covered wagons to the Petaluma River Watershed had brought dairy cows with them to provide milk for their families. On arrival, they found the coastal prairie to be natural grazing country. Thanks to the temperate climate, especially the foggy summers, the prairie's native perennial grasses stayed green year-around. Unable to safely export the milk from their cows due to the lack of refrigeration, ranchers turned to making butter, which had a longer shelf life.

To make butter, milk was poured into a hopper, strained, and set out in a wide pan to separate. The cream was then skimmed off, with the remaining skimmed milk fed to the pigs. The cream was then churned by hand until it became butter, after which it was salted, packed in wooden boxes or barrels, and shipped to San Francisco on "butter schooners" from either Petaluma or Tomales, then a port town. The ranchers were also able to make fresh cheese and cottage cheese from skimmed milk combined with sweet buttermilk. Hard cheese, however, had to be shipped around Cape Horn from the East Coast, where commercial cheese factories had only been established a few years earlier, thanks in part to the mass production of enzymes called rennet, extracted from the stomachs of calves. By the time the cheese arrived in San Francisco, it was usually moldy or rancid from the long voyage.

Shortly after her arrival in Two Rock, Clara Steele took a trip to San Francisco, where she noticed a strong appetite for hard cheese, and the high prices people were willing to pay for it. Back in Two Rock she hired a local Coast Miwok vaquero, or cowboy, to rope a few of the wild longhorn cows grazing near the farm, and tie together the cows' hind legs so that she could milk the ornery animals. After separating and skimming off the cream from the milk, she began experimenting in her kitchen with a recipe from a cookbook she had inherited from her English grandmother for making Cheddar cheese. After many tries, she perfected the recipe. Taking samples of her Cheddar cheese on a steamer down to San Francisco, she introduced it to merchants there, who immediately placed orders for the domestic hard cheese.

Returning to Two Rock, Clara and the rest of the Steele family decided to acquire a number of imported milk cows and launch California's first commercial dairy. Soon they were selling "Steele Brothers Cheddar" in San Francisco and other nearby markets. Within five years the business had become so successful that they were shipping 45 tons of cheese a year to San Francisco on their own cheese schooner, from their new 6,000-acre ranch on the Point Reyes Peninsula.

Overnight, the coastal prairie from Petaluma to West Marin was proclaimed "cow heaven." While small herds of Mexican longhorns still roamed the hills, ranchers began importing Durham, Devon, Ayrshire, Jersey, and Guernsey milk cows from the East Coast. Then in 1863 and 1864 a severe drought hit the area. Milk cows and free-grazing longhorn cattle chewed the perennial grasses down to their roots before starving to death, leaving the barren hills littered with carcasses. Some of the European settlers who had brought grass seeds with them from the old country, including Mediterranean annuals that died in summer but resprouted in the rainy season, took the opportunity to broadcast them across the prairie once the drought subsided. Unlike the native perennials, the imported annual grasses were better able to withstand excessive grazing and drought conditions. Gradually, the annuals replaced perennials across California, turning the hills and prairies golden in the summer and green in the winter.

As California's population exploded in the late 19th century, an increasing demand for cheese, milk, and butter made Petaluma the largest shipping point for dairy products in the state. By 1880, scow schooners were carrying more than 12,000 tons of butter down the river

Holstein milk cows grazing, Spring Hill Road

each year. The high demand precipitated a shift in the processing of butter and cheese from domestic farms to creameries, where mechanical milk separators replaced the old pan-separating method, and cream was churned in large rotating boxes initially turned by a horse or mule, and later by a steam- or gasoline-powered engine. Food safety concerns led to the adoption of milk pasteurization in 1882, and sealed glass milk bottles in 1886.

The dairy ranchers themselves came to the valley in different waves. In the 1850s and 1860s, they were likely to be Irish farmers leaving behind hunger and oppression in the old country. In the 1880s, the typical dairy immigrant was an Italian-speaking Swiss, primarily from a small region along the Maggia River in the Canton of Ticino. By the 1890s, they were Portuguese, mostly from the Azores, or German from the Isle of Fohr.

Operating a dairy ranch wasn't easy. Typically, the whole family pitched in, and most dairy families were large—eight to 10 children were not uncommon. Cows had to be milked by hand twice daily, generally at 4 a.m. and 4 p.m. Prior to the introduction of the mechanical milking machine in 1894, milking a cow meant strapping on a one-legged milking stool and carrying a bucket to the cows grazing in the field. Each cow took 15 to 20 minutes to milk. If she moved away while being milked, the milker had to follow.

By 1905, the average dairy in the Petaluma River Watershed had a herd of 50 cows. While imported Jersey and Guernsey cows had initially been the most popular breeds due to the high butterfat content of their milk, the black-and-white Holstein became the preferred breed by the 1880s. Thanks to selective breeding, they produced the largest volumes of milk with the highest levels of butterfat for the making of butter and cheese.

By the 1920s and '30s, sleek concrete-and-steel sanitary milking barns began to replace the venerable wooden barns, and soon trucks came to take away the fresh milk in large cans. Petaluma River Watershed and West Marin gradually became a monoculture of Grade A milk and butter production, with only a few local cheese makers. Ranchers began sending their children off to agricultural schools like the University of California, Davis or Cal Poly, where they learned modern dairy management techniques, including the benefits of selective breeding for higher milk production. After the introduction of commercial artificial insemination in the 1940s, many local ranches switched to raising only purebred herds.

In the 1960s, large factory dairies begin springing up in the Central Valley with herds of 5,000 or more cows each, many of them confined to high-efficiency, non-grazing pens. To remain financially sustainable, local ranchers turned to improvements in cattle breeding, nutrition, and milking systems to increase the efficiency of their grass-fed herds. As a result, by the early 21st century Petaluma River Watershed's 69 existing dairies, with a combined herd of 30,000 cows, were producing more milk than the area had at its earlier peak in the 1950s, but with almost half the number of cows and a quarter the number of dairies. Milk prices, though, when adjusted for inflation, were less than half of what ranchers were paid in the 1950s. To remain financially sustainable, local dairies turned to niche products like organic milk and artisan cheeses that commanded premium prices in the market. By the 2010s, the dairies had created the largest concentration of artisan cheese makers outside of Vermont—a fitting legacy for Two Rock pioneer cheese maker Clara Steele.

Holstein milk cows grazing, Spring Hill Road

Boss Chicken Town

In the 1890s, chicken mania descended upon the Petaluma River Watershed. It would consume the region for the next 70 years. The genesis came in 1878, when an ailing, 26-year-old Canadian medical student named Lyman Byce arrived in the valley, seeking the health benefits from its Mediterranean sea breezes. That same mild climate, along with the valley's rich, alluvial soil, would set the stage for the chicken rage that followed.

Byce was a born tinkerer. As a boy, he and his father had experimented with developing an artificial incubator for chickens. By accelerating the hatching of newly laid eggs, an incubator freed the hen from her maternal nesting duties, allowing her to lay more eggs.

Soon after learning that San Francisco's demand for fresh eggs was exceeding local production, Byce went to have a tooth extracted by a young dentist named Isaac Dias, who had developed an incubator prototype. The two men perfected the prototype, which became the basis of Byce's Petaluma Incubator Company in 1884.

In 1880, a Danish farmer named Christopher Nisson purchased Byce's and Dias's incubator and used it to develop a new approach to raising poultry at his ranch in Two Rock. Nisson's Pioneer Hatchery became America's first commercial egg hatchery, drawing thousands of aspiring egg entrepreneurs to the area. Thanks to Byce and Nisson, by the 1890s, Petaluma had earned a reputation as "the boss chicken town of the Pacific Coast."

Chicken ranching would reign as Petaluma's foremost industry until the 1960s, by which time new farm factory techniques reduced the feathered kingdom from 4,000 small, independent chicken ranches to merely 300.

Here are the voices of some of those who lived through the years of chicken mania in Petaluma:

"Icy" Helgason (b. 1895, Iceland): From every sailor in those days, that's all you heard—chicken ranch! Just go around and pick up eggs. It was a sailor's dream.

Hilda Tiemann Keehn (b. 1911, Petaluma): My parents, John and Amalie Tiemann, were born in Germany and came to San Francisco at the turn of the century. After the 1906 earthquake, they rented a small chicken ranch in the Liberty District outside Petaluma, and then purchased a 14-acre ranch from my uncle in 1912. It had colony houses, a granary, barn, wagon shed, egg room, and a five-room residence. There were eight of us children.

Each spring a batch of 1,500 unsexed baby chicks were bought from the Pioneer Hatchery. In the fall, the chicks were culled to separate the pullets (young hens) from the cockerels (males). We had between 4,000 and 5,000 laying hens. We'd load the horse and wagon with cases of eggs to be delivered to the Poultry Producers in town each morning, a five-mile trip that took one hour. After dropping off the eggs and picking up empty cases, we'd load up the wagon with feed for the ride home.

Maxine Kortum Durney (b. 1921, Petaluma): My father, Max Kortum, came to Petaluma in 1921 as a poultry husbandry graduate of University of California, Davis, employed by the Sperry Flour Company, a local feed mill for the area's ranchers. My father visited the poultrymen to talk about feeds and feeding, the need for ventilation in the chicken houses, diseases and inoculations, etc. He introduced the idea of the balanced formula in the mash. It changed the way chickens were fed.

Paul Hantzche (b. 1915, Cotati): There were three kinds of chicken houses. First were the brooder houses where the baby chicks lived, warmed by a heater that was at first coal- and later gas-powered. Then there were the colony houses, especially in the Two Rock area where they had free range. These small houses could be towed by a team of horses to a new location. Finally, the regular long, redwood chicken houses that were "floor operations," with boards to catch droppings below the roosts.

Jack Haberer (b. 1924, Penngrove): The colony houses had maybe 50 birds. They were built on a sled and had a hole drilled in each end of them. You'd hitch a team to move them when there was a lot of chicken manure under them. You didn't need to clean them. You just pulled them to another spot.

Anna Hansen Harringan (b. 1920, Petaluma): Toward the end of the laying season, hens were examined to determine if they were still laying. If you got three fingers between the pelvic bones, she was considered to still be a layer. Those who had stopped laying were culled and sold for soup and fricassee.

Georgina Volkerts Evans (b. 1918, Petaluma): My mother acquired an incubator, which held up to 100

White leghorns, Tara Firma Farm, 3796 I Street

eggs. The eggs had to be turned in the incubator every single day. We converted a wood shed into a brooder house with a coke stove in the center for heating the baby chicks. The first few batches of pullets and broilers were profitable, but after a while they began to contract chicken diseases like coccidiosis.

Ruby Scott Eatherton (b. 1919, Mill Valley): My father performed autopsies on some birds to determine the cause of death. Sometime he would take them to the chicken pharmacy in town for their opinion. We tried many vaccines and capsules to prevent diseases. I hated those days when we had to catch chickens—smelly things!—and vaccinate under one wing, then force a pill down their throats. When they died they were sold to a "dead man" who picked them up once a week.

Anna Keyes Nielsen (b. 1903, Butte, Montana): My father, James E. Keyes, had been taught to compound medicines. Where he got the idea to establish a chicken pharmacy, I don't know. He must have talked to poultrymen who came in to buy potassium to clean their water troughs of algae. I went to work for him at the pharmacy, filling capsules with compounds he had devised.

Prue King Draper (b. 1931, Cleveland, Ohio): I was expected to collect and clean eggs every afternoon after school, help herd chicks under the brooder in the evening, and toss young hens up on the roost after dark, to keep them from smothering themselves in heaps in the corners. After full dark, we took our dogs and made rat raids on all the chicken houses.

Maxine Kortum Durney (b. 1921, Petaluma): Rats were a serious problem to the poultrymen. They not only carried disease but chewed holes in the sacks, ate the grain, and caused enormous waste. On the trail of a rat, our rat terrier Boleybop barked sharply before crawling fearlessly under the chicken houses. Then, facing the rat head on, he would grab and shake it in one incredibly fast snapping movement, breaking its back.

Bertha Praetzel (b. 1907, Petaluma): Poultry ranching took its toll on our social life. At community gatherings, when everybody else began to pull out the goodies for the second feast of the day, my father would say, "C'mon, kids, time to go home and gather the eggs." We used big, heavy willow baskets that lasted for years. Father would come around to the brooder houses driving our old plug, which is what you called a no-good horse, and he'd pick up the eggs we'd collected and take them to the egg house, where we had to clean them by hand in cold water and pack them. It was hard work.

Marjorie Forster Sobel (b. 1920, Co. Antrim, Ireland): Holding two eggs in your left hand and a shoe-buffer covered with fine sandpaper in your right, you learned how to dry-clean eggs by turning them and sanding them lightly to remove oily bits. This method brought higher prices but at the cost of the outside edges of your left-hand fingernails.

Jan Day Thompson (b. 1908, Baltimore, Maryland): Our Sunday meal was always chicken. Sometimes chicken and dumplings, sometimes fried chicken, sometimes roast chicken. My father killed the birds, my mother defeathered them, and I cleaned them. I loved to do it, especially to see the insides with all those little eggs.

Herbert Bundesen (b. 1924, Petaluma): Many of the Petaluma poultry farmers were Germans, Danes, and Swedes. A lot of Japanese were also in the business, but not so many Italians or Portuguese. They were mostly in the dairy business.

Martin Mickelson (b. 1900, Belegrade, Minnesota): Around Two Rock there were dairies and sheep but everyone also had a brooder house and chickens, perhaps only a thousand hens, but everyone had them.

Lavelle Marie Roderick Donovan (b. 1917, Petaluma): The hen houses were lit into the evening. The idea was to give the hens a longer day so they'd lay more eggs. In the dark, the countryside looked like a city with all the lighted hen houses.

Bill Murch (b. 1916, Minneapolis, Minnesota): During the peak hatching season, from the middle of February to the first of June, up to seven Railway Express cars left Petaluma every day, carrying commercial chicks to egg producers all over California. Thirty-nine hatcheries were in business in those days. Producers were paying attention to a chick's "nickability," meaning the ability to breed true.

Plymouth Rock chickens, Open Field Farm,
2245 Spring Hill Road

Emily Light Kelsey (b. 1893, Chileno Valley): I went to work for the Petaluma Incubator Company, on Petaluma Boulevard across from Hill Plaza Park [now Penry Park], in 1910 or 1911, typing and doing secretarial work for Lyman Byce, who had invented the chicken incubator. Byce did worldwide business as the largest manufacturer of incubators and brooders in the world. Some were large enough to hold thousands of eggs.

Maxine Kortum Durney (b. 1921, Petaluma): In the hatcheries, almost all of which were in downtown Petaluma, the eggs were placed in huge incubators and individual eggs were turned over three times a day with a rocker motion, in imitation of the sitting hen. Twenty-one days later, the chicks pecked their way out of the eggs and within a day were sexed.

Anna Hansen Harringan (b. 1920, Petaluma): Before chicken sexing was perfected, we had an old brooder house that was used as a rooster house. When we bought chicks they'd be a mixture of pullets and cockerels. As the cockerels became recognizable, developing a comb, they were moved to the rooster house and sent to market as meat birds at 11 or 12 months.

Heimer Carlson (b. 1915, San Francisco): We heard in high school that the Japanese were able to "sex" newly hatched chicks with a good degree of accuracy. In the fall of 1934, my high school agriculture teacher told me that the hatcheries in Petaluma had started a chick sexing school. This fascinated me and I hurried to enroll. Classes met five days a week at the Must Hatch Incubator Company. We worked under intense lights, 200 and 300 watts. We were looking for the infinitesimal bud, the cockerel eminence, half the size of a pinhead.

Tim Talamentes (b. 1905, Petaluma): My job at the H&N Hatchery was to dispose of the cockerels after the sexers got through. My boss wanted the males disposed of immediately to prevent somebody from starting a breeding farm with the H&N Hatchery strain. I put them in the garbage can right away and put the lid on. The mink man, who came at one o'clock each day, wanted the chicks freshly dead. We dumped the dead chicks in the bed of his truck, and he'd take them to his farm in Schellville to grind them up for his minks.

Verna Hogberg Vogle (b. 1912, Minneapolis, Minnesota): I was a candler. The candler looks at the egg against a light in a black boxlike arrangement, painted white inside and containing a mirror and a magnifying glass. We'd hold two eggs in each hand and roll them in such a way as to see the inside. Working quickly, we'd sort out those with blood spots or breaks in the shell, look for the size of the air cells, which determines freshness, and grade them for overall size, cleanliness, and quality.

Hideo Shimizu (b. 1905, Waipahu, Hawaii): During the Depression, we really struggled as we were quite in debt. The feed dealers—McNear, Golden Eagle, and the Crowleys—attached the ranch, but we continued to stay and work. We finally paid them off and everything was all right. Everybody was helping; everybody pitched in.

Walter Sorensen (b. 1911, Petaluma): During the Depression, when people were going under, my job was to collect chickens from farmers who owed money to the feed mill. It was a tough thing to do. The women would be crying. In some cases I'd pick the chickens up, pay Hunt and Behrens Feed Mill with my own money, then take most of the birds and put them back in the family's chicken houses. Then they could start buying grain again, as their slate was clean. I didn't get paid right away by the ranchers, but I'd get a little money from time to time.

Herbert Bundesen (b. 1924, Petaluma): There were two chicken industries in Petaluma, meat birds and layers. It was probably 40/60 at first, but later those proportions reversed. After the World War II, California had to compete with Georgia, Arkansas, and Mississippi, all of them working with a much lower cost basis. The interstate highway system went in and everyone got refrigerator trucks to transport chickens and eggs. The industry integrated vertically, eliminating profit layers. Operators did their own hatching, feeding, and processing.

Bill Murch (b. 1916, Minneapolis, Minnesota): Large-scale commercial table egg production, as opposed to small ranch production, appeared in the late '40s and '50s. The big breeders were producing small birds appropriate for cage operations. These birds had good livability, lower feed consumption, and good laying capacity. This seemed to happen overnight in the mind of the small breeder.

Abandoned chicken houses, 1096 Middle Two Rock Road

Horse Ranches

Theodore Skillman boarded the new transcontinental railroad in Oakland in March 1876 bound for Chicago to buy some horses. Petaluma had already established a reputation as the "Big Horse Market" of the Pacific Coast, with at least a half-dozen established breeders offering a wide selection of Clydesdale and English Draft horses. Skillman though was after a draft horse not yet popular west of the Mississippi River, the French Percheron. It was a gamble, but the sort of gamble Skillman seemed constitutionally inclined to take.

At age 19, he had sailed around Cape Horn from New Jersey to strike it rich in the California Gold Rush. Like many failed miners, he reverted instead to his apprenticed trade, opening a bakery in Grass Valley. After baking for eight years, he set out for the newly discovered Comstock Lode in Nevada, but the closest he got to the silver there was hauling ore from the mines as a teamster for five years.

In 1865, he settled in Petaluma, purchasing Magnolia Farm north of Petaluma on Old Redwood Highway and Skillman Lane. The 160-acre farm included a hotel, which Skillman operated for five years before becoming a wheat harvester. Steam-powered threshing machines had just arrived on the market, and Skillman quickly made a lucrative business of harvesting in the midst of California's wheat boom. He also purchased a steamroller and began acquiring large county contracts for compacting rural dirt roads with a crust of small broken stones—a process called macadamizing—as Petaluma's official "roadmaster." With the money he made from wheat harvesting and roadbuilding, Skillman set his sights in 1876 on a new passion—horse breeding.

After his train arrived in Chicago, Skillman traveled 50 miles south of the city to the River View Stock Farm of James Perry, America's premier importer and breeder of Percheron draft horses. Also known as Norman draft horses, the breed, with its short back, broad chest, wide rump, and arched neck, conveyed an impression of power and ruggedness. Only 80 Percherons had been imported to America from France prior to 1870, but the breed was quickly gaining popularity with farmers in the Midwest as an all-work horse given their good disposition, strength, and endurance. When crossed with thoroughbreds, they also made excellent carriage horses, especially for the cobblestoned streets of hilly cities like San Francisco.

Skillman returned to Petaluma with a boxcar of five brood mares and a stallion named Superior. He wasted no time displaying them at Petaluma's Agricultural Park, where they caused an immediate sensation. Located on Fair Street and Western Avenue (the present-day site of Petaluma High School), the Agricultural Park had been created in 1867 for the annual Sonoma-Marin District Fair. The 10-acre fair site featured a half-mile track for horse racing and a large pavilion for annual exhibits of livestock, cereal, fruits, and vegetables from Sonoma, Marin, Mendocino, Lake, and Napa counties.

Skillman's big gamble began to pay off immediately after the fair. While continuing his wheat threshing and roadbuilding, he converted his Magnolia Farm into a breeding stock farm and began to compete with local breeders of Clydesdales and English Draft horses. The deck was stacked against him in that stock breeding was a rich man's sport, dominated in the 1870s by two of Petaluma's wealthiest ranchers, William Bihler and Harrison Meacham.

A German immigrant who operated a stock farm on his 8,000-acre ranch in Lakeville, Bihler had arrived in Gold Rush San Francisco in 1849 at the age of 19, apprenticing as a butcher before becoming a partner in a Napa cattle ranch. He purchased his ranch in Lakeville in 1859. That same year he began importing horse stock from England, including Young England's Glory, said to be the finest English Draft stallion in America.

Harrison Meacham had run away to the Gold Rush from his home in Iowa at the age of 15. Unlike Skillman, he had made a small fortune in the mines, which he invested in a 7,000-acre ranch northwest of Petaluma. Meacham bred Clydesdales, including a stallion named Pollock that he had imported from Scotland. Pollock was considered the best of his breed on the West Coast.

The main competitive advantage Skillman had with his Percherons was the horse's foot. Shaped like an upside-down teacup, it gave the horse the strength and stability of a mule, especially on the slippery cobblestones of San Francisco, where the English Draft horse, whose foot was shaped like an inverted dinner plate, tended to give way, resulting in crippled joints. As a result, Percherons quickly became a favorite among businesses employing draft horses in the city.

In the spring of 1877, Skillman joined with a small group of breeders to purchase the country's top-rated Percheron stallion, Duke de Chartres, from James Perry in Illinois. By the late 1870s, West Coast demand for

Horses grazing, Horick Ranch, 2170 Chileno Valley Road

Percherons was such that Perry himself began importing horses directly from France to Petaluma. Meanwhile, Skillman, having established his Magnolia Farm as California's chief Percheron importer and breeder, opened Petaluma Stables, a horse sales outlet on Petaluma Boulevard North adjacent to Main Street Plaza (present-day Penry Park). In 1884, he began traveling himself directly to France to purchase horses. The following year, with horse breeding having become one of the largest sources of revenue in Sonoma County, Skillman was elected vice president of the National Association of Importers and Breeders of Norman Horses.

By that time, Agricultural Park had outgrown its Fair Street location and was beginning to pose traffic problems on the west side of town. More importantly, the park's racetrack, only a half-mile long, had a rock stratum beneath its surface that many horsemen considered unsafe, deterring racing entries. In 1882, the Sonoma and Marin Agricultural Society purchased 60 acres of a ranch on the east side of town along Payran Street formerly owned by Judge Stephen Payran, an early justice of the peace in Petaluma during the 1860s. At the new park they constructed a mile-long track. While not ideal for winter racing because of its adobe soil, it was one of the fastest summer tracks in the state, reviving horse racing in Petaluma.

In 1895, with California in the midst of a national recession, the newly elected governor, James Budd, eliminated the state subsidy paid to district fairs such as Petaluma's as part of a new tax reform initiative. The Sonoma and Marin County Agricultural Society raised enough private funding to mount one last fair in 1895, after which they closed down the annual fair at Agricultural Park. Shortly thereafter, Theodore Skillman moved his stock farm to the San Joaquin Valley, where he resided until his passing in 1910.

With the increasing use of tractors and automobiles in the early 1900s, the need for draft horses rapidly declined, and the horse industry shifted to entertainment and competition shows, including rodeos. In 1902, Harry Stover, a well-known California racehorse owner, purchased Petaluma's dormant 60-acre Agricultural Park, along with 50 adjacent acres, for breeding and training his horses. He renamed the facility Kenilworth Park in honor of his champion racehorse Kenilworth. In 1909, Stover died while attending a horse race at his track in Salt Lake City. Two years later, Petaluma approved a 20-year, $20,000 bond to purchase Kenilworth Park, converting it into a municipal park for baseball games, horse racing, rodeos, and a public campground. The Sonoma-Marin District Fair returned to staging annual fairs at the park in 1936, converting the horse race track to auto racing.

During the 1960s and 1970s, the Petaluma area saw another brief boom in horse breeding, thanks in part to a tax law that allowed part-time horse ranchers to write off horse show expenses as an alternative business. After the tax law was changed, many people sold their horses, and attendance at local shows declined. Beginning in the 1990s, an influx of wealthy horse owners drawn to the area led to an increase in horse ownership and equestrian events, once again making Petaluma and the rest of Sonoma County a key West Coast equine center.

Pegasus Ranch, 6525 Lakeville Highway

Sheep Ranches

When the Great Depression hit in the 1930s, Bernard Groverman scrambled like other ranchers to diversify. Oversupplied markets kept prices so low for eggs, milk, and produce that ranchers saw little or no financial return for their efforts. Small ranchers who had borrowed money to purchase their ranches or to fund expansion during Petaluma's egg boom in the 1920s were especially vulnerable. Many lost their ranches by foreclosure to the banks and grain mills, or else became sharecroppers, working for larger landowners who had swallowed up their ranches in foreclosure.

Bernard Groverman was 10 years old when his family moved from San Francisco to Petaluma following the 1906 earthquake. His father, a German immigrant, drove a brewery wagon for Rainier Beer. His distribution route extended north to Petaluma, which had been relatively untouched by the quake. Leaving behind the devastation in San Francisco, the family relocated to a chicken ranch northeast of downtown Petaluma on Corona Road. When America entered World War I, Bernard, who was 21, enlisted in the army, and sailed off to France to join in the fight. Upon his return in 1919, he purchased 50 acres of land on Ormsby Lane, adjacent to his father's ranch on Corona Road, and for the next 10 years rode the egg boom, eventually expanding his flock to 8,000 laying chickens.

After the bottom fell out of the egg market in the early 1930s, Groverman added meat birds, horses, milk cows, veal, hay, and vegetables to his ranch. He even tried his hand at sheep ranching, acquiring six Shropshire ewes, an English breed raised primarily as meat lambs. It would prove a fateful decision.

Sheep were first introduced to the Petaluma River Watershed in 1823 by the Franciscan padres who had established the Mission San Francisco de Solano in Sonoma. Sheepmen in Spain, concerned about potential overseas competition, refused to send the Franciscans their fine-wool Merinos, and instead provided them with sheep of very coarse wool. Upon secularization of the Sonoma mission in 1834, Mexican comandante Mariano Vallejo of the Petaluma Adobe assumed ownership of the mission's sheep flock. He also sent the mission's administrator, an Irishman named Timothy Murphy, to England to purchase purebred sheep of medium-coarse wool. Unlike the fine wool of Merinos, sheep with medium-coarse wool were capable of shedding water, which was important in Petaluma's foggy climate. Their wool was also more suitable than heavy coarse wool for weaving blankets and clothing.

Vallejo's flock quickly grew to 3,000. Well fed and tended, they were guarded by day and herded into corrals at night as a defense against marauding grizzly bears. Annual shearing time was marked by a large fiesta, after which the clipped wool was tied in bundles and taken to Vallejo's Petaluma Adobe, where it was woven by Coast Miwok women into blankets, rugs, and cloth. A portion of the flock was also slaughtered each year for their meat and pelts, which were then exported on Yankee ships to Europe for the making of shoes and leather goods.

By the 1840s, the domesticated sheep population in all of California numbered more than two million head. With the discovery of gold in 1848, the sudden influx of fortune seekers created an enormous demand for fresh meat, raising the price of sheep to $12 a head ($350 in early 21st-century-currency). Within two years, there were only 17,000 head of sheep left in the entire state.

As settlers descended upon California in the 1850s, half a million sheep were imported on overland drives from the southwest or on ships from Australia. Enterprising ranchers also began importing sheep with finer wool from Vermont, New York, Ohio, and Pennsylvania. By 1875, there were six million head of sheep in California, producing 56 million pounds of wool per year. That same year, a German immigrant named Sol Dannenbaum built the Petaluma Woolen Mills beside McNear Canal, serving as an anchor for grain merchant John McNear's dream of a factory district in Petaluma. The three-story mill quickly became known for its quality flannel and woolen blankets.

In the 1880s and 1890s, local sheep flocks began to decline due to increased competition on the international market and to competition for grazing lands from local cattle and dairy ranchers. Petaluma Woolen Mills burned down in 1898 and was not replaced. After the turn of the century, sheep ranchers began moving away from wool production to raising meat lambs, relying on advances in selective breeding to enhance their flocks. By the time Bernard Groverman purchased his Shropshires in 1934, lamb constituted about 65 percent of a sheep rancher's income, with the remaining 35 percent coming from wool.

During the 1930s, in addition to declining prices for eggs, dairy products, and produce, ranchers like Bernard Groverman also faced labor challenges. Beginning with

Flock of sheep, Lakeville

the Santa Clara pea harvest in the spring of 1933, worker strikes erupted throughout California as each crop ripened that year for picking—cherry, grape, peach, pear, sugar beet, tomato, and cotton. The strikers—some of whom were earning less than 75 cents a day ($13 in early-21st-century currency) and, according to a federal commission, living in "filth, squalor and an entire absence of sanitation"—were demanding better wages, improved living conditions, and a unionized hiring hall. In 1934, a large strike of lettuce and vegetable workers was followed by the legendary longshoremen strike that lasted 83 days, crippling West Coast shipping of agricultural goods and leading to a general strike in San Francisco that ground the city to a virtual standstill.

In response, alarmed growers and ranchers formed an alliance called the Associated Farmers. Though publicly appealing to the interests of small farmers and ranchers, the group was in fact funded by the large corporate farms that produced more than 50 percent of the state's agriculture, along with many of the state's largest businesses and utilities, including the California Packing Corporation, the Bank of America, Pacific Gas & Electric Company, and the major railroad companies that transported agriculture products. With their backing, the Associated Farmers quickly became a significant political force in California, advocating for anti-union laws, ensuring passage of anti-picketing and strike ordinances, and seeing to it that striking laborers were denied federal public relief, an initiative known as "No work – No eat."

In association with the Chamber of Commerce and fraternal organizations such as the American Legion, the Elks, the Moose, and the Native Sons of the Golden West, the Associated Farmers used the strikes as a pretext for cracking down on radicalism, which they defined as factions of the labor movement aligned with the Communist and Socialist parties, both of which were legal voting parties at the time in California. They mobilized vigilante groups to take up arms against the striking workers, racking up a record of brutality across California that was characterized by the *Nation* magazine as "organized terrorism."

In 1935, Sonoma County found itself at the center of the laborer-grower battle. That same year, the newly created Congress of Industrial Organizations (CIO) split off from the American Federation of Labor (AFL) in an effort to organize California's 250,000 unskilled agricultural workers. The CIO called for a $3 minimum daily wage ($50 in early-21st-century currency), an eight-hour day with time and a half for overtime, a 25-day month, adequate housing, and a union shop.

During a strike of Sebastopol apple pickers in July 1935, vigilantes violently broke up a meeting of labor organizers at Santa Rosa's Germania Hall with clubs and sticks. Weeks later, on the eve of a threatened strike by hop pickers, vigilantes abducted five labor organizers from their homes in the dead of night, beat them, and demanded that they kneel and kiss the American flag. When two of the men refused—World War I veterans Sol Nitzberg, a Petaluma chicken rancher, and Jack Green, a Santa Rosa sign painter—they were stripped of their shirts, doused in crankcase oil and pillow feathers, and then marched through Santa Rosa's Courthouse Square as a mob of drunken vigilantes circled the square in cars, honking their horns and firing guns in the air.

Among the 23 prominent Sonoma County men arrested and charged with kidnapping, assault with a deadly weapon, and other felonies was Petaluma businessman Robert J. McClain. Charges were subsequently dropped against McClain because he was undergoing a medical operation in San Francisco. In December 1936, four months after his surgery, McClain was elected president of the newly formed Sonoma County unit of the Associated Farmers. Joining him as officers were John Watson, a Petaluma dairyman, and Bernard Groverman.

By that time Groverman had become one of the most prominent farm leaders in the county, serving as an officer of the Sonoma County Farm Bureau and president of the Petaluma branch of the Poultry Producers of Central California, a marketing cooperative. Along with McClain and Watson, Groverman hit the county speaking circuit as a spokesman for the Associated Farmers. Their position was that while that the group had no problem with "old-time trade unionism," by which they meant the collective bargaining of skilled laborers, when it came to unskilled farm workers they felt that wages should fluctuate with farm commodity prices, making workers share the same risks as the farmers who employed them. They portrayed the efforts of the CIO as "labor racketeering" and an encroachment of socialism on the American way of life.

Also having a great impact on California agriculture in the 1930s was the Dust Bowl, which spawned an epic migration of refugees from Texas, Oklahoma, Kansas, New Mexico, and Colorado. At first, growers and ranch-

Sheep on Open Field Farm, 2245 Hill Road, Chileno Valley

ers were happy with the surplus of labor flooding into the state, which made it easier to push down wages on the state's 200,000 seasonal laborers, most of whom were either contracted Mexicans or Mexican-Americans. But as labor tensions built, Mexican and Mexican-Americans became targets of discrimination, blamed by the immigrating whites for the high unemployment. Busloads were repatriated to Mexico. Their replacements, derisively referred to as "arkies" and "okies," were accustomed to a mode of independence as farmers themselves. Finding the wages too low to support themselves and their families, many mustered their courage to support the labor movement. Their struggle was profiled in John Steinbeck's 1939 *The Grapes of Wrath*, a book the Associated Farmers dismissed as "lies" and "communist propaganda," and destroyed in public book burnings.

Meanwhile, farmworker strikes continued. In 1936, West Marin milkers went on strike demanding two days off per month instead of no days, and $2.16 a day for each milker who handled 30 cows ($35 in early-21st-century currency). Dairy ranchers resorted to hiring scabs and transporting their milk to San Francisco in armed convoys. In 1938, Bernard Groverman addressed the Sonoma-Marin Wool Growers Association, whose members were facing a strike by teamsters. The sheepmen decided to circumvent the teamsters' strike by shipping their wool via rail. In 1940, Petaluma poultry workers staged a strike demanding to be recognized as part of the butchers union. As president of the local Poultry Producers co-op, Groverman pushed back.

By 1940, Petaluma dairyman John Watson had been elected state president of the Associated Farmers, and Bernard Groverman president of the Sonoma County unit, with businessman and accused vigilante Robert J. McClain serving as his secretary. All three men found themselves under investigation that year by the LaFollete Civil Liberties Committee of the U.S. Senate over the Associated Farmers' anti-union activities. Watson argued in the press that the LaFollete Committee had it wrong—it was rights of the farmers, not the workers, that had been violated. When the committee asked Groverman to produce records of the Sonoma County unit, Groverman was evasive, informing them that the records were in the hands of Secretary McClain, who had "gone east to buy a new car."

Following America's entry into World War II in 1941, most labor unions agreed to a "No-Strike Pledge" for the duration of the war. With 10 percent of the population in the military, and West Coast shipyards and defense plants generating thousands of new jobs, the country reached its highest level of employment in American history. The wartime economy also brought new prosperity to agriculture for the first time in a decade. With the commencement of the Cold War following World War II, Congress passed the Taft-Harley Act, which limited strikes and required unions to sign anti-Communist affidavits. With these legislative changes, the Associated Farmers diminished in importance, eventually folding up in the mid-1960s.

After the war, Bernard Groverman transitioned to raising turkeys on the ranch, while also continuing to expand his flock of Shropshire sheep. In 1950, working with veterinarians from the University of California, Davis, he bred his sheep with a purebred Shropshire ram from England, making his flock among the oldest line of Shropshire in the world. The following year, Groverman died unexpectedly, leaving his 17-year-old son, Fred, a freshman at the University of California, Davis, to run the ranch. After finishing college, Fred Groverman returned to Petaluma, where he became a well-known veterinarian, sheep rancher, and civic leader.

In the mid-20th century, local sheep ranchers were faced, like local dairy and chicken ranchers, with the rising cost of feed and increased competition from factory feedlots in Central California. They also faced stiff foreign competition from New Zealand and Australia. Beginning in the 1980s, new predators, like coyotes, resulted in ranchers importing Great Pyrenees dogs and llamas for protecting their flocks.

In the early 21st century, with the price of wool barely covering the cost of shearing, sheep ranchers moved to balancing economic viability with environmental stewardship, relying on natural, grass-fed meat lambs and niche boutique products to remain financially sustainable. Bellwether Farms in Two Rock began raising East Friesen, a breed of Northern European milk sheep whose milk was good for cheese making. Haverton Hill Creamery, also in Two Rock, specialized in pasteurized sheep milk. Petaluma River Watershed and West Marin became part of the first designated Fibershed, a regional network comprising local sheep ranchers and clothing designers, weavers, knitters, and natural dyers working with wool. Meanwhile, Fred Groverman continued to maintain his flock of purebred Shropshires.

Shropshire sheep, Groverman Ranch, 400 Ormsby Lane

The Petaluma Gap

In 1823, Padre José Altimira, a 36-year-old Franciscan priest in charge of Mission San Francisco de Asis, or Mission Dolores, led an expedition of 20 soldiers across the marshlands of San Pablo Bay into the hills of present-day Lakeville in search of a suitable site for a new mission for converting the local natives. There he found a freshwater lake covering more than 300 acres. The natives camped beside the lake called it Tolay, after one of their former chiefs. The padre, worried that the lake was surrounded by too many tules to provide easy access to drinking water, continued east with his party until they came to the Sonoma Valley, where they found a freshwater creek and nearby springs. On that site he built Mission San Francisco de Solano.

Padre Altimira's stay at the new mission lasted only a few years before his religious zealotry and harsh treatment of the natives provoked an uprising. But prior to his sudden departure in 1826, he planted Sonoma County's first small vineyard of Mission grapes. Imported to California from Spain by Franciscan missionaries in the 1780s, the Mission grape was used primarily for making sacramental wine.

When the Mexican government decided to secularize the California missions in 1834, Lieutenant Mariano Vallejo of the San Francisco Presidio was sent to assume charge of Mission San Francisco de Solano in Sonoma. He was also granted 66,600 acres of land extending from the Sonoma Estero west to the Petaluma River that he named Rancho Petaluma. The next year, Vallejo sailed up the Petaluma River with 80 cavalrymen and disembarked at the Lakeville landing, then known as the Padre Ventura, where he made a treaty with members of the local Lekituit tribelet before sailing back down to San Pablo Bay and making his way up the Sonoma Estero to Mission Solano. There he built a new pueblo and presidio for his troops. Using cuttings from the mission's grapevines, he started his own vineyard, moving winemaking from the altar to the dining table, and becoming one of the county's top wine producers.

During the 1840s and 1850s, Mission grapevines began taking root throughout Sonoma County, with the exception of the Petaluma River Watershed, where the Mission grape had trouble maturing. This was thought to be because of the Petaluma Gap—an opening in the coastal mountain range northwest of the valley that allowed fog to drift in from the Pacific during the summer. The valley's rich, sandy loam soil was also considered a problem. Grapes flourish best in poor soil, where the roots are made to work harder in sending nutrients to the fruit and not the foliage. The Petaluma River Watershed's soil yielded too much foliage on the vines, shading the grape clusters and stunting their growth.

Then, in 1856, winemaking in Sonoma County took a dramatic turn with the arrival of Agoston Haraszthy, a Hungarian nobleman who purchased a vineyard in Sonoma from Mariano Vallejo's brother, Salvador, renaming it Buena Vista. One of the first things Haraszthy did was plant vines on the hillsides, disproving the belief of the Franciscans padres that irrigation was required for growing grapes. Commissioned by the state legislature in 1861 to study European viticulture overseas, Haraszthy returned to Sonoma County a year later with nearly 200,000 rooted vines and cuttings taken from 300 grape varieties in France, Germany, Italy, and Spain. The vastly better wines made from Haraszthy's European vines set off a "grape rush" in the county among the influx of farmers seeking riches form the land.

Many of the early grape growers in Sonoma County were German immigrants, among them a cattle rancher named William Bihler. Bihler immigrated to America with his parents at age nine. His family settled in Baltimore, where the young William apprenticed as a butcher. In 1848, at the age of 20, Bihler sailed via Cape Horn to San Francisco, continuing in his trade as a butcher for two years before becoming a partner in a Napa County cattle ranch. In 1859, he purchased 8,000 acres of Vallejo's former Rancho Petaluma, creating a ranch that included Tolay Lake and extended east from Lakeville almost to Sonoma. He anchored the ranch with a large Italianate Victorian home in Lakeville.

A lifelong bachelor, Bihler set out to raise cattle and draft horses on a large scale, importing some of the best-bred stock in the county, including Durham bulls and a celebrated draft stallion named Young England's Glory. Not satisfied with the number of potatoes he planted on the land around Tolay Lake, he dynamited the southern end of the lake's natural dam, allowing the water to run out into the San Pablo Bay where it created "Bihler's Slough." On the 300 acres of fertile dry lakebed he planted a potato and beet patch.

OPPOSITE: *Keller Estate, 5875 Lakeville Highway*

OVERLEAF LEFT: *Site of Tolay Lake, drained in the 1860s*

OVERLEAF RIGHT: *Italianate Victorian home built by William Bihler, 6614 Lakeville Highway, circa 1871*

By 1880, California winemakers were producing more than 10 million gallons of wine, 90 percent of which were foreign varieties. Looking to join the grape bonanza, Bihler set out to dispel the belief that grapes grown in the Petaluma Gap would not mature in time for winemaking. In 1874, he successfully planted 90 acres of early grapes such as Zinfandel and Malvoisie on the tidewater banks of the Petaluma River and in the hills and dry bed of Tolay Lake, expanding the vineyard to 200 acres in 1881. He was joined in his quest by two Petaluma farmers, J.W. Cassidy, known for his large cherry orchard in West Petaluma's Cherry Valley, and J.G. Staedler. In 1881, the *Sonoma Democrat* heralded their efforts, singling out Cassidy:

> Standing in front of the American Hotel was a wagon load of grapes, brought to market for table use, grown on the farm of J.W. Cassidy on the Bloomfield Road about two miles from Petaluma. This impromptu exhibit of Petaluma grapes gave a flat contradiction to the oft-repeated assertion that the climate and soil in the neighborhood of Petaluma is not adapted to grape culture. Finer specimens of the products of the vine we have nowhere seen, than those in Mr. Cassidy's wagon.

By 1884, the same newspaper was also applauding Bihler for having one of the finest vineyards in the county. Clouding Petaluma's emerging wine industry however, was an infestation called *Phylloxera vastatrix*, or root louse, which arrived in Sonoma County in 1873, destroying numerous vineyards. Bihler maintained that the deep soil in Lakeville prevented phylloxera, a theory supported at the time by Sonoma County's wine commissioner, Isaac DeTurck. While the outbreaks in California were largely localized and initially slow to spread, in Europe phylloxera devastated millions of acres of vineyards after the French imported California vines in an attempt to produce a hybrid able to combat another fungal disease called *oidium*. Swallowing their pride, the French restored their vineyards by grafting their vinestocks to a phylloxera-resistant California rootstock.

In 1891, Bihler, struggling with health issues, sold his Lakeville ranch to James G. Fair, an Irish immigrant who had tried farming in the area earlier before striking it rich in the Comstock silver mines. Fair had also served as a U.S. Senator of Nevada. He added 300 acres of vines to Bihler's 200 acres, and imported a state-of-the-art distillery from France that he installed on the site of an old brick armory built by Mariano Vallejo along the Petaluma River. By 1893, the winery had a capacity of 600,000 gallons. A year later, in 1894, Fair died. Ten years after his death, his daughters sold the ranch to Arthur W. Foster, president of the Northwestern Pacific Railroad, who operated it for the next two decades.

By 1911, California was producing almost 90 percent of the 50 million gallons of wine made in America, much of it coming from Sonoma County. At the time Prohibition was imposed in 1920, Sonoma County had 256 wineries with more than 22,000 acres of grapes in production. Only 50 wineries survived Prohibition's 13-year ban on the production, sale, and transportation of alcohol. Those that did were restricted to making "sacramental" wine for churches and "medicinal" wine prescribed by doctors for the epidemic of "sore throats" that accompanied Prohibition. James Fair's winery and cooperage built along the river reportedly became a speakeasy that nighttime patrons traveled to by boat.

Thanks to a legislative loophole in the Volstead Act of 1920, 200 gallons of wine were permitted yearly for home production and consumption. Grape growers continued to flourish during Prohibition largely because of the demand for grapes from home winemakers. In 1930, 21,300 acres of grapes were in production in Sonoma County, almost reaching pre-Prohibition figures. After Prohibition ended in 1933, the return of viticulture in the Petaluma Gap was dealt a lethal blow by another outbreak of phylloxera. Grapes didn't substantially return to the area until the 1990s, when the Gap's similarity to the nearby Carneros grape-growing region along foggy San Pablo Bay convinced ranchers to begin replacing their grazing lands with vineyards. More than three-quarters of the acreage was planted with pinot noir grapes, and the rest with chardonnay and syrah.

In 1996, the Hendricks family purchased 150 acres of the original Bihler ranch, restoring Bihler's Italianate Victorian house on the property and constructing a Spanish mission-style home on the original Fair Winery site. In a nod to Bihler's legacy, they planted 50 acres of grapes and installed a large horse facility on their Rockin' H Ranch. In 2017, the Petaluma Gap, comprising 4,000 acres of wineries in Lakeville and the Petaluma area, was formally recognized as Sonoma County's 18th appellation.

In the foreground, the Rockin' H Ranch (formerly part of the Bihler Ranch), 6614 Lakeville Highway

Part III: The River Town

Petaluma lay like a jewel, glowing in the sunlight on the plain. The white cottages of the residential district spilled into town from the rolling slopes of the mesa west of the creek.

William T. Ortman

Downtown Petaluma looking west

The River Town

Like most cities, Petaluma began as a market town along a trade route. In October 1850, Tom Lockwood, a meat hunter, rowed up the Petaluma River in a whaleboat with two companions in search of wild game to feed the throngs of people pouring into San Francisco. The men set up camp along the river at an abandoned Coast Miwok village, where they built a trading post. They were joined a few months later by other hunters and an enterprising squatter named Garrett Keller.

Although the land along the river was part of a 13,000-acre Mexican land grant known as the Rancho Arroyo de San Antonio, the brazen Keller made his own claim to 158 acres of it, and with the help of Lockwood and a surveyor named J.E. Brewster, laid out the streets for a town he called Petaluma (the name derived from a nearby Coast Miwok village of the same name). Keller then opened a real estate office on the riverbanks at Washington Street, and began selling property to unsuspecting new settlers for $10 a lot.

The Treaty of Guadalupe Hidalgo, which ended the Mexican-American War in 1848, honored the legal standing of the Mexican land grants. But squatters, like Keller, believed it their right to stake homestead claims on any unused land they found, as was the practice in other parts of the American frontier. They were encouraged by one of California's two newly elected U.S. senators, William McKendree Gwin, who in 1851 pushed through Congress the Act to Settle Private Land Claims in California. A bonanza to Yankee lawyers, the act set up a three-man land commission to review all Mexican land claims under American law, subjecting grantholders to a laborious legal appeals process. Along with predatory property taxes imposed by the new state of California, the act forced many Mexican grant holders to sell out to their Yankee lawyers or else to scheming land speculators. Others abandoned their claims altogether. Those who chose to pursue the appeals process often spent a decade or two in litigation before usually losing out in court. Despite the injustices inflicted by the act, under the framework of American law, the great California land grab was all perfectly legal.

In the case of Petaluma, it would take the courts 20 years to sort out the city's tangled legal ownership. In the meantime, the city of Petaluma was incorporated in 1858, as its new citizens set out to build a market town in accordance with Keller's original map.

The city's location on the banks of the Petaluma River, a tidal slough that extended south to the San Pablo Bay, made it the primary port for shipping surplus crops from Sonoma County's agricultural lands to San Francisco. Initially, a shipping run to the city required up to three days to navigate, as the 16 miles of tidal slough contained 88 bends, and the tide rose and fell twice a day, making the shallow stretches impassable for hours. As farmers went about reconfiguring the valley floor, rechanneling tributary creeks and reclaiming freshwater wetlands and tidal marshes, they contributed to a buildup of silt and debris in the slough, further impeding boat passage. Efforts to straighten and dredge the slough—formally known as the "Petaluma Creek" until 1959, when an act of Congress designated it a "river" in order to qualify it for federal dredging funds—began in 1859. It would remain an ongoing effort into the 21st century.

While Petaluma remained a vibrant agricultural center for its first century, its primacy as an agricultural port changed in 1870 after the new San Francisco & North Pacific Railroad bypassed the town as its southern railhead. The city stagnated until the 1890s, when the local invention of an innovative egg incubator set off an egg boom. Eggs, along with a thriving dairy industry, drove the city's prosperity and growth for the next half century. By the time of Petaluma's official centennial in 1958, however, the dairy and poultry industries were in serious decline, victims of the rise of large factory farms in the Central Valley and American South. The loss of its agricultural base set the city on a downward spiral.

U.S. Highway 101, which opened in 1956, offered Petaluma a chance to reinvent itself as a bedroom community for commuters working in San Francisco. Tract houses and shopping malls sprang up on the flat ranchlands along the new freeway east of the downtown. After the city's population dramatically tripled from 10,000 in 1950 to 30,000 by 1972, Petaluma applied the brakes, becoming the first city in the nation to successfully impose growth controls to protect its livability. In the mid-1970s, an effort began to restore the city's historic downtown. To further protect the city's heritage as an agricultural market town and its surrounding greenbelt, the city voted in 1998 to adopt a 20-year urban growth boundary.

Iron-front buildings along Western Avenue, built 1880s

Main Street

Three of Petaluma's early settlers responsible for building the city were John McNear, Issac Wickersham, and Hiram Fairbanks. A successful gold miner, Fairbanks invested his riches in building the Golden Eagle Mill and the Petaluma Savings Bank, before serving three terms as president (mayor) of the city trustees. Wickersham also made his fortune in the Gold Rush. A lawyer by training, he opened Sonoma County's first bank in Petaluma in 1865, and became an early investor in many rail and industrial enterprises. McNear, a Maine sea captain, started out in town as a grain mill merchant before opening the Bank of Sonoma County and helping to develop a number of Petaluma's early factories.

One night in the late 1890s, the three men gathered with Galen Burdell, one of the area's largest landowners, at the Liberty Street home of Burdell's nephew, George Ortman, to reminisce about the town's early days. Ortman's son, William, captured their conversation.

Hiram Fairbanks: When I arrived in Petaluma in November of 1853, a pall of smoke hung over the place from burning brush and leaves. About the first ones I became acquainted with were Tom Baylis and Dave Flogdell. They were partners and had a store on the bank of the creek opposite the Odd Fellows Hall. They took up with Tom Lockwood and his companions, Pendleton and Levi Pyburn. These men all hunted for the San Francisco market.

John McNear: When I arrived during the year 1856, there were but 12 houses in the settlement, and little more than 1,200 souls in the entire valley. I remember the little trading post on the bend of the river, just above the Washington Street Bridge built in 1851 by a man named Lemarcus Wiatt. He had a partner named John Lemus. These two men were not the first in the area by any means. There was Dr. August Heyerman—a lot of you remember Gus—who built the first log cabin. That was in the early part of 1850. Later that same year—in October—Tom Lockwood and the two other men camped in the oak grove after coming to the area to hunt for game.

Isaac Wickersham: Being a lawyer, I immediately hung out my shingle when I arrived in 1852. There were not many people living in the hamlet at the time, but there were a number of settlers on farms in the valley. Land was plentiful and cheap. Money was scarce and hard to come by. I had money accumulated while practicing law in Keokuk, Iowa. That money, I loaned out.

The law business wasn't much in those days, so I did various other work. In the summer of 1854, I cut 300 tons of wild hay on the flat just north of the Washington Street Bridge. There was a good profit in the crop. I had heard there was in San Francisco a machine someone had brought by ship from the East. It was a sickle-bar mower—the first in Northern California. I bought it and a horse. That mower amazed me with its speed and ease.

Hiram Fairbanks: Speaking of cutting that 300 tons of hay, I have been waiting to hear you speak of that German fellow who cut wild oats down south of town. His named was Adolph Gericke. He did the job alone and heaped the hay in stacks along the creek for shipment to San Francisco. For some reason or other, the hay didn't sell. He left it standing. That is how the place got its name of the Haystacks.

Isaac Wickersham: Petaluma was carved from a wilderness. Tree stumps dotted the settlement. I remember that for many years a huge redwood stump occupied the spot which is now the center of Main and Washington streets. No one ever did anything about it. A time came, however, when civic pride rebelled and the unsightly thing was removed.

In 1854, being a lawyer, I was elected district attorney of Sonoma County. I mention it because I had to earn money and that was one way of doing it. I bought a lot on Main and Washington streets. It was in close proximity of the redwood stump. When the redwood stump was burned and the two streets were lined up at right angles, it turned out that I had a corner lot, although it did contain other stumps which had to be burned off.

Galen Burdell: Petaluma was a busy little town when I first visited in December of 1863. There was much shipping going on. I remember standing on the creek bank and watching a scow being loaded with hay. A schooner, loaded with sacks of grain, was being maneuvered about in a high tide, to be in position to leave.

The bank of the stream was stacked high with sacks of potatoes. Much fruit, vegetables, grain, hay, and varying kinds of meat were shipped to San Francisco by sloop, steamer, scow, and schooner.

Petaluma Boulevard North and Western Avenue

Cedar Grove

In 1904, Adolph Bloom returned to Petaluma from a long honeymoon in Southern California with his new bride, Eva, and purchased a home on 34 acres north of downtown known as Cedar Grove. Only 31 years old, Adolph was already one of the wealthiest men in Petaluma. The oldest son of Swiss immigrants, he had grown up on a large cattle ranch in Chileno Valley established by his father. Following his father's death, Adolph, then only 20, assumed charge of the ranch and along with his younger brother, Americo, formed the Bloom Company. By the turn of the century, the company's holdings had grown to include a couple of thousand acres of ranchland, 10,000 white leghorn chickens, herds of milk cows, cattle, goats, and horses, and a creamery that turned out some of the finest-quality butter and cheese in the area.

Adolph's marriage to Eva and his purchase of Cedar Grove were his first steps in breaking out of the family ranching business and becoming a man of importance in Petaluma. Cedar Grove was a trophy home of significant historical importance. Originally a Coast Miwok trading village called Lekituit, the site was widely celebrated as the first Yankee settlement in the Petaluma River Watershed (although it was in fact the third). Tom Lockwood, a failed gold miner, had piloted a whaleboat up the Petaluma River in 1850 with two companions, Levi Pyburn and a man named Pendelton, in search of wild game to sell to hungry miners in San Francisco. The men set up camp at the site of the old Lekituit village, depopulated like most native villages for more than a decade due to smallpox and syphilis transmitted by the Spanish and Mexican colonists. They were soon joined by a handful of other enterprising Yankees, and together established a small trading post.

After Petaluma was platted into real estate lots in 1852, the Lekituit property changed hands a couple of times. In the early 1860s, one of the owners built a Carpenter Gothic Victorian house on the site. In 1876, a German immigrant named Frederick Starke purchased the property, by then known as Cedar Grove. Starke had first entered the Petaluma River Watershed in 1848 with a party of men from Sonoma intent on rounding up what Coast Miwok natives remained in the area for slave labor. He returned in 1849 and built a shack along the estuary near where Petaluma Boulevard South lies today, becoming Petaluma's second white settler—the first had been a German doctor named Johann Frederick August Heyerman, who constructed a log cabin in 1847 near the present-day McNear Park.

When the rail lines of the San Francisco & North Pacific Railroad were laid through Petaluma in 1870, they ran adjacent to Cedar Grove. Recognizing an opportunity, Starke converted the property into an amusement park, complete with a bowling alley, shooting range, picnic grounds, baseball diamond, restaurant, and large dance pavilion. Starke's Park, as he called it, became a popular destination for San Franciscans taking country excursions north of the city aboard the train.

The park was shut down by the time Adolph Bloom purchased the property in 1904. Leaving his brother Americo in charge of the family ranching business, Bloom ventured into banking, serving as the president of the California Savings Bank of Petaluma, located at the northwest corner of Western Avenue and Petaluma Boulevard North. He also purchased the Petaluma Opera House at 149 Kentucky Street, which originally had been built in 1870, hiring Petaluma architect Brainerd Jones to convert it to retail and office use.

By 1937, Adolph had retired from the bank to his home at Cedar Grove. In September of that year, he received a subpoena to testify as a government witness against his brother Americo, who along with 10 other prominent Petalumans had been named in an illicit liquor ring, and accused of defrauding the government of a million dollars in taxes. Suspicions were also raised of money laundering.

In the early morning hours of September 29th, just days before his scheduled court appearance, Adolph's wife, Eva, found her husband dangling from a rope inside the chicken coop near their house. His body and clothes were soaking wet with salt water, apparently from a failed attempt to drown himself in the nearby Petaluma River.

After Adolph's death, Cedar Grove changed hands a few more times before Elizabeth Tunstall purchased the Blooms' house in 1957. In the early 1960s, all but seven acres of the original site were developed into the Linda Del Mar subdivision of tract homes. The only remnants of Petaluma's early birthplace were a handful of uncovered Lekituit artifacts and the boarded-up Bloom-Tunstall House.

Bloom-Tunstall house at Cedar Grove, built circa 1860s

The McNear Buildings

Brothers John Augustus McNear and George Washington McNear called it quits as partners in 1874. Since arriving in Petaluma in the late 1850s, they had been fortunate to tap into the wheat boom that had transformed the entire state of California into an agricultural powerhouse. Their grain mill and shipping company had made them the wealthiest family in Petaluma. But once Petaluma's monopoly as the transportation hub of Sonoma County was undercut by the arrival of the San Francisco & North Pacific Railroad in 1870, the two brothers both began looking for new opportunities—John locally, and George in San Francisco.

Born into a Maine family that boasted six generations of sea captains, the McNear brothers had migrated to Petaluma at the recommendation of John's father-in-law and second cousin, George Williams, a gold miner who had built two of the first hotels in the frontier town, the Washington and the American. The brothers were both intent on breaking free of their seafaring destinies and making their fortunes in the West.

John was the first to arrive, in 1856. At the age of 24, he had already sailed before the mast on ships around New England and across the Atlantic to Liverpool. After joining a family-related expedition to Mississippi to build a sawmill on the Gulf Coast, John had become superintendent and part owner of the mill, piloting a schooner that made lumber deliveries to New Orleans. When he departed for Petaluma with his new wife, Clara, John left his Mississippi schooner in the hands of his 19-year-old brother, George.

Although downtown Petaluma consisted at the time of only a handful of homes, hotels, and bars, John McNear quickly recognized its potential as a major shipping terminus to San Francisco. With a $3,000 stake from his profits at the lumber mill ($90,000 in early 21st-century-currency), he started privately lending money, as there were no commercial banks in town, and investing in real estate. In 1857, he purchased a livery stable and hay yard. After selling his interest in the stable three years later, he sent for his brother, George, extracting him from Mississippi just before the start of the Civil War. Together, they set up McNear & Brother, a commission and grain merchant business with a fleet of scow schooners headquartered on Washington Street and a branch office in San Francisco.

By 1864, the business was so successful that the McNears built California's largest grain warehouse, on the east side of Washington Street Bridge, installing the first concrete floor in the state. To speed up deliveries of their schooners to San Francisco they straightened a number of the bends on the Petaluma River. In 1867, they began exporting their shiploads of grain to Europe.

While the Gold Rush of 1848 had initially spawned California agriculture to feed a burgeoning San Francisco, it was the Australian gold rush of 1852—launched by prospectors who had returned to Australia from the California goldfields empty handed—that generated a demand for wheat in Australia to feed its growing population of miners. That demand was amplified by the outbreak of the Crimean War in 1853, which disrupted Russia's supply of grain to the world markets, creating an international shortage that drove grain prices skyward.

Wheat quickly became California's boom commodity in the 1850s, filling the valleys and hillsides of Sonoma County. Easy to grow, it did not require irrigation, which was important given California's long dry season, and once harvested it could be stored in the fields during summer without fear of rotting. As international demand grew, new innovations in mechanized farm implements allowed larger acreages of wheat to be planted, harvested, sacked, and shipped. In Petaluma, flour-milling companies like the McNears began springing up along the Petaluma River.

During the 1850s, more than 50 percent of California's wheat and flour exports went to Australia and New Zealand. In 1860, the export market shifted to Europe, as millers there learned how to grind California's hard and glutinous wheat, often blending it with local varieties to produce popular hybrid flours. International demand for California wheat was further increased by the Civil War's disruption of grain production in the Midwest. By 1867, 80 percent of California's wheat and flour exports were being shipped to grain markets in Liverpool.

Back in Petaluma, the McNear brothers were making a fortune. Tight-fisted teetotalers, the two men made a formidable team. John McNear, known for his kind and unassuming manner, possessed a quick and shrewd mind for business, well matched by the cool judgment and determined energy of his younger brother, George.

While George focused increasingly on the company's dealings in San Francisco, John devoted his attention to Petaluma, becoming the city's largest landowner and one of its most powerful citizens. He served as the

The adjoining McNear Buildings built by John McNear in 1885 and in 1911

founding president of the Bank of Sonoma County and of the Sonoma County Water Works, and at his own personal expense helped fellow banker and capitalist Isaac Wickersham secure Walnut Park for the city.

To break the passenger steamship monopoly on the river held by an unpopular fleet owner, Charles Minturn, John built the steamer *Josie McNear*, charging passengers one half of Minturn's exorbitant rates. After his wife, Clara, died following the birth of their fifth child (only one of their children would survive to adulthood), John created Cypress Hill Cemetery on Magnolia Avenue in her honor. A year after her death he remarried, and with his second wife, Hattie Miller, moved into a newly constructed estate that occupied almost an entire city block at 4th and D streets.

Although the McNears invested in many businesses throughout California, their initial fortune was dependent on Petaluma's monopoly as Sonoma County's primary shipping terminus. With the coming of the railroad to California in the 1860s, that position was suddenly in jeopardy. Developers in San Francisco and Oakland were particularly anxious to gain rail access to the virgin redwood forests of the Russian River Valley, having depleted other timber stands around the bay. Recognizing both a potential opportunity and a threat, John McNear set out to ensure that any railroad built in Sonoma County would make Petaluma its railhead for steamboat access to San Francisco. Between 1865 and 1870, he and other Petaluma business leaders, most prominently banker Isaac Wickersham, attempted to launch two railroad companies, the Petaluma & Healdsburg Railroad and the Petaluma & Cloverdale Railroad.

Due to the failure to raise sufficient public contributions for financing, both initiatives failed.

In 1868, Sonoma County officials offered a subsidy of $5,000 per mile to the first railroad company able to build a track connecting the county's southern and northern borders. The two main contenders were the Vallejo & Sonoma Valley Railroad, which would run north through the Sonoma Valley, bypassing Petaluma, and the Sonoma County Railroad, a new venture backed by John McNear and Wickersham, which would run from Petaluma to Cloverdale. After winning the bid, the Sonoma County Railroad transferred its interest to the better-financed San Francisco & North Pacific Railroad (SF&NPR), which began actual construction.

The original owner of the SF&NPR succeeded in building a railbed from Petaluma to within three miles of Santa Rosa when his shipment of rails from England sunk off the coast of Chile. The railroad was then taken over by Peter Donahue, the owner of Union Iron Works in San Francisco. He completed laying the rails to Santa Rosa, and opened regular rail service in 1870. Donahue had originally planned to make Petaluma the railhead for connecting with steamboats, but after Petaluma business leaders rejected his request to run a track down the middle of Petaluma Boulevard, Donahue chose instead to construct his own shipping terminus at a new town below Lakeville he named Donahue, relegating the depot in East Petaluma to a mere way station.

Angered, John McNear and Wickersham set out again in 1872 to organize another rail company, the Sonoma & Marin Railroad, with a line that extended from Petaluma to San Rafael, bypassing the town of Donahue. After this venture went belly up, Donahue purchased the line and folded it into the SF&NPR, eventually extending it to Tiburon at the expense of his railhead at Donahue, which he folded in 1882, moving most of the buildings to Tiburon.

The consequences of not securing a railhead in Petaluma were significant. While steamboats and scow schooners continued to ply the river with passengers and freight—primarily wheat, flour, hay, lumber, paving stones, and eggs, making Petaluma the third busiest river port in California in terms of tonnage—by the late 1870s Santa Rosa had become the new shipping center of Sonoma County, the railroad providing the town with a passport to prosperity that the steamboat had previously delivered to Petaluma. With rail service stimulating construction of canneries, dryers, and fruit packing plants, Santa Rosa's population surged from 900 people in 1870 to more than 6,500 by 1900. Petaluma, its shipping monopoly ended, began to stagnate, barely increasing from 3,300 residents in 1880 to 3,800 in 1900.

George McNear clearly saw the writing on the wall. While his brother John was busy with railroads and banking in Petaluma, George had become more focused on the exportation end of their grain business. In 1874, after the McNear brothers dissolved their partnership, George assumed control of the partnership's export assets. His timing was fortuitous. An economic depression in 1875 followed by a crop failure in 1877 provided

The McNear Canal, constructed by John McNear in 1893 for his Factory District, with the Rivertown Revival festival at Steamboat Landing Park in the foreground

him with the opportunity to shift the export grain business away from San Francisco's costly ports to the less expensive Port Costa on the Carquinez Strait.

The gamble paid off, and by the early 1880s Port Costa was the West Coast's leading grain port, earning George McNear the crown of California's "Wheat King." But instead of passing the cost savings on to farmers, McNear and other Port Costa shippers attempted to corner the market by stockpiling wheat to drive up prices. After the initial price bubble they had generated burst, wheat prices began a precipitous decline in the late 1880s. That, along with soil exhaustion and growing competition from Great Plains farmers, led to a complete bust for the California wheat market by 1900.

Meanwhile, back in Petaluma, John McNear was making new plans. In 1870, he had purchased a flour mill on Petaluma Boulevard North across from Penry Park. Facing a critical management crisis at the mill in 1876, John pulled his son, George Plumber McNear, or "G.P.," out of Petaluma High School, just two weeks shy of graduation and placed him in charge of the mill. It was the first step for the 19-year-old toward becoming his father's new business partner. G.P. proved to be a quick study, turning the mill around in a relatively short time, and eventually transforming it into a feed operation.

In the mid-1880s, the younger McNear spotted Lyman Byce selling a new egg incubator that he had invented with Isaac Dias at a blacksmith's shop across the street from his feed mill. He joined with others in helping Byce establish an incubator factory right next door to the mill. As demand for chicken feed increased, G.P. McNear began making private loans to people starting chicken ranches. When the poultry industry began to revive Petaluma's economy in the 1890s, G.P. McNear moved into banking, becoming president of the Sonoma County National Bank, and helping to finance future expansion of the industry. After a fire destroyed his feed mill in 1902, McNear relocated to B Street and Petaluma Boulevard, site of the present-day Great Petaluma Mill. For the next three decades, G.P. McNear would reign as one of Petaluma's most prominent capitalists and philanthropists.

Having passed the reins of his grain enterprise onto his son, John McNear set his sights on making Petaluma into the manufacturing hub of the North Bay. The arrival of the railroad, along with the introduction of such new inventions as the telephone in 1880 and electric lighting in 1889, were ushering in a second industrial revolution that offered to diversify small communities like Petaluma away from their agriculture-reliant economies. Young farm women, as well as a steady flow of immigrants to the area—mainly Irish and Chinese, many who initially came to work on the railroads before taking up work in the fields or in the trades—provided industry with a ready source of cheap labor.

John McNear devoted much of his time to recruiting factories to town—a silk mill, a shoe factory, a tannery, a creamery, a cold storage plant, a woolen mill, a box factory, a lumber mill, a petroleum plant—offering them attractive financing as well as property on the vast tract of land he owned along the east side of the Petaluma River. In 1890, he began the three-year construction of McNear Canal, a waterway basin with 20 feet of depth that ran parallel to the Petaluma River, hoping one day to extend it all the way to Black Point and so eliminate the narrow twists and turns of the river, allowing large ships to service the many factories he foresaw lining the banks of his canal downtown.

After the turn of the century, John McNear continued to be a prominent force in Petaluma, launching in 1903 with his son, G.P., the Petaluma & Santa Rosa Electric Railway that replaced horse-drawn railways, promoting his industrial center, and expanding his real estate holdings. In 1886, he had cleared the shanties of a Chinese colony on Petaluma Boulevard at B Street after the Anti-Chinese League drove many of the Chinese out of town, building in its place one of the most prominent historic landmarks in town, the Victorian Italianate Armory Building that extended from Petaluma Boulevard to 4th Street. In 1911, he built an adjoining building in a more modern style designed by local architect Brainerd Jones. It included the Mystic Theater, a vaudeville house and one of the first silent movie houses in California, run by his eldest son, Dr. John McNear, Jr.

John McNear's dream of making Petaluma a diversified factory town, however, never fully materialized. In 1918, the year he died, the Chamber of Commerce voted to abandon the idea making the city an industrial center and instead placed all its efforts behind championing Petaluma as "the egg basket of the world." After John McNear's death, G.P. McNear created McNear Park in his memory, and donated part of his father's home estate at 4th and D streets to the city for building the main post office.

The Great Petaluma Mill, 6 Petaluma Boulevard North

The Train Depot

Miners who struck it rich during California's Gold Rush fell roughly into two camps—adventurers and visionaries. What distinguished one from the other was how they used their newfound wealth. Adventurers gambled, visionaries plotted. No one exemplified the differences better than the two men responsible for bringing the first railroad to Petaluma, Ashbury Harpending and Peter Donahue.

Harpending was the adventurous type. In 1857, at the age of 15, he ran away from his Kentucky home to join an armed militia bound for the conquest of Nicaragua. After the group was thwarted by federal agents, Harpending set sail for California. With a grubstake of five dollars that his father had given him, he purchased the purser's fruit supply and then auctioned it off to passengers on the boat at a premium. Once in California, he used his profits from the fruit sales to acquire an abandoned hydraulic mining claim in the goldfields. He relentlessly worked the mine until he hit paydirt.

With his new treasure, the now 17-year-old Harpending sailed to Mexico. Teaming up with a Mexican partner, he became a millionaire at the age of 20, mining gold in the treacherous Mexican Sierras. At the outbreak of the Civil War, he returned to San Francisco and joined in a conspiracy to align California with the Confederacy. When that effort failed, he traveled back East to serve under the rebel commander General P.G.T. Beauregard at the battle of Shiloh. Granted a captain's commission in the Confederate Navy by Jefferson Davis, he returned once again to San Francisco, where he invested his money in converting a clipper ship to a warship that would be used to raid Union vessels carrying gold from California to the U.S. Mint. Captured and convicted of treason, he spent four months on Alcatraz before being pardoned at the war's end by Abraham Lincoln.

After the war, Harpending set out with a group of fellow Confederate copperheads to Kern County, where he founded the town of Havilah, named after the land cited in the Book of Genesis as "where there is gold." Within a year, he had turned Havilah into a booming mining town, netting himself $800,000 in the process ($11 million in early 21st-century-currency). Returning to San Francisco in 1865, Harpending began investing in real estate development along Market Street with William "Billy" Ralston, founder of the Bank of California and one of the richest men in the state thanks to his financing of Nevada's Comstock Lode. Together, they developed much of New Montgomery Street. In 1868, at the age of 29, Harpending decided to sail up the Petaluma River in pursuit of the next big thing, railroading.

He wasn't the only one who had caught railroad fever. During the 1850s California had been filled with prospectors looking to exploit and extract its natural bounty of minerals and agriculture. By the 1860s, properous capitalists like Harpending realized that the real money lay in controlling monopolies. Nothing spoke monopoly like a railroad company. Railroads held the power of economic life and death over many communities, opening up access to landlocked natural resources, agriculture, and manufactured goods. California's legendary "Big Four"—Leland Stanford, Collins P. Huntington, Mark Hopkins, and Charles Crocker—caught the railroad fever early, breaking ground in 1863 on the Central Pacific Railroad. By 1869, it would link up with the Union Pacific from the East to form the first transcontinental railroad, creating a bonanza for California's economy.

In Petaluma, the city fathers were anxious to protect the city's position as the shipping hub of Sonoma County. They were led in their quest by two of the town's wealthiest men, John McNear and Isaac Wickersham. Wickersham, a Pennsylvania lawyer who struck it rich in the gold mines, was a visionary type, using his riches to create Sonoma County's first bank. McNear, a Maine sea captain and another visionary, arrived after the Gold Rush, quickly established a shipping monopoly on the Petaluma River, and opened a bank across the street from Wickersham's. With their hands on the local purse strings, Wickersham and McNear were at the center of most major new developments in town, including railroads. Their first joint venture was the Petaluma & Healdsburg Railroad Company in 1865, which died an early death because of their inability to raise sufficient local capital.

In 1867, to incentivize railroad builders, Sonoma County offered a subsidy of $5,000 per mile of track ($85,000 in early 21st-century-currency) for the first railroad to extend between the county's southern and northern borders. McNear and Wickersham promptly formed another paper railroad, the Sonoma County Railroad Company, to run from Petaluma to Healdsburg, and started looking for investors. John Frisbie, the founder of the city of Vallejo and son-in-law of the former

Petaluma Train Depot, 210 Lakeville Street, built 1914

Mexican Commandant of Northern California, Mariano Vallejo, announced that he too would build a competing railroad extending from Vallejo to Healdsburg by way of Santa Rosa, completely bypassing Petaluma. County officials asked voters to decide which company should be awarded the subsidy. After a boisterous campaign of torch-lit rallies and mudslinging articles in rival county newspapers, McNear and Wickersham won the vote. To celebrate, they held a groundbreaking ceremony on July 4, 1868.

Two months later, still unable to raise sufficient capital from a public offering, they sold their rights to the county subsidy to another paper railroad, the San Francisco & Humboldt Bay Railroad Company, with the stipulation that the new owners lay 10 miles of track from Petaluma to Santa Rosa by November 16, 1869, or else forfeit their rights. Backed by a group of investors led by the publisher of San Francisco's *Alta California* newspaper, Fred McCrellish, the new company's plan was to run a rail line from Sausalito to Humboldt County, giving them access to the virgin redwood timber in the Russian River and Eel River valleys, the true prize for railroad investors. Within a few months, McCrellish's group also came up short on financing, and so sold out to Ashbury Harpending.

Harpending wasted no time embarking on his latest grand adventure, breaking ground on laying a railroad bed from Petaluma to Santa Rosa, lobbying for federal permits to the redwood groves, and entertaining the idea of building a suspension bridge across the Golden Gate. In May 1869, the grading of the railroad bed came to a halt within just two miles of Santa Rosa—Harpending had run out of money. For a quick infusion of funds, he and his real estate partner, Bank of California founder Billy Ralston, held an auction of their New Montgomery Street holdings in San Francisco. Ironically, with the arrival of the transcontinental railroad that spring, cheap goods began pouring into San Francisco from Chicago and St. Louis, undercutting many local businesses, and driving down real estate prices. Harpending and Ralston were severely disappointed with the sale, but pushed ahead in placing an order for 22 miles of iron rails for the tracks.

Unable to come to terms with San Francisco's main rail manufacturer, Union Iron Works, Harpending placed his order with a supplier in England. In September 1869, word came that the ship carrying the rails from England had gone down in the harbor of Valparaiso, Chile. Up against the deadline imposed by McNear and Wickersham to lay track to Santa Rosa by November 16th, Harpending reorganized his company under a new name, the San Francisco & North Pacific Railroad, allowing him time to negotiate a new contract with the two men, and to order new rails.

In the meantime, Harpending faced new competition from John Frisbie, who had partnered up with Milton Latham, chairman of the California Pacific Railroad and a former California governor and U.S. senator, to run a rail line from Vallejo to Petaluma, and then north to Cloverdale. Sonoma County voters, frustrated by Harpending's delays, approved a set of subsidies in June 1870, intended to spur construction. First, they issued Latham's California Pacific Railroad an incentive of $25,000 in bonds for every five miles of track that they laid between the Napa County line and Petaluma. Second, they amended their earlier subsidy offer of $5,000 per mile to be awarded to the first railroad company able to lay track between Petaluma and Santa Rosa, and separately, between Santa Rosa and Healdsburg.

Shortly after the vote, California's railroading Big Four—Stanford, Huntington, Hopkins, and Crocker—called in their chits with Harpending's partner, Billy Ralston, to force Harpending to sell his San Francisco & North Pacific Railroad to Peter Donahue, a co-founder of Union Iron Works. In late July 1870, Harpending threw in the towel.

Like many ruthless capitalists, Peter Donahue had serious talents. Unlike the bold, adventurous Harpending, he was a shrewd operator, known for being able to read the cards of any rival and carefully outmaneuver them through planning and calculation. An Irish immigrant reared in Glasgow, Scotland, Donahue had arrived in America with his family at age 11, and apprenticed with his brothers, James and Michael, as a machinist in a New Jersey iron foundry. At the age of 25, he caught a steamer bound for the Gold Rush in California, making a quick $1,000 repairing its boilers in route. His two brothers soon joined him, and after a short stint in the goldfields, they opened up a blacksmith shop in San Francisco in 1849. Soon after, they founded California's first iron casting foundry, the Union Iron Works, at 1st and Mission streets. In 1852, they erected San Francisco's first gasworks, bringing gaslit street lamps to the city.

Stable House and Dance Hall, Donahue township, 5268 Lakeville Highway, built 1870

They held a monopoly on gas lighting in the city until 1870, when Harpending's partner, Billy Ralston, formed a rival company and then forced Donahue into a merger.

As San Francisco grew, Donahue moved into transportation, first with ship repair and shipbuilding, and then with construction of the first steam locomotives on the West Coast. He built San Francisco's first horse-car rail system, and in 1860 the San Francisco & San Jose Railroad. When Billy Ralston brought him the San Francisco & North Pacific Railroad deal in July 1870, he wasted no time seizing the opportunity. By early August, schooners began arriving in Petaluma with rails, redwood ties, and hundreds of Irish laborers, replacing Harpending's Chinese crew. Donahue laid the first spike for the railroad on September 3rd.

The one snag in the deal was the location of the railroad's southern terminus. The money to be made on the train would come from hauling tons of grain, fruits, vegetables, livestock, and lumber, not necessarily passengers. As a thriving river port, Petaluma was the obvious choice, but Donahue's demands for a right-of-way through town on Main Street were rejected by McNear, Wickersham, and city officials. In a huff, Donahue decided to build a new town along the river some eight miles south of Petaluma to serve as the southern terminus. He modestly named the town Donahue.

The new township of Donahue went up overnight, with housing for 200 of Donahue's crew. It featured a machine shop, a blacksmith shop, a two-story hotel, a firehouse, a one-room county school, two laundries, a saloon, and a stable that doubled as a dance hall. To connect his trains with San Francisco, Donahue put together a fleet of four veteran steamers to run from San Francisco's Embarcadero to the landing. On New Year's Eve, 1871, four months after laying the first spike, Donahue staged a "first-class blowout" for the railroad's inaugural run, laying claim to the first part of the county's rail subsidy.

The subsidy for extending a railway from Santa Rosa to Healdsburg remained. Milton Latham, owner of the rival California Pacific Railroad, hired a few hundred Chinese laborers, who frantically began laying track out of Santa Rosa, in an attempt to beat out Donahue. Donahue rushed more Irishmen to Santa Rosa. The race was on, with Chinese and Irish crews working side by side on parallel tracks, and many citizens in Sonoma County setting wagers on their progress.

Then, suddenly, it was over. This time, Billy Ralston stepped in to convince Donahue to sell out to Latham. As part of the deal, Donahue agreed to finish laying track to the Russian River in Healdsburg using his Irish crew. The San Francisco & North Pacific Railroad (SF&NPR) became a division of Latham's California Pacific Railroad. Two years later, as Latham found his expansionist plans in California thwarted by the Big Four, Donahue bought the SF&NPR back from him.

In Petaluma, the fears of McNear and Wickersham were quickly realized, as thanks to the railroad, Santa Rosa soon replaced Petaluma as the county's main transportation hub for agriculture, setting off a massive boom for the city of Santa Rosa. With the township of Donahue now serving as the terminus to the Petaluma River, Petaluma stagnated. Its population would remain relatively flat until the 1890s, when the local invention of an efficient incubator set off an egg boom for the town.

John McNear tried one last time to launch a new rail line extending from Petaluma to San Rafael that bypassed the town of Donahue. After going bust, the line was consolidated into Donahue's SF&NPR in 1877. Five years later, Donahue extended the line from San Rafael to Tiburon, which became the permanent terminus of his SF&NPR. He loaded the buildings at the township of Donahue onto barges and moved them to Tiburon, where the surviving two-story terminal called the "Peter Donahue Building" still remains. All he left behind in the township of Donahue was the stable and the dance hall.

In 1885, Donahue caught a cold while making an inspection tour of his SF&NPR, and died. His 26-year-old son, Mervyn, succeeded him, but also died from a severe cold four years later. The railroad then passed out of the family, and was sold at auction.

Ashbury Harpending and Billy Ralston went on to more adventures, including the Great Diamond Hoax, a notorious scheme called "the most gigantic and barefaced swindle of the age." After Ralston's Bank of California dramatically collapsed following the financial Panic of 1873, Ralston was found drowned in the San Francisco Bay. Harpending died in 1923, after writing one of the most colorful autobiographies of the age.

The Cinnabar railroad trestle north of Petaluma

Hatcheries

Like many others who had found their way to the Petaluma River Watershed in the late 19th century, Christopher Nisson fell for the lure of raising chickens. With a little thrift, hard work, and a minimum of capital, here was an opportunity to make a good living without having to surrender to the drudgery of punching a clock in an urban factory.

Nisson's timing couldn't have been better. Industrialization was ramping up across the country, and the processes of mass production were beginning to redefine the character of American society, especially in the growing demand for cheaply processed foods. Chickens, by their nature, appeared to defy this transformation. Pastoral creatures, they ranged the barnyard and the farm, leaving their eggs in mangers or under porches until the farmer's wife, ready to go to town, would send the children out to scare up any available eggs to sell for what was called "pinmoney," or cash squirreled away for non-essentials. If chickens were to become part of the new industrialization, someone would have to figure out how to efficiently produce them and their eggs in steady supply and then safely transport both to market.

Christopher Nisson, it turned out, was that someone. Fortunately for him, he was in the right place at the right time. The scows and steamers plying the Petaluma River in the late 1880s could make the run to San Francisco in a day, safely ferrying eggs to market. As San Francisco's population grew and inexpensive sources of protein became hard to come by, eggs emerged as one of the most profitable goods aboard the market-bound boats. All that remained was figuring out how to improve the low productivity of the laying chickens.

Nisson, troubled by the unhealthy practice of leaving undated eggs lying around for casual gathering, set out in a methodical manner to bring a more intentional approach to "chicken ranching."

Nisson had arrived in Petaluma in 1864 at the age of 19, having sailed round Cape Horn from his native Denmark. For a decade he worked as a landscape gardener until he was able to save up enough money to purchase a 100-acre ranch in Two Rock. After trying his hand at potato farming and then dairy ranching, Nisson began adding chickens to the farm once the demand for eggs in San Francisco began to grow. Taking advantage of the area's sandy soil and year-round mild and airy climate, he placed his free-ranging chickens into large outdoor pens, where he could manage their egg laying.

Noticing that the caged hens stopped laying eggs once they became broody—inclined to incubate eggs for hatching—Nisson realized that the time his hens spent sitting on and hatching their eggs, and then tending to their chicks, was time not spent laying more eggs. Removing the eggs soon after they were laid increased the hens' fecundity, but it didn't provide him with new chicks to grow or replenish his flock.

Luckily for Nisson, two Petaluma men, Lyman Byce and Isaac Dias, had recently perfected the first practical egg incubator. By heating a coal-oil lamp with an electric regulator, Byce and Dias found that they could maintain the temperature in their device at a steady 103 degrees, the same as a brooding hen's body. To simulate the hen's regular turning of her eggs with her beak, the eggs had to be manually rotated in the incubator three times a day. The small, primitive machine created by Dias and Byce caused a sensation at the local county fairs. Skeptics initially refused to believe it wasn't wily sleight of hand, with chicks concealed in a hidden part of the odd-looking box and allowed to emerge through a trick door.

Nisson quickly recognized the commercial potential of the incubator machine. Purchasing several from Dias and Byce, he began using them to propagate his flock, which left his hens to lay eggs for the market, uninterrupted by maternal cares. To provide the hatched chicks with a mother hen surrogate, Nisson invented a separate brooder house with a stove to keep the chicks warm. For his laying hens, he developed a colony house, with a slatted floor, which rested on skids, meaning it could be moved by a team of horses once the ground beneath became fouled by droppings. Those droppings were then collected for fertilizer.

Thanks to these innovations, by 1881 Nisson had grown his flock to 2,000 laying hens. Seeing this growth, neighbors began hiring Nisson to hatch their eggs in order to rapidly expand their own flocks. As San Francisco's demand for eggs increased and more chicken ranches sprang up around the area, Nisson shifted his operation from producing eggs for the market to producing chicks to sell to other ranchers. After designing his own incubator, he established America's first commercial egg hatchery at his Pioneer Hatchery Breeding Farm in Two Rock.

Meanwhile, in 1885, the incubator inventor Lyman Byce—his partner Isaac Dias having died in a duck

Christopher Nisson's original Pioneer Hatchery Breeding Farm, 4381 Middle Two Rock Road

hunting accident in 1884—opened the Petaluma Incubator Company at 242 Petaluma Boulevard North across from Hill Plaza (present-day Penry Park), and began marketing the apparatus he had created with Dias around the country. After winning multiple prizes against rival incubators at state and county fairs, Byce began to attract orders from around the world, leading to an unmet demand.

By the 1890s, six egg hatcheries were operating in Petaluma, many of them having developed their own incubators patterned after Byce and Dias's early breakthrough. Nisson joined them in 1898, moving his Pioneer Hatchery from Two Rock to downtown Petaluma at 6th and G streets. Also that year, the Must Hatch Incubator Company was launched by Alphonse Bourke at 7th and F streets. By 1929, it was the largest commercial hatchery in the world.

Riding the egg boom, flour mills in Petaluma began converting to storing and mixing chicken feed, and a dedicated chicken-boat started a daily run down the river to San Francisco, returning full of feed. Sales of hatchery chicks were at first limited to ranchers in the immediate vicinity, until hatcheries realized they could ship chicks by rail express to within a two-day radius of Petaluma, or as far away as 300 or 400 miles, since newborn chicks did not require food or water for their first 48 hours.

All that remained to complete the transformation of the chicken from farm animal to industrialized commodity was the bird itself. After years of competitive breeding, the white leghorn emerged as Petaluma's egg-laying champion in the 1890s. Producing a large egg with a pure white, smoothly textured shell and a desirable light yellow yolk, the bird was christened the "Pride of Petaluma," and quickly became the town's agent of wealth and fame. As the egg industry grew, local poultry journals sprang up, offering "scientific" information about improvements to feed that included kale as a staple; ways to combat common diseases; and further advances in the design of long-row, redwood chicken houses.

By the 1920s, Petaluma was host to 33 hatcheries and shipping out an estimated 264 million eggs a year, making the Petaluma River Watershed the largest poultry-producing region in America, and providing its citizens with one of the highest incomes per capita in the country. To promote its continued growth, the Petaluma Chamber of Commerce hired a public relations man named Bert Kerrigan, who rebranded Petaluma as "The Egg Basket of the World," a moniker that would define its image for the next half century.

The Must Hatch Incubator Company at 7th and F Streets, designed by Brainerd Jones, built 1926

Towers of Grain

The lure of the American Dream blared from Petaluma like a siren's call in the early 1900s. For anyone working long hours for low wages in a dead-end job on a factory line, the idea of owning a chicken ranch and having to engage in only a few light chores to produce a daily abundance of eggs—"making every day a payday"—sounded like heaven on earth.

For a relatively small investment of $3,500 ($90,000 in early-21st-century currency), you could purchase five acres with a four-bedroom house, 10 chicken houses, a heated brooder house for newborn chicks, an incubator, and a thousand white leghorn laying hens. If you lacked the upfront capital, you could start out as a ranch hand on a chicken ranch for $25 a month with free room and board, until you saved up enough money to rent a ranch, and then, after a few years, enough money to buy your own place. Chicken ranching provided a good home for your family in the healthy outdoors, where you'd be free of the big cities with their strife, filth, and overcrowding and released from the never-ending struggle to pay the bills. At least, that was the story told in real estate brochures sent out across the country from Petaluma.

Between 1900 and 1920, aspiring poultry entrepreneurs descended upon the Petaluma River Watershed in droves, nearly doubling the town's population from 3,800 to 6,300, with another estimated 6,000 residing in the surrounding valley. Drawn largely by word of mouth, the new converts came from all over the world—Germany, Sweden, Denmark, Japan, and Russia, as well as from factory towns back East, all of them looking to reap the just rewards of their labor and faith.

With the outbreak of World War I, demand for eggs soared to an all-time high, lifting Petaluma's income per capita to the highest in the country. Looking to capitalize on the egg boom, the Chamber of Commerce hired a San Francisco public relations man named Bert Kerrigan to brand Petaluma as the "Egg Basket of the World."

Suddenly, there was National Egg Day with a parade. Egg queens and chicken dances. A 400-member male chorus. A chicken rodeo. A professional chicken impersonator. A 15-foot egg basket at the railroad station. The Order of the Cluck Clucks. An egg-laying contest. In San Francisco, above the corner of 3rd and Market streets, two sacks of chicken feathers were dropped from a plane with a small card attached to each feather granting the bearer three dozen of Petaluma's finest eggs.

If things sounded too good to be true in the Egg City, they were. As Walter Hogan noted in his 1913 treatise *Call of the Hen,* raising poultry was appealing because it appeared to be easy work with a big return. The reality was that for every person who succeeded with a chicken ranch, a hundred failed. Along with the challenges of battling fowl disease, shoveling manure, and tending to broody hens, the price of eggs fluctuated wildly depending on market conditions, making chicken ranching a risky gamble. Still, new believers kept coming, blindly replacing those who had fallen by the wayside.

Meanwhile, the people making money hand over fist were the owners of the hatcheries, feed mills, shipping companies, banks, and wholesalers. The chicken ranchers, looking to improve their odds, formed a cooperative in 1916 called the Poultry Producers of Central California. Members sold their eggs to the co-op at a guaranteed minimum price, and in turn the co-op sold them feed at a lower cost than the mills.

Price controls became even more important when the Great Depression hit in the 1930s. Still, many ranchers were reduced to swapping eggs for vegetables, food, and labor. Others were foreclosed on by the banks or the feed mills. By 1937, 60 percent of Petaluma's eggs were sold through the co-op. That same year the co-op constructed its own towering feed mill with an 11-story grain elevator in downtown Petaluma. Chicken feed, which had been scientifically enhanced by local mills over the years, became Petaluma's most critical commodity.

With the start of World War II, the egg market rebounded. By 1945, Petaluma's annual egg output peaked at 624 million eggs. However, new innovations were on the horizon, including climate-controlled facilities with wire cages suspended from the ceiling that allowed tractors to sweep away manure droppings below while conveyor belts transported newly laid eggs away.

Soon, modern factory farms were springing up in the Central Valley and American South, leading to the collapse of Petaluma's small ranching model, and leaving the countryside dotted with thousands of abandoned chicken houses. The final blow came in 1964 when the Poultry Producers went under, taking with them the life savings of many of their remaining members.

After sitting vacant for almost 20 years, the co-op's towering grain mill was purchased in 1982 by Dairyman's Feed, a local co-operative established in 1959 by Russian immigrant Dave Soren, and put back into operation.

Dairyman's Feed & Supply Co-Operative,
323 East Washington Street, built 1937

LEFT: *R.O. Shelling Grain and Feed at the corner of Magnolia Avenue and Petaluma Boulevard North, established in 1948*

RIGHT: *Inside the Hunt & Behrens mill*

Hunt & Behrens Mill, originally established in 1921, moved to its current location at 30 Lakeville Street in 1947

The Silk Milk

On July 16, 1892, a group of women led by Ida Belle McNear, wife of local grain merchant George P. McNear, gathered at city hall to form the Petaluma Women's Silk Association. The women were hoping to corner the market on raw silk produced in California. They set out to purchase the 80,000 pounds of cocoons produced by domestic silk worms, reel the silk out of them, and then sell the silk to the new Carlson-Currier Silk Mill about to open its doors in East Petaluma. The one hitch in their plans was that the man who had lured the new mill to town, local grain and shipping magnate and Ida's father-in-law John McNear, was still short on the funds needed to subsidize the mill's construction.

"There is yet about $2,000 to be raised before we can run up the flag that shall proclaim victory," McNear announced in the *Petaluma Morning Courier* newspaper. "It is strange to me that in a world so wide, and where life is so short, that some of our capitalists should be so very miserly about putting up some coin. Yet, they are all good folks, and I am led to the conviction that when the necessities arise, they will not hesitate when it comes down the question of 'ground hog, or no supper.'"

It was a strong condemnation coming from McNear, who was well-known for being a tight-fisted, money-pinching, teetotaler himself. But McNear was also a man of vision. With Petaluma's preeminence as a primary shipping port having been displaced in the 1870s by the arrival of the San Francisco & North Pacific Railroad, he was on a mission to transform the city into the manufacturing hub of the North Bay, creating a Factory District east of the river. McNear himself was already an experienced factory owner, having operated a brick manufacturing plant since 1868 at McNear Point 20 miles south of Petaluma.

To expanding factories in San Francisco and Oakland, he offered inexpensive land along the east side of the Petaluma River (that he personally owned); financing from the town's largest bank (that he presided over); and easy shipping access on the McNear Canal (that he was in the process of dredging out). McNear's other big selling point was access to cheap labor. Prior to the 1890s, he and other local capitalists had relied primarily on Chinese laborers, but following passage of the Chinese Exclusion Act in 1882 and the rise of Anti-Chinese Leagues that imposed boycotts on businesses employing Chinese labor, the local factory labor market shifted to young women 16 and older from town and the surrounding ranches. They already filled the factory floors of Nolan-Earl Shoe Factory and Adams Box Factory that McNear had helped to establish in his new Factory District, as well as the new poultry hatcheries springing up around town.

The latest factory that McNear was attempting to lure to Petaluma, the Carlson-Currier Company, was the West Coast agent of one of the country's largest silk manufacturers, Belding Brothers & Company, based in Michigan. J.P. Currier, a former Belding Brothers manager, had joined with Edward Carlson, California's former deputy state treasurer, to form the San Francisco-based Carlson-Currier Company in 1877, shipping wholesale silk thread all along the Pacific Rim from British Columbia to Central America, and across the Pacific to the Hawaiian Islands, New Zealand, and Australia.

McNear's timing was perfect. The American economy's recovery from the national recession of the early 1870s marked a new boom for American-made silk. The domestic market had been originally established in 1830 with the introduction to America of the Chinese Mulberry tree, the leaves of which when eaten by silkworms produce a high quality silk. American sericulture, or silk farming, skyrocketed in the 1830s with a "Mulberry Craze" that rivaled Holland's infamous "Tulip Bulb Craze" in the 17th century, giving rise to a number of silk factories in New England and Michigan. Overspeculation and a mulberry blight caused the bubble to burst in the 1840s, forcing domestic silk factories to start importing raw silk from China. By the 1870s, most of the imported raw silk was shipped by steamer from China to San Francisco, where it was placed on trains to the East.

In the early 1890s, Carlson-Currier decided to create a large West Coast factory, which brought them to John McNear. After McNear successfully finished raising the local money needed for a subsidy, Carlson-Currier built their silk mill at the corner of Jefferson and Erwin streets, making it the crown jewel of McNear's Factory District. Designed by San Francisco architect Charles I. Havens, its Georgian Colonial Revival Industrial Style harkened back to the brick textile mills of New England. The brick itself was supplied by McNear's brickyard at McNear Point in Marin County. Operating with its own steam-powered electric system, the mill was able to manufacture 250 pounds of raw silk into thread each day. Following the building's opening dedication in 1892, a

Carlson-Currier Silk Mill, Jefferson and Erwin streets, built 1892

grand ball was held inside the mill, attended by a who's who list of Petaluma's elite. The only ones disappointed were Ida Belle McNear and her Petaluma Women's Silk Association. Their scheme to corner the domestic production of raw silk on the West Coast was foiled when they discovered that the could not compete with the cheap labor in China for reeling silkworm cocoons into raw silk for the mill.

Unfortunately for John McNear, the Carlson-Currier Silk Mill was to be the zenith of his dreams for the Factory District. As Petaluma's egg boom took off at the turn of the century, local capitalists ignored McNear's advice to diversify into various manufacturing industries, and instead put their money into egg-related ventures like hatcheries.

In 1915, Belding Brothers and Company assumed controlling interest of the silk mill, dropping the use of the Carlson-Currier name. The head of the Michigan-based firm, Alvah Belding, became a frequent visitor to Petaluma, staying at the 6th Street home of his cousin Frank Snow, publisher of the local *Poultry Journal*. In 1922, Belding decided to expand manufacturing capacity at the mill, hiring Petaluma architect Brainerd Jones to double the size of the factory to 40,000 square feet by seamlessly adding a second tower and extension to the south end of the building. The call for additional factory workers set off a temporary housing crisis in Petaluma. To manage the expansion, Belding hired Jasper Woodson to serve as superintendent of the mill. Woodson would go on to serve as a city councilman and later mayor of Petaluma during the 1930s.

As silk demand grew during the fashion-conscious Roaring Twenties, Belding Brothers entered into a $20 million merger with Heminway Silk in Connecticut. The onset of the Great Depression, however, decimated the luxury fabric market, leading to consolidations among the mills. In 1932, the owners of the Petaluma factory merged with another prominent East Coast mill, Corticelli Company, becoming the Belding-Heminway-Corticelli Company. The increasing popularity of cheaper synthetics like rayon and nylon in the 1930s further accelerated the decline in demand for silk, as did Japan's embargo on silk exports in the years preceding World War II.

Petaluma's silk mill, which at its peak had employed 200 workers, was down to 35 employees when it closed in 1939. The building was sold the next year to Sunset Line and Twine, makers of fishing line and cordage, which relocated their machinery and employees to Petaluma from a factory in San Francisco. During the 1960s, Sunset Line and Twine became known for manufacturing parachute line for NASA's Apollo and Gemini command modules.

Thanks to the efforts of Petaluma historian Lucy Kortum and others, in 1986 the silk mill was granted national historic landmark status. Production at Sunset Line and Twine came to a halt in 2006 after the company decided to relocate to Kansas. South Bay hotelier B.B. Patel eventually purchased the mill and redeveloped it into a boutique hotel that opened in 2018.

Machinery left behind in the silk mill building after the shutdown of Sunset Line and Twine in 2006

The Creamery

Gene Benedetti wasn't planning to spend his life as a milkman. Having recently returned from naval service in World War II, 26-year-old Benedetti was newly married, expecting his first child, and happily adjusting to civilian life as a history instructor and assistant football coach at Santa Rosa Junior College.

But George Dondero, the manager of the Petaluma Cooperative Creamery, had a different idea. Dondero was recruiting young veterans to buy milk from dairy ranchers, especially vets who could speak Italian since many the local ranches were run by families of Swiss-Italian immigrants. Gene Benedetti was already a local war hero, having skippered the lead landing craft in the D-Day invasion of Omaha Beach. After hearing Benedetti speak at a sports banquet, Dondero offered him a job. Benedetti knew nothing about the dairy business aside from milking a few cows on his family's small farm in Cotati. That was not important to Dondero. He saw potential in the former University of San Francisco football star—perhaps even a successor at the creamery.

Commercial creameries first emerged in the Petaluma River Watershed at the end of the 19th century to meet the rising demand for dairy products in San Francisco. Because milk was highly perishable, dairy ranchers had turned to making butter and cheese on their ranches. The need for greater production led to the establishment in 1887 of Sonoma County's first commercial creamery on the Denman Ranch near Penngrove.

But while creameries made production more efficient, they also reduced ranchers to mere producers of milk, leaving middlemen to process and market their butter and cheese. In 1913, 37 dairy ranchers formed the Petaluma Cooperative Creamery at Western Avenue and Baker Street. With a combined herd of 1,980 cows, their plan was to control their dairy products from the cow to the grocery shelf. Adopting the brand name "Clover," they began to exert their collective bargaining muscle.

George Dondero signed on as the co-op's manager in 1922. An innovator, Dondero upgraded and expanded the facility, introducing bottled milk in 1927 and cottage cheese in 1933. Largely self-educated, he successfully navigated the co-op through the roller coaster of fluctuating milk prices during the Depression and World War II.

When Dondero made Benedetti a job offer in 1946, the co-op was on a growth spurt thanks to the thriving postwar economy. To sweeten the deal for Benedetti, Dondero offered to help him start a semipro football team in Petaluma called the Petaluma Leghorns.

By the early 1950s, the creamery occupied a full city block. Its 1,100 members, with a collective herd of 30,000 cows, annually produced 15 million gallons of "Grade A" milk, a million pounds of cottage cheese, and more than two million pounds of sweet cream butter. By 1951, Dondero asked Benedetti to give up his sideline as a football coach and become assistant manager of the creamery. (The champion Petaluma Leghorns continued playing without Benedetti until 1958, when televised pro football essentially put an end to the semipro leagues.) In 1955, Dondero retired, leaving Benedetti to run the creamery.

For the next two decades, Benedetti oversaw the co-op through advances that doubled the average amount of milk produced by a single cow. Those decades were also overshadowed by the growth of dry-lot dairies in the Central Valley and Southern California, where large herds were crowded onto small acreages and fed exclusively on feed, as opposed to grazing in pastures. The factories drove down the price of milk, making it difficult for smaller, less efficient ranchers to compete. By the mid-1970s, membership in the Petaluma Cooperative Creamery had dropped to 120 ranches, with larger ranchers buying up their smaller neighbors.

In 1975, tragedy hit when a fire destroyed the creamery's processing and bottling operations. The creamery's board decided not to rebuild, instead selling the Clover brand to Gene Benedetti and five of his partners, who merged the company with Stornetta Dairy in Schellville, together forming Clover-Stornetta Farms. In the mid-1980s, Benedetti turned operations over to his son Dan. In 1991, Clover-Stornetta moved into a new state-of-the-art facility at the former site of the Reif & Brody chicken processing plant on Lakeville Avenue and Madison Street. In 2006, the company passed to third-generation Marcus Benedetti.

Meanwhile, the old co-op plant on Western Avenue lived on as the California Cooperative Creamery, expanding its membership to 500 dairies across Northern California under the brand "Cal-Gold," before merging in 1998 with a number of other co-ops to form Dairy Farmers of America, the nation's largest dairy cooperative. In 2004, after the co-op announced plans to shut down and sell the Petaluma facility, Larry Peter, of Spring Hill Jersey Cheese in Two Rock, stepped in to save the plant from the wrecking ball, rechristening it the Petaluma Creamery.

The Petaluma Creamery, 621 Western Avenue, built 1913.

The Railroad Trestle

After arriving in Petaluma in 1856, John McNear spent the next three decades amassing a fortune from grain sales, banking, and riverboat shipping during California's wheat boom. Once the boom ended in the late 1880s, McNear set out on a new vision to turn Petaluma into an industrial center—the Oakland of the North Bay.

The one thing that McNear lacked for his grand new vision was a railroad. After three unsuccessful attempts to launch a rail line from Petaluma, McNear and other local investors had lost out in 1870 to the San Francisco & North Pacific Railroad. The SF&NPR bypassed Petaluma as its main shipping railhead, ending the city's dominance as the North Bay's primary port.

In the 1890s, McNear's attention was drawn to the introduction of the electric interurban trolley in San Francisco, where it replaced the horse-drawn trolley system. First introduced in Richmond, Virginia, in 1888, electric trolleys ran relatively quietly and required a crew of only one or two men, making them cheaper to operate than a steam locomotive. Not having to bear the weight of a locomotive, their roadbeds were less expensive to build and could be laid out more easily, especially over rolling terrain.

Electricity had first come to Petaluma in 1889 with the arrival of the Petaluma Electric Light and Power Company, located on Weller and East Washington streets. Generating electricity from a coal-fed steam engine, the plant gradually put an end to the gaslights that had lit the town since the 1860s. The company's founder, 21-year-old Will Pierce, was owner of one of the most prosperous dairies in the area, the 2,200-acre Pierce Ranch at the north tip of the Point Reyes Peninsula.

Will Pierce had been just 15 years old when his father, Abram Pierce, died, making him one of the wealthiest dairymen in the county. But the young Pierce's true passion was electrical innovations. In addition to the power company, he also launched one of Petaluma's early phone companies, the Pierce Telephone Company, in 1894. Pierce's life was tragically cut short in the spring of 1895, when he was electrocuted during a rainstorm while trying to fix a broken power line on Main Street in front of the present-day Putnam Plaza.

Not long after Pierce's death, John McNear brokered the sale of Pierce's power plant to Mary Burdell, owner of the 15,000-acre Burdell Ranch that stretched from Mount Burdell to Point Reyes Station. McNear also sold Mrs. Burdell a lot at the southeast corner of Lakeville Avenue and East D Street to construct a new building for the power plant. Located across from the train depot and the docks of McNear Canal, the Burdell Building was built with bricks from McNear's brickyard. In addition to a new power plant, it also featured the town's first creamery and first ice and cold storage plant, making it possible to keep eggs, milk, butter, and cheese fresh while awaiting their transport to San Francisco. Mary Burdell held 100 percent of the stock in all three companies.

In 1903, two entrepreneurs from San Francisco, Alfred Bowen and Charles Towne, approached McNear about backing an electric rail service in Sonoma County. By that time, the electric grid for Petaluma and the rest of Sonoma County was being powered by a hydroelectric dam built in the Sierra foothills. (Pacific Gas & Electric Company would begin buying up small regional power companies like the Burdell's power plant in 1907.) McNear jumped at the opportunity, helping to pull together a consortium of investors, including Santa Rosa banker Frank Brush, Bay Area sugar tycoon Rudolph Spreckels, and his own son, Petaluma grain merchant George P. McNear, to help finance a third of the railway's million-dollar capitalization. The remaining two-thirds was funded by 20-year mortgage bonds. McNear also assumed presidency of the new company, which was named the Petaluma & Santa Rosa Railway.

Dubbed "the juice line" because of its use of electricity, the P&SR anchored its railhead at Weller and East D streets in Petaluma, across from both the train depot and the docks of the McNear Canal. At its outset, the line purchased the river steamer *Gold*, and later a companion steamer, *Petaluma*. The two passenger boats departed twice daily to San Francisco, carrying with them a cargo of eggs, chickens, fruit, and incubators, and returning with household goods, glass, paper, wagons, farm implements, and hardware.

Service between Petaluma and Santa Rosa via Sebastopol began on December 1, 1904, with stops along the way at the junctions of Cinnabar, Corona, Denman, Liberty, Live Oak, and Stony Point near the Washoe House. From Sebastopol, one branch of the line ran to Santa Rosa, and a second branch to Forestville. A third branch line was later added in 1911 that stretched from the Liberty junction at Pepper Road to Two Rock.

The train moved on steel rails laid out upon redwood

The West Petaluma Spur and Trestle along the west bank of the Petaluma River, built 1922

ties, with two trolley wires overhead—one wire for each direction—connected every 600 feet by copper jumpers. Initially the cars—known as "windsplitters" due to their rounded corners—were painted white, but after being mistaken for rolling chicken houses, they were repainted yellow. Trolley cars departed from Petaluma every half hour at a fare of two cents per mile (50 cents in early 21st-century-currency). Traveling at a speed of 18 miles per hour, the trolley took an hour and a half to travel the 23 miles from Petaluma to Santa Rosa. Although the line was immediately popular with passengers, especially rural residents and children commuting into town for school, the P&SR's primary revenue came from hauling freight. It stopped at every farmer's crossing to pick up cans of milk, crates of eggs or fruit, or boxes of live chicks, earning it the nickname "The Cows and Chickens Line."

The main challenge for the trolley was John McNear's old nemesis, the SF&NPR, which by the early 1900s was known as the California Northwest Railway, and owned by Arthur W. Foster, a wealthy Irish immigrant who had made his fortune at a young age operating a brokerage firm in San Francisco. Foster, along with two partners, had purchased the SF&NPR at a bankruptcy auction in 1893. The rail line ran from Tiburon to Cloverdale, stopping in Petaluma, Santa Rosa, and Healdsburg, with a branch line from Santa Rosa to Sebastopol. Foster, who lived in San Rafael, wielded significant influence in the area, having developed a number of resorts along the Russian River after it was logged of its redwoods in the late 19th century, as well as a 10,000-acre sheep ranch that extended from Lakeville to the San Pablo Bay.

McNear initially approached Foster about investing in the electric trolley, but Foster passed, preferring to put his capital into expanding his California Northwest Railway line to Willits, where he planned to establish a lumber company. But once McNear launched the P&SR in 1904, Foster viewed it as a competitive act of war. First, he denied P&SR the right to cross CNW tracks at Weller Street in Petaluma, an action quickly overruled by the city. Then, in December of 1904, as the P&SR was completing laying its tracks into Santa Rosa, where it planned to connect with Santa Rosa's new street rail system, Foster refused to allow P&SR to install a grade crossing at the CNW tracks that ran across Sebastopol Avenue near the CNW depot, meaning they would have to go either over or under his rails.

With either option too costly for the fledgling P&SR, the line was forced to load and unload passengers and freight at the grade crossing on the edge of town. Outraged, a group of 92 Santa Rosa merchants signed a petition threatening to boycott the CNW for freight hauling. They also initiated a successful passenger boycott. In response, Foster slashed his rates for passenger travel between Santa Rosa to Sebastopol to 10 cents, or 5 cents below the rate charged by P&SR. Still, his cars ran empty.

On January 3, 1905, P&SR's general manager, William Bowen, sent a flatcar loaded with rails, a crew of gandy dancers, or track laborers, and guards armed with clubs to the end of the line on Sebastopol Avenue. Once there, the gandy dancers began sawing through CNW's rails to install the crossing. They were met by two of Foster's steam engines, which came rolling down the track from opposite directions, spraying the men with jet blasts of scalding hot steam. After chasing off the gandy dancers, the steam engines retreated to the CNW roundhouse to refuel. Meanwhile, back at the crossing, no one paid much attention to the arrival of a regularly scheduled P&SR trolley as it pulled up, until out jumped another bunch of gandy dancers. Grabbing railway ties from the flatcar, the men secured them to the CNW rails with spiked chains to block the steamers' return, and then quickly began installing the grade crossing. By the time Foster's steamers returned, the crossing was in place and a team of horses and mules had pulled the P&SR trolley across it.

P&SR had won what came to be called the "Battle of Sebastopol Avenue," but the war between the steamer locomotive and the juice line waged on. To connect with Santa Rosa's street rail system, the P&SR still had to cross a CNW spur track that ran to the Grace Brothers Brewery on 3rd Street. This time Foster took the battle to the courts in San Francisco, obtaining an injunction to stop P&SR from passing over his tracks on the grounds that doing so would endanger public safety. For the next two months, the P&SR trolley that had crossed the CNW tracks in the earlier battle sat stranded in downtown Santa Rosa until a judge dismissed the injunction.

When Bowen's gandy dancers arrived on March 1st to place the newly allowed grade crossing on CNW's spur track, a large crowd of onlookers gathered to watch.

Site of the "Battle of Sebastopol Avenue" in Santa Rosa

As the *Petaluma Argus* breathlessly reported:

> There is a hot time in Santa Rosa. It is the greatest day in the history of the county seat. Since early morning Santa Rosa has deserted the work bench, counter, desk, and even the family fireside, and its population of 10,017 souls is congregated at the tracks to watch a red hot fight.

Foster showed up at the crossing with two steam locomotives approaching from both sides of the track, each specially fitted with steam pipes and several rail gondolas loaded with sand and gravel. As the P&SR crew began digging beneath the CNW track, the steam locomotives drove them away with jets of hot steam while Foster's men refilled the freshly dug holes with the sand and gravel. After a few rounds back and forth, P&SR pulled two wagons filled with sand across the tracks in the path of the locomotives. They were smashed to splinters as Foster's two steam locomotives drew closer together in an attempt to close off the crossing. The opposing crews resorted to engaging in fistfights and throwing rocks at each other.

Finally, McNear's partner in the P&SR, Santa Rosa banker Frank Brush, threw himself down upon the rails in front of the two approaching locomotives. The locomotives stopped within inches of his prone body. As Brush clutched the rails, a tug-of-war broke out over his body. It ended when one of the steamers blew Brush off the rails with a blast of hot steam, burning his skin. A large brawl then ensued until police arrived and ordered Foster's men to stop their obstruction of the trolley crossing. A number of Foster's men who ignored the order were arrested and taken away in paddy wagons.

At 5 p.m., Foster returned to the crossing with a special train from Marin filled with 150 fighting replacements. He also brought with him two Marin County sheriffs prepared to arrest any Santa Rosa police officer or Sonoma County sheriff who tried to stop him. Upon disembarking, Foster was served with a legal restraining order, forcing him to call off his men. After Foster retreated, P&SR's gandy dancers worked through the night to complete the crossing over the spur track and connect their line to Santa Rosa's street rail system by sunrise.

Shortly after the battle, CNW was absorbed into the Southern Pacific Company, a deal Foster had initiated prior to his fight with P&SR. A jubilant John McNear promptly announced plans for line extensions of the P&SR to Tomales, Dillon Beach, Guerneville, Healdsburg, and even to McNear's Point in Marin. Those expansion dreams ended in 1906 after the San Francisco earthquake and the financial panic that followed put a damper on investment capital.

The P&SR had a successful 10-year run until 1915, when it found itself unable to pay off the interest on the 20-year mortgage bonds used for its initial financing. Following a foreclosure sale, the railway was reorganized in 1918. That same year, John McNear died at the age of 86. Following his passing, McNear's son, George P. McNear, became P&SR's largest stockholder and vice president. In 1922, he built the West Petaluma Spur and Trestle that ran along the west side of Petaluma's new turning basin, connecting the trolley to his feed mill (the present-day Great Petaluma Mill) and other businesses along the west side of the river.

The growing popularity of the automobile in the 1920s eroded passenger traffic on the juice line. Trucks had a similar impact on hauling freight from outlying farms. Losing money, the P&SR was purchased in 1928 by the Northwestern Pacific Railroad, which ceased passenger service after 1932. In the mid-1940s, following World War II, diesel locomotives replaced the trolley's electric engines. The opening of the Golden Gate Bridge in 1937 introduced long-distance trucking to San Francisco, reducing riverboat traffic. In 1940, the P&SR's steamer *Gold* was retired from service. Its companion steamer, *Petaluma*, made its last run on August 24, 1950.

The P&SR rail line continued to be used for freight hauling until 1984. By 1987, all of P&SR's tracks were torn up, with the exception of the West Petaluma Spur and Trestle along Petaluma's turning basin. In 1990, the Petaluma Trolley Living History Railway Museum opened on Baylis and East Washington streets, across from the former P&SR rail yard, with the dream of one day returning electric trolley service to Petaluma.

Train car from the Petaluma & Santa Rosa Railway, Western Railway Museum, Suisun City

Plazas

Petaluma's prosperity as a bustling river port in the mid-19th century was largely the doing of a handful of industrious city fathers—among them John McNear, Isaac Wickersham, William Hill, Ezekiel Denman, and Hiram Fairbanks—who capitalized on California's explosive wheat boom. But as the city's fortunes shifted in the 1890s with the declining wheat market and the emergence of a local poultry industry, a watershed moment occurred in Petaluma's development. On May 28, 1896, a group of Petaluma women, prompted by a local bicycle race, gathered to set a new future direction for the city.

Independence Day was approaching, and the usual local boosters—fraternal clubs, patriotic societies, and school marching bands—were gearing up for the annual Fourth of July celebration. With cycling having become the new craze of the Gay Nineties, the Petaluma Wheelmen were looking to stage the largest bicycle race ever held in the county. The leader of the Wheelmen, a young lawyer named Frank Lippitt, obtained an agreement from local businessman John McNear to build a new circular bicycle track along Vallejo Street near Kenilworth Park on spec, with the promise that the race would attract enough fans to pay for it.

Rena Shattuck, editor of the *Petalumian* newspaper, felt that in their zeal to build a racetrack that would attract thousands of visitors, the men were overlooking two of the city's biggest eyesores—Main Street Plaza (present-day Penry Park) and D Street Plaza (present-day Walnut Park)—where the Fourth of July festivities were being staged. The two plazas were littered with garbage, overgrown with weeds, and ringed with decrepit picket fences. Shattuck, the daughter of Frank Shattuck, one of the first Sonoma County judges and the founder of the *Petaluma Courier* newspaper, argued that the plazas were not only a public disgrace but unsafe for any woman or child who dared to enter them.

As a longtime *Courier* society columnist writing under the pseudonym Polly Larkin, Shattuck had covered the comings and goings of Petaluma's social elite since 1881. Despite her social connections and journalistic influence, Shattuck failed to get the attention of the men in town on the matter of the plazas, and so resorted to issuing a call-to-action among her female coterie—the middle- and upper-class wives and daughters of Petaluma's prominent Protestant elite, which was composed of businessmen, doctors, lawyers, newspaper editors, and bankers. And so on May 28th, the women gathered in Shattuck's newspaper office above a print shop in the McCune Building at Washington Street and Petaluma Boulevard North, where they agreed to form the Petaluma Ladies Improvement Club to clean up the plazas.

The club was the first of its kind on the Pacific Coast. While women's clubs had begun gaining popularity among middle- and upper-class women during the late 19th century, most of them, like the Petaluma Women's Club founded in 1895, focused on self-improvement through literary reading clubs, music performances, and lectures. With the dawning of the Progressive Era in the 1890s, some women's clubs began to step into community service, looking to temper the capitalistic drive of city fathers with values of beautification and civic consciousness. Doing so, however, meant pushing against the Victorian boundaries that had restricted women to the domestic sphere. According to historian Paige Meltzer, the women justified their entry into the community arena as "municipal housekeepers," working to clean up their cities and tend to the health and well-being of their neighbors without directly challenging the paternal order of their husbands and fathers. Still, in some quarters, women who took their activities into the public sphere were looked upon suspiciously, as if their ambitions somehow undermined social propriety.

In adopting the cause of the plazas, the Petaluma Ladies Improvement Club was stepping into a political hornets' nest. For while Petaluma's first city planner, the squatter Garrett Keller, had established Main Street Plaza in 1852 as part of the layout of the new town he called Petaluma, some of his fellow settlers weren't as enthusiastic about leaving a fallow piece of land undeveloped in the heart of the downtown. As the town built up based upon Keller's layout, the attitude of the business community toward his Main Street Plaza was perhaps best summed up by *Petaluma Argus* newspaper editor Henry L. Weston, who declared it "a waste and a nuisance."

To register their displeasure, the city's trustees (precursors to the city council) purposely left the plaza barren, with no paths, benches, trees, or water for decades. In 1859, barely a year after Petaluma was incorporated, the city's first board of trustees wasted no time proposing that the plaza be sold as a means of raising money for straightening the Petaluma River. Throughout the 1860s and 1870s they pursued one proposal after another

Penry Park, originally created as Main Street Plaza, 1852

to turn the plaza into something "useful," whether it be homes, businesses, a city hall, a courthouse, or a jail. In 1886, the trustees shaved off 40 feet of the plaza abutting Mary Street to appease downtown merchants concerned about parking for horses and buggies. They also constructed a stone wall along the eastern edge of the plaza to end complaints of winter mudslides clogging up Petaluma Boulevard North. Later that same year, the trustees pushed through a bond initiative with the Board of Education to build a high school on the plaza site. As excavation of the plaza began, an influential plaza neighbor named J. E. Gwinn filed a lawsuit that resulted in a court order stopping the city from repurposing the plaza.

At the first meeting of the Petaluma Ladies Improvement Club in 1896, Addie Atwater was elected club president. Atwater lived in an elegant Italianate Victorian on the corner of 4th and E streets, directly across from the D Street Plaza. She had moved to Petaluma in 1859 from New York with her husband Henry, the "cashier" or general manager of the Wickersham Banking Company. They purchased their home in 1875 from Henry's boss, Isaac Wickersham, one of the richest men in town, who had originally built the house for his son, Captain Jesse C. Wickersham, and his wife, Sarah.

In 1873, Isaac Wickersham had created D Street Plaza (present-day Walnut Park), along with John McNear, another wealthy man in town. The two men convinced the city to purchase the land from Wickersham, with McNear agreeing to donate half of the $2,500 purchase price ($50,000 in early-21st-century currency). For Wickersham and McNear, it was clearly a development investment. McNear's own private estate sat kitty-corner from the plaza on the northwest corner of 4th and D streets (now the site of the Post Office and Methodist Church), encompassing nearly an entire city block. In 1874, the two men privately graded the streets adjoining the new plaza, and in 1876 hired Edward S. Lippitt, a local educator and prominent attorney, to design the plaza. For reasons unknown, they stopped short of implementing Lippitt's design, aside from planting a handful of eucalyptus trees.

The city trustees, in keeping with their utilitarian outlook, then converted D Street Plaza into a pasture for horses and cows. In the 1880s, city trustees made some halfhearted efforts to improve the plaza, planting a hundred walnut trees on the site and installing a water fountain in the center of the plaza. By the time the Ladies Improvement Club formed in 1896, however, the plaza had reverted to a neglected wasteland.

The first task for the Ladies Improvement Club was to quickly raise money for the cleanup of the plazas in time for Independence Day, five weeks away. Within a week, Rena Shattuck and Addie Atwater succeeded in converting William Robinson, the president of the city trustees, to their cause. The owner of Robinson & Farrell, a blacksmith and wagon-making company, Robinson begrudgingly explained to his fellow trustees that he had started working with the ladies "to avoid being talked to death." He invited Shattuck, Atwater, and Kittie Weston, daughter of former *Petaluma Argus* editor and state senator Henry L. Weston, to address the trustees at their June 10th meeting. There, the three women laid out the club's rationale for improving the parks.

Beautification had been a main objective of the urban parks movement since its arrived in America from England in the early 19th century, along with providing green "lungs" for cities blighted by the ubiquitous filth of industrialization. Beginning with the Progressive Era in the 1890s, the urban parks movement expanded to promoting parks as a means of fostering public interaction, social coherence, and democratic equality.

These objectives fell on deaf ears among Petaluma's trustees. Instead, they peppered the ladies with explanations of "the cold facts," and repeatedly questioned them about where they expected the money to come from. Ultimately, the trustees agreed to temporarily provide water to the plazas at the city's expense, but for the upcoming summer only. Atwater assured them that once they saw how attractive and beautiful the women had made the plazas, they would want to provide water year-round, every year.

The Ladies Improvement Club quickly set about organizing themselves into various committees, with Addie Atwater overseeing D Street Plaza, and Daisy Reed, a pianist and wife of physician Clarence Reed, overseeing Main Street Plaza. They were joined by a number of single young "society belles" from Petaluma's finest families, including Zoe Fairbanks, Gertrude Hopkins, Lizzie Wickersham, Sallie Jewell, Sarah Cassiday, Ella Johnson, Estelle Newberg, Angie Tibbets, and Emma Palmer. Being ladies, they did not plan to do the physical work themselves, but instead solicited bids for the labor. To raise money, the club formed a women's minstrel group and staged a benefit concert in the

Walnut Park, originally created as D Street Plaza, 1873

Petaluma Opera House at 149 Kentucky Street, generating $181.75 ($5,000 in early-21st-century currency).

The cleanup quickly proceeded with the removal of old tree stumps and cartloads of garbage and discarded tin cans. Emma Palmer, the daughter of a furniture merchant, proved an especially shrewd financier, selling off 10 sacks of cut grass to poultry men as well as the decrepit picket fences surrounding the plazas to cattle ranchers. The plazas were cleaned up by July 4th, in time for the 2,000 visitors who descended upon the city for the Wheelmen's bicycle race.

Encouraged by their accomplishment, the Ladies Improvement Club pressed on after Independence Day, raising more money by hosting masquerade balls, minstrel shows, carnivals, and baseball games. They used the money to improve the plazas with pathways, flowerbeds, iron benches, curbs, gutters, and velvety grass lawns, and outfit D Street Plaza with a well, tank house, windmill, and water fountain donated by the Women's Christian Temperance Union. At Main Street Plaza, they planted 50 date palms, 42 of them a gift from Mary Burdell, owner of the 15,000-acre Burdell Ranch south of town. The remaining eight were donated by local nurseryman and city trustee William Stratton. The club was also instrumental in renaming D Street Plaza "Walnut Park," and Main Street Plaza "Hill Plaza," ignoring critics who sarcastically compared their efforts to rechristening "Chicken Hill" as "Poultry Highlands."

One advantage of the Ladies Improvement Club was media access. Rena Shattuck, known as the "mother of the club," was an experienced journalist who ran the *Petalumian,* one of Petaluma's three newspapers. Of the other two newspapers in town, the *Courier* had been founded by Shattuck's father, and the *Argus* had been run at different times by the fathers of club members Kittie Weston and Sara Cassiday. In 1901, the Ladies Improvement Club put out a special Thanksgiving edition of the *Argus,* edited by Shattuck and completely staffed by club members, who also wrote all the articles. The front page was devoted to covering the accomplishments of the club under the women's leadership.

The Petaluma Ladies Improvement Club managed their showpieces, Walnut Park and Hill Plaza, until 1911, when they turned them over "to the tender mercies" of a new parks commission created by the city council. By that time, few improvement projects could be found in town that didn't have the personal touch of the club, including trees lining residential streets, cement sidewalks, the purchase of the first city ambulance, the opening and paving of A Street, the painting of water hydrants and telephone poles, and the nighttime illumination of the town clock at Western Avenue and Petaluma Boulevard North to mark the time for errant, barhopping husbands. The club also raised money for the new Carnegie library at 4th and B streets, the land for which Addie Atwater sold to the city at half its market value, and inspired the formation of other women's civic clubs like the Oak Hill Improvement Club, which raised the money in 1908 to create a third city park at the city's abandoned burial ground at Oak Hill on Howard Street. In 1909, even the more staid Petaluma Women's Club elected to begin engaging in civic improvements.

Perhaps most importantly, the ladies demonstrated to the city fathers the value of city beautification in terms they could understand—money. Residences built adjacent to parks or along tree-lined streets with good sidewalks commanded premium prices in the real estate market, resulting in higher property tax revenues for the city, which in turn paid for the improvements. Known as the "proximate principle," the approach gained national acceptance after having been successfully demonstrated by Frederick Law Olmsted in his design of Central Park in New York City. In Petaluma, it had been the half-baked impetus behind Wickersham's and McNear's creation of Walnut Park in 1873, and the basis of the judge's ruling in the 1886 lawsuit that had prevented the city from building a school at Hill Plaza.

After Addie Atwater passed away in 1912 at age 75, the Ladies Improvement Club was inactive until the World War I, when they regrouped one last time to raise money for the Red Cross. Their spirit of progress, however, inspired ongoing improvements to the city parks.

The city council, however, never ceased in their efforts to convert Hill Plaza (renamed Penry Park to honor hometown Congressional Medal of Honor winner Richard Penry in 2001) into something useful. In 1948 and again in 1960, the council put forth proposals to turn the plaza into a parking lot. During city council hearings on the proposal in 1960, a doctor named L.J. Snow stood up in council chambers and, quoting the poet John Keats, delivered what some considered the turning point of the evening: "A thing of beauty is a joy forever."

The Ladies Improvement Club would have been pleased.

Oak Hill Park, created 1908, from the city's first cemetery

Places Called Home

When 35-year-old Brainerd Jones was chosen in 1904 to design Petaluma's new Carnegie Public Library, the *Petaluma Argus* announced the appointment with a prophecy:

> Great honor fell upon the city when the library trustees, after examining the plans submitted by the leading architects of California, accepted those of a Petaluma boy, a man young in years but old in experience who will be among the great builders of his day.

Over the next three decades until his death in 1945, Jones would in fact become Petaluma's most prominent builder, designing school buildings, banks, churches, fraternal halls, business blocks, and fire stations. His creations—well-built, simple yet sophisticated—composed 80 percent of the significant commercial and municipal structures in town during the early 20th century, according to Sonoma County historian Katherine Rinehart. Nine of his buildings are listed on the National Register of Historic Places. Aside from the iron-front buildings lining Petaluma Boulevard and Western Avenue which predated Jones, the sheer volume and scope of his work make him the dominant storyteller of Petaluma's historic downtown landscape.

Yet the assortment of work that perhaps best captures Jones's versatility is his residential home development, which extended over one of the most exciting periods in Bay Area architecture, an era known as the First Bay Area Tradition.

Jones, who had originally moved to Petaluma from Chicago at the age of 6 with his recently widowed mother, apprenticed at the prominent architectural firm of McDougall Brothers in San Francisco. Best known for their construction of public libraries, schools, and municipal buildings, the firm's senior partner, C.C. McDougall, genially networked the social clubs, fraternal societies, and commercial organizations for business. It was a valuable art of hobnobbing that Jones wisely adopted once he moved back to Petaluma in 1899 and hung out his shingle.

Jones's timing was fortuitous. Following half a century as a prosperous river port, Petaluma was at the very beginning of its second financial boom as the self-proclaimed "Egg Basket of the World." With the new prosperity came new wealth. It was one of the two ingredients considered by architects to be essential in influencing architectural style, the other being books.

In 1842, a New Yorker named Andrew Jackson Downing published a book titled *Cottage Residences* that popularized the Carpenter Gothic style of home. Mixing romantic architecture with the English countryside's pastoral picturesque, the book had a large influence on homes built in the Bay Area following the Gold Rush. Downing, who propagated the philosophy that "a good home will lead to a good civilization," popularized the Victorian Italianate style in his second book, *Architecture of Country Houses,* promoting the use of wood to simulate stone house fronts from the Italian countryside.

In Petaluma during the mid-19th century, the wealthy class that arose from shipping and agriculture interests viewed elaborate home ornamentation as an expression of new wealth. As developers amplified the curb appeal, increasing amounts of ornamentation were thrown against the walls, in an apparent fear of plain, vacant surfaces. Along with Italianate, other ornate Victorian styles including Greek Revival, Stick Style, and Queen Anne gained popularity, some on very grand scales.

The egg boom that began in the late 19th century gave rise to a new professional class in town with less rococo tastes—bankers, lawyers, doctors, dentists, and merchants. It also coincided with the start of a new fertile period for architecture, beginning with a major pivot in 1890 toward the Arts and Crafts style. The style was inspired by the books of English critic John Ruskin who, in reaction to the urbanization and mechanization of the Industrial Revolution, advocated for a return to medieval design and handcraft. Taking up Ruskin's challenge, English designer William Morris launched the Arts and Crafts movement, defining its characteristics as a link to nature, the use of locally sourced materials, and an emphasis on craftsmanship, volume, form, and asymmetry.

In America, a number of young architects in the late 19th century were inspired to create local versions of the movement, grounded in simplicity, rigor, and thought. One of the most prominent versions was the First Bay Area Tradition, popularized most notably by Bernard Maybeck, Julia Morgan, and Willis Polk. They established a look that was warm and woodsy, with an unpretentious value placed on honesty and authenticity, and yet also witty, sophisticated, and willing to take chances.

Craftsman-style home, 1197 East Washington Street, designed by Brainerd Jones for rancher John Ellis, 1911

Their designs—with an emphasis on natural woodwork, attention to the building site, large rooms in a horizontal orientation, and logical planning—gained quick popularity among the new moneyed classes in contrast to the stylistic excesses of the late Victorian era.

While some of San Francisco's most prominent First Bay Area Tradition architects designed buildings in Petaluma, including Julia Morgan, Albert Farr, and Ernest Coxhead, the most prolific practitioner was Brainerd Jones. Like his contemporaries, Jones was adept at many styles, employing the tradition as more of an attitude than a set of specific stylistic attributes. Among both the wealthy and the middle-class, Jones found a ready demand for his work. While not necessarily a great architect, he was a competent one who excelled at creating houses well-suited to their individual owners. Sonoma County historian Jeff Elliott, owner and restorer of a prominent Santa Rosa home designed by Brainerd Jones, points out that Jones's genius was fashioning living portraits of the lifestyles of the owners for whom he designed homes.

Jones began designing homes in the Queen Anne style, which was the only Victorian style that carried over into the Arts and Crafts period. With its gables, signature corner turrets, and broad volumes of space both inside and out, the Queen Anne style was a bit of a collection bin of the styles that had preceded it. As demand for the Arts and Crafts style grew locally, Jones began to design homes with Craftsman and Shingle Style influences. The Shingle Style was an American variation on the English shingle homes advanced by the Bay Area's Bernard Maybeck, with a nod to Frank Lloyd Wright's Prairie Style design.

Many of Jones's houses designed during this period had Craftsman details, but they also had steeply pitched, dominant gable roofs, mixed with shingle surfaces, and elements of Queen Anne and Colonial Revival styles, resulting in a style referred to as Transitional.

Jones enjoyed tweaking the formula of each style, playfully adding amusing, idiosyncratic details, all the while emphasizing strong, simple, and well-proportioned forms. A signature touch, especially on his Transitional homes, was a roof that flared out at the edges like a Chinese pagoda, giving his homes a slight Asian flavor.

By the 1920s, Jones had moved on from the Transitional style, designing homes in various revival styles in vogue from European sources, including Mediterranean Revival, Spanish Colonial Revival, Tudor Revival, and Mission Revival. His habit of ingratiating himself with the local fraternal and business organizations kept him steadily employed. His local ties famously helped him beat out prominent architect Julia Morgan, whose mother lived in Petaluma, on a commission to design the Woman's Club at 515 B Street in 1913.

What distinguished his buildings was that they were beautifully proportioned and detailed, with wide doorways, plenty of windows, and simple floor plans for ease of movement. By the time of his death in 1945, Jones had designed more than 150 buildings, including 55 homes. Almost everyone who has lived in a house designed by Brainerd Jones says that it feels like home—a fitting memorial to a local boy the *Petaluma Argus* dubbed "the man who built a city."

A sampling of Petaluma homes designed by various architects, including Brainerd Jones:

FIRST ROW (LEFT TO RIGHT)
Gothic Revival, 619 Prospect Street, built 1856

Greek Revival, 6 6th Street, built for Hanna Stewart Smith, 1865

Italianate, 222 4th Street, built by contractor L.G. Nay for banker Capt. Jesse C. Wickersham and his wife, Sarah, 1871

SECOND ROW (LEFT TO RIGHT)
Stick Style, 516 Prospect Street, built 1888

Queen Anne, 600 B Street, built for Dr. Harry S. Gossage and his wife, Edna, 1898

Shingle, 617 C Street, deigned by Julia Morgan for grain merchant Ezekiel Denman McNear, 1910

THIRD ROW (LEFT TO RIGHT)
Transitional, 319 Keokuk, designed by Brainerd Jones, 1912

Spanish Revival Style, 625 D Street, designed by Brainerd Jones for hardware merchant Americo F. Tomasini and his wife, Esther, 1929

Colonial Revival, 14 Martha Street, designed by Julia Morgan for banker J.H. Gwinn and his wife, Josephine, 1930

161

St. Vincent's Church

Upon arriving in Petaluma in 1915, Father James Kiely found himself facing the chance of a lifetime. A tall, imposing man with a quick wit and a lilting Irish brogue, Kiely had been among a wave of young Irish priests sent to America in the late 1890s to minister to the country's growing flock of Catholic immigrants. In the 18 years since his arrival in the Bay Area, he had distinguished himself as a tireless builder, constructing new churches in Oakland and San Francisco, and rebuilding churches in Olema and Bolinas destroyed by the 1906 earthquake. Now, as the newly appointed pastor of St. Vincent's church, he was faced with demands that exceeded the parish's ability to address them.

In the midst of a prosperous egg boom, Petaluma's citizens were enjoying one of the highest average incomes per capita in the country. An affluent middle class of Protestant doctors, lawyers, bankers, and merchants displayed their good fortune and status by constructing stately homes along D Street, the most elegant street in town, or stamping their names on new commercial buildings going up along Kentucky Street downtown.

Meanwhile, the dairy and cattle ranches ringing the town were largely owned and operated by Catholic immigrants from Switzerland, Italy, and Portugal. Looking to get their fair share of the local prosperity, in 1913 a group of 37 Swiss-Italian ranchers had formed the Petaluma Cooperative Creamery at Western Avenue and Baker Street, cutting out the middle man to market their milk, butter, and cheese directly to the consumer under a common brand called Clover.

The influx of Catholic immigrants at the turn of century had expanded St. Vincent's parish to 2,000 members, overwhelming its Victorian-era church and packing its parochial school. The sisters at the school were forced to live in the same cramped quarters that they taught in. For the enterprising Kiely, such challenges spelled opportunity for not only putting his mark upon the parish, but also upon the town of Petaluma.

St. Vincent's parish had begun in the 1850s, at a time when Petaluma was but a small village with a few homes and a handful of stores scattered along the sidewalks of wooden planks that lined Main Street. As the town grew into a bustling river port, it became largely dominated by Protestant merchants and entrepreneurs from back East, who congregated in fraternal civic lodges like the Masons and the Odd Fellows, where immigrants were not welcomed.

Irish Catholics began arriving in Petaluma in the 1850s, many of them escaping the potato famine back home. Others had come to California in 1846 as Union soldiers in the Mexican-American War and then stayed behind to mine for gold before settling on farms in Sonoma County. A number of them followed Irishman John Keyes to west Sonoma County, where he began growing potatoes, or "Irish diamonds," the first big boom crop for feeding San Francisco. Others settled on wheat and dairy ranches in Lakeville and on the western slopes of Sonoma Mountain, also known as "Little Ireland."

In the early 1850s, a grocery store merchant named James Daly opened his house on Keokuk Street to a small band of Irish families for celebrating Holy Mass on Sundays. Catechism for the children was conducted in Daly's stable. In 1857, the parish of St. Vincent de Paul was officially founded, and the first church was built near Daly's house at the southeast corner of Keokuk and Prospect streets. The Rev. Louis A. Auger from the Catholic parish in San Rafael served as St. Vincent's first visiting priest. St. Vincent's opened its first parochial school in 1865 under the Daughters of Charity of St. Vincent de Paul, a zealous order of nuns, at Howard and Union streets. In 1870, the church created Calvary Cemetery on Magnolia Avenue adjacent to the Protestants' newly established Cypress Hill Cemetery.

By that time, St. Vincent's parish had grown to 40 families, most of them Irish. In the 1870s, a number of Irish laborers laying tracks for the San Francisco & North Pacific Railroad settled in Donahue, the railroad's company town in the Lakeville area. After the tracks were installed, some of them stayed behind. The U.S. Census at the time counted the Irish as the largest single immigrant group in Sonoma County. (They also composed a third of San Francisco's population of 100,000.)

In 1873, a new priest, Rev. James Cleary, arrived at St. Vincent's parish. He built a new Gothic-style church on a block bounded by Bassett, Liberty, and Howard streets and Western Avenue, and then, in 1888, replaced the small parochial school at Howard and Union streets with the two-story St. Vincent's Academy, offering boarding to students from ranch families located outside town. By the turn of the century, many of the Irish had moved out of the area. They were replaced by Swiss-Italian immigrants from the Canton of Ticino and Portuguese immigrants from the archipelagos of the Azores

St. Vincent's Church, Bassett and Howard streets, built 1928

and Madeira, who grew the parish to 385 families.

Father Kiely replaced the retiring Rev. Cleary in 1915. He wasted no time establishing himself as a man about town, making a point of getting out daily, either on foot, horseback, or behind the wheel of an automobile—which he was known for driving somewhat recklessly around town—to visit parishioners, often stopping at homes unannounced for a brief visit. He also made daily trips to the hospital to comfort the sick, regardless of creed. A convincing pulpit speaker, he was noted for his clarity and candor, but sometimes got caught up in his sermons, trying the patience of altar boys anxious to get his focus back on the mass.

Kiely brought the same single-minded determination to fundraising. Shortly after arriving in Petaluma he began soliciting "assessments" from parishioners for parish improvements. The first initiative was building a new convent on the grounds of St. Vincent's Academy for the sisters to live in. The convent was followed by construction of a two-story parochial hall at Western Avenue and Howard Street and the remodeling of Calvary Cemetery.

In 1921, Kiely announced plans to build the premier church in all of Northern California, a landmark that would serve as a beacon from every corner of the city and for many miles around. By 1926 he had raised sufficient funds to sell off the Catholics' old Gothic-style church to Elim Lutheran Church. The Lutherans carefully dismantled the church board by board, and then reconstructed it as their new church at the corner of Baker and Stanley streets.

The opening of the new St. Vincent's church in 1928 was a watershed moment for both the Catholic community and Petaluma. Designed by San Francisco architect Leo J. Devlin, its Spanish Romanesque style recalled cathedrals and churches from Europe. The interior seated 800, and was laid out in a cruciform with a nave, transepts, and three altars made of imported Italian marble. The church was illuminated by 56 stained-glass windows: In the clerestory there were 16 windows of the Apostles and evangelists, and along the aisles there were 40 windows of saints, with men on the right, women on the left. Kiely had the windows made in Bavaria by Mayer of Munich Studios. A giant bell salvaged from the old church rang out from the eastern steeple of the church's twin towers, its peals audible for miles around. The $250,000 Kiely spent on construction ($3.3 million in early-21st-century currency), was completely funded within a year after the church's completion, just prior to the stock market crash in 1929.

The Great Depression didn't slow down the indefatigable Kiely. By the 1930s, there were 4,000 baptized Catholics living in the Petaluma River Watershed. St. Vincent Academy was again overrun with students. In 1937, Kiely remodeled the academy and also broke ground on a new grammar school adjacent to it that was opened to all religious denominations. Following World War II, San Francisco-based Catholics began moving to town as part of the suburbanization of Petaluma, creating crowded conditions once again at the parochial school. In 1956, after a California ballot initiative made private schools tax exempt, Father Kiely launched a fundraising drive to build a new high school. It opened in 1962 at Keokuk Street and Magnolia Avenue.

By that time, Kiely had assumed pastor emeritus status, turning the parish over to Monsignor Clyde Tillman, a priest he had baptized as an infant in Oakland in 1911. In the mid-1960s, St. Vincent's parish, which had grown to 7,000 members, was split in half, with parishioners living on the east side of town assigned to the new St. James Church on Ely Road.

The oldest practicing priest in California, Father Kiely continued doing what he liked best: celebrating eight o'clock morning mass each weekday and taking his famous walks around town, greeted by a noisy chorus of children and honking car horns, until he passed away at the age of 97. His passing came just as a third wave of Catholic immigrants began arriving in Petlauma from Mexico and other Latin American countries. Like the Irish immigrants before them, they initially held mass in private homes (in their native language), and then in the gym of the Catholic high school, before Spanish masses were incorporated into St. Vincent's Sunday service.

In 1994, the Spanish Romanesque church that Father James Kiely built in 1928, and where he had celebrated more than 25,000 masses and baptized, married, and buried multiple generations of the congregation, was beautifully restored inside and out.

Interior of St. Vincent's Church

The King of Hardware Stores

JUST A TEENAGER when he hopped a freight train in his native Kansas in 1902, Ernest Hobbie was keen on riding the rails west to visit his uncle, a chicken rancher in Petaluma. Once he arrived, his uncle helped him get a job at one of the largest businesses in town, the Schluckebier Hardware Company. It was a plum position for a young man in a farming community where family hardware businesses served as anchor stores, passed down from generation to generation.

Schluckebier was Petaluma's oldest hardware store, having been established by a German immigrant named Carl Bauer and his partner, Conrad Temple, as Temple & Bauer Hardware in the 1860s. In 1884, Carl Bauer's daughter Florentine married Henry Schluckebier, a German immigrant and bookkeeper, who soon became a full partner in his father-in-law's store. By the 1890s, Schluckebier took over the business from his retiring father-in-law and affixed his own name to the store.

Located at the northeast corner of Petaluma Boulevard North and Washington Street, the store extended down to the Petaluma River, with a large warehouse annex across the river on East Washington Street. Schluckebier boasted the North Bay's largest selection of hardware, plumbing, agricultural implements, carriages, and wagons. He was also the founding president of the Petaluma National Bank at the corner of Western Avenue and Petaluma Boulevard North.

While working at Schluckebier's, the adventurous Ernest Hobbie fell in love with Hanna Lohrman, the daughter of a German and Danish couple who had immigrated to Petaluma during the chicken craze in the 1890s. After marrying Hanna, Hobbie decided at the age of 27 to venture out on his own in business. In 1907, he and two partners opened Rex Hardware Merchandise, "The King of Hardware Stores," at the northwest corner of B and 4th streets. Catering specifically to poultrymen, Hobbie's store offered fencing, heated brooders for chicks, and an array of egg contrivances.

After buying out his partners, Hobbie expanded his wares to include home appliances, kitchen goods, and Bavarian china. The additions were made to compete with another new hardware store in town, A.F. Tomasini's. The founder, 25-year-old Americo Tomasini, had grown up in a Swiss-Italian ranching family in Nicasio. He opened his hardware store at 120 Kentucky Street in 1905, specializing in supplying local dairymen.

All three hardware stores—Schluckebier's, Rex, and A.F. Tomasini's—prospered as Petaluma grew with the egg boom from 3,900 residents in 1900 to more than 6,000 by the 1920s. Then came the transitions to the next generation of hardware men. In 1917, 30-year-old Ludwig Schluckebier took over Schluckebier's Hardware upon the death of his father, Henry. In 1930, 25-year-old George Hobbie, holder of a master's degree from Harvard, assumed the reins at Rex Hardware from his ailing father, Ernest. Finally, in 1940, 20-year-old George Tomasini suddenly found himself at the helm of A.F. Tomasini's Hardware upon his father's unexpected death.

The onset of the Depression in the 1930s presented major challenges to local hardware merchants, nearly driving them all out of business. As egg and milk prices dramatically dropped, the stores had to extend credit to thousands of ranchers. Many ranchers went bankrupt, forcing merchants to take on debt themselves to stay afloat. With the onset of World War II, the local agriculture economy began to pick up. George Hobbie, who had enlisted in the U.S. Navy, was serving as an aide to Admiral Chester W. Nimitz in the Pacific when he got the news that Rex Hardware had caught fire and burned to the ground. Instead of rebuilding, he relocated the store across the street to his longtime warehouse, originally constructed in 1851.

The postwar years were turbulent for the local poultry and dairy industry due to the introduction of large factory farms in the Central Valley. After 100 years in business, Schluckebier Hardware closed in 1959. A.F. Tomasini's Hardware relocated in 1956 to smaller quarters at 140 Keller Street, before closing its doors for good in 1961. George Hobbie operated Rex Hardware until 1964, at which time he sold the store to Henry Tomasini, founding CEO of Northbay Savings and Loan and a nephew of Americo Tomasini, who had started A.F. Tomasini's Hardware in 1905.

In the family tradition, Henry Tomasini passed Rex Hardware on to his son, Jeff, in 1984. Jeff Tomasini renamed the store Tomasini's Rex Ace Hardware and Country Store, uniting two local family heritages. In 2006, an electrical short ignited a blaze that burned the store down. Tomasini rebuilt the store on the same footprint and in the same centuries-old style as the original building, including its signature stairstep roofline. It remains Petaluma's only surviving family-owned hardware store from the turn of the century.

Tomasini's Rex Ace Hardware and Country Store at the corner of B and 4th streets

The Last Tugboat Company

Petaluma's ability to reign as the "Egg Basket of the World" largely turned on two natural assets: its mild Mediterranean climate and its sandy soil. The soil was important because chickens lack teeth. Instead of chewing their food, chickens swallow their food whole. The food then moves into their gizzard, a muscular organ where, with the help of small stones or grit that the chicken has also swallowed, it is ground up for digestion. Petaluma's foggy climate allowed chickens to freely roam outside, and its sandy soil provided them with grit as they foraged for food on the ground.

Still, the one thing Petaluma chickens lacked in their diet was calcium. If they were going to lay an egg a day, a supplement was required, otherwise calcium would be drawn from their bodies, leaving them with brittle bones and soft-shelled eggs. As a solution, chicken ranchers turned to oystershells.

Oysters had once been abundant in the San Francisco Bay. Ohlone and Coast Miwok tribes who lived in small villages beside the bay's creeks, streams, and tidal wetlands for many millennia, enjoyed an abundant shellfish population of oysters, mussels, and clams. Seventeenth-century Spanish explorers reported finding middens, or shell mounds, as long as football fields and as tall as two- and three-story buildings.

For reasons still unknown, the population of native oysters, scientifically known as *Ostrea lurida*, peaked 2,000 years ago. When the forty-niners arrived for the Gold Rush, there were no oysters to be found anywhere along the California coast. That presented a need, as raw oysters were a regular staple of working people on the East Coast, providing an inexpensive, high-quality source of essential nutrients for their otherwise poor diet. John Stillwell Morgan, an oysterman from New York City who had come to San Francisco originally looking for gold, set out to change that.

Discovering that *Ostrea lurida* oysters were available in the Puget Sound of Washington Territory, Morgan began shipping them to San Francisco. He branded them "Olympias," after the town of Olympia, Washington, to provide them with some of the sophistication of the varietals on the East Coast. For a fresh oyster in San Francisco during the 1850s, Morgan could fetch an equivalent of $12 in early-21st-century currency. To expand his supply, Morgan tried getting oysters to spawn in the San Francisco Bay, but was unsuccessful, forcing him to keep importing them from Washington.

That changed once the Transcontinental Railroad arrived in the Bay Area in 1869, and Morgan was able to transport young Atlantic oysters in barrels of seawater by rail across the country. He would then seed them in beds along the tidal marshlands of the South San Francisco Bay until they had fattened up enough to sell at an enormous markup. By the 1870s, oyster farming had made John Stillwell Morgan one of the richest men in San Francisco.

Oyster shells became popular in the early 1890s for lining garden walks. In the 1920s, as poultry raising in Petaluma evolved into more of an agricultural science—much of it covered in the *Petaluma Poultry Journal*—the Agricultural Lime and Compost Company began mining oyster shells from Morgan reefs in the South San Francisco Bay and shipping them on barges up the Petaluma River to the company's plant, where they were ground up for feed.

The Morgan reefs proved to be a short-lived bonanza, however. Beginning in the 1890s, pollution began to build up in the bay from coal-fueled steamboats, city sewage, effluents from tanneries and slaughterhouses, and sediments from hydraulic mining in the Sierra foothills, making the waters uninhabitable for oysters. In 1923, Morgan Oyster Company sold its beds to the Portland Cement Company, which used them for dredging purposes. Live oyster beds moved to the cleaner waters of Drakes Bay and Tomales Bay in Marin County, where the popular Pacific oyster from Japan was first introduced in 1931.

Meanwhile, as the egg industry in Petaluma churned through a 70-year cycle of boom and bust ending in the 1960s, the Agricultural Lime and Compost Company went through a number of name changes and diversification efforts. A family-owned company known as Lind Marine by the early 21st century, it was Petaluma's last remaining tugboat and barge business, hauling 20 tons of oyster shells a year from the South San Francisco Bay for livestock feed and bocce ball courts, as well as more than a million tons of sand and aggregate for use in construction.

Lind Marine tugboat docked outside its oyster shell milling plant at 300 East D Street

The Speakeasy

Silvio Volpi was intent on becoming a musician, not a grocer. Twenty-four years of age, he had been working in the Oakland shipyards following the death of his father, Giovanni, an Italian immigrant who had worked in the rock quarries near Lodi, California, and studying accordion with San Francisco's vaudevillian virtuoso Angelo Cagnazzo. Then, in 1925, his widowed mother, Giovanna, purchased a corner grocery in Petaluma called Solari's, making him the manager, and life changed.

Thanks to his talents as an accordionist, the outgoing Volpi quickly became a well-liked figure around town, teaching accordion and playing with a group called the Petaluma Minstrels at gatherings for local social clubs such as the Sons of Italy, the Elks Club, the Druids, and the Danish Sisterhood and Danish Brotherhood. In 1934, he married one of the most popular young women in town, Mary Oberto, the Egg Day Queen of 1925, and set his sights on one day owning a dairy ranch.

Meanwhile, by day he managed Volpi's Grocery at the corner of Keller and Washington streets. Originally established by Louis and Emilia Solari, the grocery was well known for its imported goods, including the area's largest stock of Italian salami, Swiss cheese, and macaroni. In 1909, the Solaris had moved their grocery into the newly built Canepa Building from their former location down the street. They brought with them a bar they had salvaged in 1899 from the fire-damaged Exchange Saloon on Petaluma Boulevard North, which they installed in a small saloon at the back of the grocery.

In those days, a small grocery with a backroom tavern was so commonplace that the Women's Christian Temperance Union declared the corner grocery an evil, claiming it afforded the opportunity for "covert indulgence in the drink habit to many who would never go into a rum shop." That all changed with America's entry into World War I in 1917. Congress, which had come to rely on taxes from the manufacturing and sale of alcohol, passed the first national income tax in 1916, creating a substitute source of revenue. That combined with the war effort to save grain for the troops, and a patriotic campaign to associate beer drinking with Germans, resulted in wartime prohibitions imposed on the manufacture of distilled liquor, beer, and even wine, although it was not derived from grain. In Sonoma County, at the time the state's largest wine producer and the country's second-largest hop producer, the prohibitions were largely ignored, especially among Italian immigrants, who struggled to understand how such a common aspect of life could be called a crime.

In 1919, the 18th Amendment to the Constitution was ratified, making it a crime to produce, transport, or sell intoxicating beverages. Exceptions were made for wine used in religious sacraments or as medicine subject to a doctor's prescription, specifically the "hot claret wine gargle" for treatment of a sore throat. With its rural population, dairy manufacturing know-how, and rugged coastline, Sonoma County became a vast underground of basement winemakers, secret whiskey distillers, and smugglers of imported Canadian whiskey, who paid off local law enforcement and played an ongoing cat-and-mouse game with the Feds.

After 1920, the backroom saloon at Solari's Grocery was converted to a hidden speakeasy. Allegedly, the back door to the alleyway provided patrons with a quick escape if needed, but it's doubtful it ever was. Most liquor busts followed a standard procedure: the seller was given a few hours notice to move their liquor off premises, leaving one pint on hand so that local law officers, or "drys," would have something to show for their trouble. The fines collected replaced the annual liquor license fees previously charged tavern owners by the city before Prohibition. In 1922, Solari's Grocery experienced such a raid. A bottle of "jackass brandy," or grappa infused with burnt sugar to give it a brandy appearance, was found beneath the bar. Louis Solari was taken two blocks away to City Hall, charged his fine, and given a suspended sentence.

In 1925, Louis and Emilia Solari retired, selling the corner grocery and speakeasy to Giovanna Volpi. She and her son operated the backroom speakeasy only during daytime grocery hours, most likely paying off the drys to avoid raids. When local ranchers came into town for supplies, they would leave a grocery list at the front counter and then step into the secret backroom for drinks while waiting for their orders to be filled.

When the government's need of tax revenues at the onset of the Great Depression brought about the repeal of Prohibition in 1933, Volpi's Grocery was among the first establishments in Sonoma County to be issued a liquor license. Yet, bootlegging did not end once the county became "wet" again. Federal and state agents remained flummoxed by the seemingly endless supply of illegal alcohol flowing from the Petaluma area by

Volpi's Ristorante & Bar, 124 Washington Street, built 1909

bootleggers looking to evade taxes. Finally, in the spring of 1937, agents succeeded in trailing a couple of sugar shipments used in the manufacture of jackass whiskey from a warehouse in San Leandro to the dairylands west of Petaluma, where the trail went cold.

The sugar shipments were made in inconspicuous but souped-up sedans that were outfitted with oversized tires and heavy springs, and stripped of all seats but the driver's, giving them the storage capacity of a small truck. The sugar was delivered to relay stations on dairy ranches, where it was stored before being moved to a still. After the alcohol was made, the automobiles transported five-gallon tins of "alky" back to the relay ranches, where they were eventually taken into San Francisco via the Sausalito ferry, or driven as far north as Oregon, Washington, and Idaho.

The breakthrough lead for the Feds came with a tip about the phenomenal growth of a clump of oak trees on an abandoned poultry ranch owned by Morris Sibalowsky north of town. They discovered the trees had been nourished by waste mash piped down from a still 1,500 feet away on the ranch. Over the next six weeks agents quietly trailed other sugar shipments to various ranches in the area. On April 13, 1937, they followed a sugar delivery from the ranch of George Silva on I Street Extension to a warehouse on Hopper Street in East Petaluma. By the time they obtained a warrant, the bootleggers had hastily fled the site, leaving behind a partially dismantled, 1,500-gallon still.

Consisting of two 50-foot towers, the still was designed to be quickly disassembled for transport to a new location in the event of an impending raid. The towers each contained multiple distillation plates that were able to produce alcohol with a purity of 98 percent, or 196 proof. To preserve its purity, the alcohol was immediately placed in airtight containers, preventing it from absorbing water from the air. Sodium succinate was added as a catalyst to speed up fermentation. Confiscated records showed that at peak production the still was generating about $1,500 worth of liquor a day ($25,000 in early-21st-century currency).

An agent driving along East Washington Street after the Hopper Street raid spotted the car of one of the suspected bootleggers, 30-year-old Louie Boitano, who owned a nearby welding company. The agent followed Boitano to a dog food packing plant, owned and operated by the bootleggers' ringleader, Charlie Garzoli. A member of a large pioneer dairy ranching family in Two Rock, 35-year-old Garzoli had begun the liquor ring in the early thirties. By 1933, he had amassed enough money to build a palatial Mediterranean Revival-style home at 5865 Old Redwood Highway in Penngrove, just beyond the Twin Oaks Roadhouse. He operated the dog food plant as a front for his liquor operations.

As agents raided the dog food plant, Garzoli and Boitano slipped out a side door, but were soon apprehended nearby. Silvio Volpi put up the $5,000 for Garzoli's bail. While being arraigned, Garzoli proclaimed his innocence, asserting, "They haven't got a damned thing on me." After the raid, another dozen people believed to be associated with the liquor ring were arrested, a number of them from prominent Petaluma families, including Americo Bloom. Like Garzoli, Bloom was the son of a pioneering Swiss-Italian rancher, and head of the family ranch in Chileno Valley. His brother, Adolph Bloom, was a prominent Petaluma banker. Subpoenaed as a government witness, Adolph Bloom hung himself just days before the trial.

Charlie Garzoli and Louie Boitano were convicted of having defrauded the government of $1,000,000 in taxes ($17 million in early-21st-century currency). They were sentenced to two years in the McNeil Island Penitentiary in Washington, and fined $10,000 each. A number of other ring members were given lighter sentences or saw their cases dismissed. After his release from prison, Charlie Garzoli bought a 220-acre dairy ranch on Tomales Road, which he operated as a gentleman rancher with his wife until 1971. He eventually received a full pardon, and died at his Penngrove home in 1997.

In 1956, Silvio Volpi realized his lifelong dream of owning a dairy ranch, but died shortly after purchasing it. His 19-year-old son John assumed operation of the ranch, while Silvio's wife, Mary, and his daughter-in-law, Mary Lee, operated Volpi's Grocery. The arrival of big chain supermarkets in the 1960s put an end to most small corner groceries in town. The Volpi family converted their grocery into a deli and tavern. In 1992, they added the space next door that had housed Eliot's Candyland for 40 years, and expanded into a successful Italian family-style restaurant. The old speakeasy in the backroom of Volpi's remained a popular hangout, with John Volpi, an accomplished accordionist like his father, Silvio, entertaining patrons at the bar most evenings.

John Volpi playing the accordion in the backroom bar of Volpi's Ristorante & Bar

Brothels

The play *Camille* opened for a one-week run at Petaluma's Hill Opera House on May 1, 1905. Performed by the acting troupe of the renowned "queen of drama," Georgia Harper, the performance was a high-water mark for the theater. Only five months since its grand opening, the Hill Opera House was being heralded as one of the finest playhouses in the state, a testament to the vision of Josie Hill. The recent widow of banker William Hill, one of the richest men in town, Mrs. Hill had spared no expense in creating what she called "a temple of the thespian" at the corner of Keller and Washington streets.

Adorned with luxurious side boxes, orchestra stalls, and an interior fashioned of ivory, buff leather, and gold, the 600-seat playhouse was filled for *Camille*'s opening night with the crème de la crème of Petaluma, or what one reporter called "representatives of pure womanhood and decent manhood." The vestibule of tile and marble that led to the dress circle was a virtual runway of women in fine gowns, sweeping down the aisles on the arms of their escorts like "poetry in motion."

The poetry came to an end when a local madam—most likely Georgie Herbert—and two of her "girls" traipsed into the vestibule and took their seats in a prominent front side box. Herbert was well known to most members of the audience as a "woman of ill-fame"—a euphemism for any woman who strayed from the Victorian code of true womanhood, which called for domesticity, submissiveness, piety, and sexual purity. The operator of a brothel at 2nd and C streets since the early 1890s, Herbert's appearance at the opera house coincided with an incident the night before, during which a neighboring madam, 35-year-old Fannie Brown, had been arrested after reports of loud noises coming from a "midnight orgy" at her boarding house. Brown was jailed and fined for serving liquor without a license, a violation imposed upon brothels by the city as a de facto operating tax. Brown, Herbert, and other local madams had repeatedly applied for liquor licenses, only to be denied by the city trustees, or city councilmen, who feared a public backlash if they appeared to sanctify prostitution.

After the curtain went up for *Camille*—Alexandre Dumas's tragic love story of a tubercular prostitute, and the basis of Verdi's opera *La Traviata*—Herbert and her two companions continued drawing attention to themselves throughout the evening by conspicuously moving about their box and receiving repeated visits from a male admirer. The outrage expressed on the front page of the *Petaluma Argus* the next day was scathing, a measure of the fear among the town's middle-class elite of the changing times, when brothels run by smart and capable businesswomen like Georgie Herbert and Fannie Brown were raising prostitution to a new level, one that demanded public recognition of the trade as a regular commercial enterprise.

Brothels had had their place in the dark corners of society in the late 19th century, unofficially sanctioned under a Victorian belief that while the sex drive of the male was strong, the female's was virtually nonexistent. In relieving a man of his desires, a prostitute served to protect the virtue of the man's wife, assuming the prostitute stayed in the shadows and did not cross any cultural, class, or racial lines, nor spread disease into the home.

With the turn of the century and the dawning of the Progressive Era, such repressive attitudes were beginning to change. New definitions of what was permissible and normal were beginning to evolve, driven in part by middle- and upper-class women who were demanding greater personal autonomy for themselves and a larger role in public life. With the broader changes came changes in attitudes about prostitution. While Victorian and religious moralists tended to portray the prostitute as either a seductress or a victim, Progressives viewed her as a fatality of poverty, surrounded by degradation, disease, and violence, while women suffragists saw her as the embodiment of oppression under the shackles of deviant patriarchs.

These differing perspectives were not new to the trade. During the Gold Rush era, writers like Bret Harte had stereotyped prostitutes as "hookers with a heart of gold," possessing both a good woman's kindness and warmth and a bad woman's sensuality and vigor. It was a portrait that resonated with the cultural mythology developed about the American West, one that celebrated rugged, self-reliant individuality in contrast to the compliant role demanded of women under the Victorian code of true womanhood.

Such conflicting viewpoints were nothing new to those in the prostitution trade. Although prostitution had been legal during the Gold Rush, it's status began to change in 1855 when the California state legislature passed its first anti-prostitution bill. As the number of women in the state grew during the 19th century, further

The Lan Mart Building, 35 Petaluma Boulevard North, built 1911

attempts to regulate prostitution was correlated with efforts to more closely proscribe the roles of women in general, placing limits on what constituted acceptable gender, class, and sexual behavior. During the industrialization that took place in the second half of the century, prostitution saw a steady increase as more unmarried women left the economic and social protection of their immigrant families to work in factories or as domestic servants, where they were subjected to low wages and, often, sexual exploitation. Some of the women, unable to find sustainable employment or else abandoned or abused by their husbands or families, entered the world of prostitution.

By the turn of the century, prostitution in Petaluma was part of a thriving vice industry that included numerous illegal gambling and drinking establishments. A handful of roadhouses, including reportedly the Washoe House and the Penn Grove Hotel, boarded prostitutes for travelers and ranch hands, while hidden bordellos in places like the second floor of the Lan Mart Building on Petaluma Boulevard North (then Centennial Livery Stables) provided discreet services for guests staying at the adjacent Continental Hotel.

Petaluma's formal tenderloin district was located along the river, between 1st and 2nd streets and C and D streets. In the early 1900s, the tenderloin hosted five bordellos, listed on Sanborn maps as "F.B." for female boarding house. They drew local customers as well as visitors to town who arrived by train or steamboat. Fannie Brown's house at 101 C Street, locally known as the "101 Ranch," was the largest, featuring between one and two dozen prostitutes. Unlike the small, windowless "cribs" provided for liaisons in places like the Lan Mart Building, houses like Brown's typically consisted of a suite of small rooms. The prostitutes paid the madams 50 cents per john ($15 in early 21st-century-currency) for "room rent," plus a monthly fee of five dollars per month, in return for which they received room and board. Brown also provided the women with contraception and a monthly health checkup by a physician, and saw to it that they were well dressed by a local tailor.

Brown rotated her sex workers regularly with fresh replacements from San Francisco, the new arrivals discreetly announced by train conductors who received kickbacks. Other out-of-towners found their way to the tenderloin thanks to small "blue books" that were sold behind the counters of local bars and cigar shops. The outside money from sexual tourism benefited many in town, including the owners of bars, restaurants, and hotels, the landlords who charged the madams exorbitant rents, the police who pocketed bribes to look the other way, and the city treasurer who collected regular fees for illegal liquor sales. Fannie Brown herself lived in style. An Austrian immigrant, she also went by her maiden name, Fannie Ciran, and her married name, Fannie Mardorf, while residing with her German-born husband, William (who also went by the nom de guerre William Brown), in a well-appointed home at on Walnut Street. She reportedly was chauffeured to and from work each day.

The Progressive Moment at the turn of the century sought to reform society by applying rational and scientific methods to everything. It also sought to employ the government in policing behavior that during Victorian times was thought to be exempt from the bright lights of public scrutiny, including prostitution, alcohol consumption, and entertainment. Progressive reformers found themselves joined in this initiative by the nation's largest women's organization, the Women's Christian Temperance Union.

Initially launched in the 1870s as a moral crusade against men who spent their paychecks at the saloon and then came home to beat and rape their wives, by the turn of the century the W.C.T.U. had expanded their crusade into a "social purity" movement that included the moral reform of prostitutes. Their membership was made up predominately of middle-class women from evangelical Protestant churches like Josie Hill, founder of the Hill Opera House. The group refused to accept women of the Catholic or Jewish faith, or women not born in America.

Following Georgie Herbert's scandalous display at *Camille's* opening night, Progressive and W.C.T.U. reformers combined their efforts to eradicate prostitution from Petaluma altogether. Their opportunity came in 1907 after the Santa Rosa City Council passed an ordinance legalizing prostitution as a means of making the brothels comply with city licensing, taxation, and hygiene laws. The backlash from Progressive and religious reformers was thunderous, leading Sonoma County's ambitious new district attorney, Clarence Lea, to initiate a countywide crackdown on brothels. Both Georgie Herbert and Fannie Brown were arrested for keeping houses of ill-repute. Herbert, reading the writ-

Wickersham Building, 168 Petaluma Boulevard North, built 1910

ing on the wall, promptly relinquished her business to Johanna Kohler, a British woman, and left town. Kohler was arrested shortly afterward under a newly adopted law against white slavery, for importing a woman to her brothel from England "for immoral purposes."

The Santa Rosa City Council reversed its ordinance legalizing prostitution, after a judge ruled in a lawsuit filed by a local citizen that the city couldn't license something already illegal under state law. In the same lawsuit the judge ruled that boarding houses couldn't be rented or leased for purposes of prostitution. This placed landlords in legal jeopardy for the first time. Some madams like Fannie Brown already owned their houses outright. Others like Johanna Kohler stayed in business by signing lease-to-purchase agreements with the landlords that legally made them owners of the houses. Other brothels shut down.

In navigating their way through these turbulent times with the added burden of class and gender restrictions placed on women, madams like Georgie Herbert, Fannie Brown, and Johanna Kohler demonstrated that they were not helpless victims but women capable of exercising agency. Even so, the life of a madam was a life marked by intrusions of violence, arrests, illness, and even death. Fannie Brown's predecessor at 101 C Street, Frankie Duval, was a prime example. Petaluma's leading madam in the 1890s, Duval, whose real name was Frances Gaffney, died in 1898 at the age of 29 after succumbing to a debilitating illness most likely related to her line of work. She left behind a small fortune, but caused a minor scandal when her will was published in the local newspaper. In it she specified that the men in her life—her father, brothers, and the husband who had abandoned her years before—were only entitled to receive $1 each.

In 1914, the W.C.T.U. and the Progressive reformers succeeded in getting the Red Light Abatement Act enacted in California. Under the act, owners of buildings where prostitution took place were fined by the city. This inadvertently led to discriminatory rental practices, such as not allowing single women to rent a first-floor apartment. In some places, women could not rent an apartment at all. New laws criminalizing prostitutes and the act of prostitution followed during World War I, as troops fighting overseas experienced massive outbreaks of venereal disease, raising fears of venereal disease spreading through military training camps in the States. During this period, Fannie Brown and Johanna Kohler were repeatedly jailed with fines of up to $400 ($10,000 in early-21st-century dollars) by District Attorney Lea, who rode his prostitution-busting campaign to election to the U.S. Congress in 1917.

In 1919, Johanna Kohler died after a long illness of dropsy and complications, bringing an end to the storied brothel at 2nd and C streets. Her obituary called her "a good-hearted woman, known for her honesty and square business sense." Fannie Brown continued to operate the 101 Ranch at 1st and C streets until the spring of 1925, when the author of California's Red Light Abatement Act, Edwin C. Grant, made it his last act as head of the California State Law Enforcement League to close down Brown's house for good. She resided in Petaluma until her death in 1938.

As a result of the Red Light Abatement Act, prostitution increasingly moved to the streets, where the madams were largely replaced by pimps, increasing the danger for prostitutes, who were further criminalized and shunted to the margins of society.

From the 1930s through the 1950s, other low-key brothels periodically sprung up around Petaluma, including the upstairs of the Wickersham Building at 170 Petaluma Boulevard North and the Green House on Lakeville and Madison streets. Owned and operated by Helen Walker, the nondescript Green House was known for the prominence of its clientele. It opened in 1939, a year after Fannie Brown's death, and operated as a "necessary evil" unofficially sanctioned by local police as a means of containing streetwalkers and potential sexual assault. In 1953, a crusading exposé in the Santa Rosa's *Press Democrat* succeeded in shutting the Green House down. When questioned by a *Santa Rosa Press Democrat* reporter about allowing the Green House to operate, Petaluma police chief Melvin Del Maestro unapologetically explained that the Green House had been in place since the time he was a kid, implying that as far he was concerned, it was part of the community.

Former Penn Grove Hotel, 10056 Main Street, Penngrove, built 1906

Theaters

ALAN FINLAY REALIZED HIS DREAM of becoming Petaluma's sole movie theater mogul in February 1973, when he signed a 10-year lease on the Showcase Theater at Keller and Washington streets. The Showcase's owner, Dan Tocchini, had already sold him the town's other two theaters, the State and the Parkway Drive-in, six years earlier. Now, with a monopoly of local cinemas, Finlay was ready to embark upon a bold new strategy, one that he promised would put Petaluma on the map.

A small, thin man with a club foot, Finlay spent his evenings in the projection booth of the Parkway Drive-in Theater changing film reels and watching television with his mother, who had turned the booth into a makeshift living room. Based in Sonoma Valley, he still operated the first theater he had purchased in Boyes Hot Springs in 1954.

In the 20 years that had passed, the movie business had been in steady decline, its audiences lured away by the growing popularity of television. One bright spot had been the introduction of rural drive-in theaters. Initially targeted at working-class families with station wagons full of pajama-clad kids, the drive-ins also found popularity with young couples as "passion pits." In 1964, Dan Tocchini, a second-generation theater operator from Santa Rosa, opened the Parkway Drive-in at Old Redwood Highway and Highway 101. Featuring a 50- by 100-foot screen, the theater accommodated 800 cars but was plagued from the beginning by flooding in winter and fog in summer, moving Tocchini to sell it to Finlay in 1967.

Meanwhile, the movies themselves were changing. After the U.S. Supreme Court recognized movies as a form of artistic expression protected by the First Amendment in 1952, the censorship restrictions movies had operated under regarding language, sexuality, and violence began to loosen up. With the arrival of the sexual revolution in the 1960s, the Motion Picture Association of America decided to drop the Hays Code that had defined decency standards since 1930, and introduce in 1968 a system of film ratings that allowed moviegoers to largely make their own decisions of what level of censorship they wanted. The original ratings were G for General Audiences, M for Mature Audiences, R for those under 16 requiring an accompanying parent or adult guardian, and X for no one under 17.

Meanwhile, television remained heavily censored, giving movies a new advantage. As riskier content began drawing adult audiences back to the theaters in 1969, sexually explicit films, led by Andy Warhol's *Blue Movie*, began showing in mainstream cinemas, ushering in a 15-year period that came to be known as the "Golden Age of Porn."

In 1971, Alan Finlay began running X-rated films intermittently at the Parkway Drive-in and the State Theater. They were the only mainstream theaters north of San Francisco to do so. The films drew large audiences from the far reaches of Sonoma, Marin, Mendocino, and Napa counties. After leasing the Showcase from Tocchini in 1973, Finlay unleashed his grand plan. He continued to show mainstream films at the Showcase while running X-rated films exclusively at the State. His first double billing was *Deep Throat* and *Behind the Green Door*, two new X-rated films that quickly became a local sensation, packing in audiences night after night.

Local religious and civic leaders mounted a petition drive to shut down the theater. On June 11, 1973, Sonoma County's district attorney charged Finlay with six counts of exhibiting obscene matter and assisting persons to expose themselves. Dan Tocchini, who continued to operate theaters outside of Petaluma, came to Finlay's defense, arguing in a letter to the *Petaluma Argus-Courier* that "movies do not corrupt a society, they only reflect a society." Ten days later, on June 21st, the U.S. Supreme Court issued a ruling that appeared to support Tocchini's position, redefining obscenity as that which lacked "serious literary, artistic, political, or scientific value," as determined by "community standards."

The moral debate over what constituted community standards in cinema had raged since 1912, when the State Theater—then called the Mystic—first opened its doors. At that time, the powerful Women's Christian Temperance Union made a case for judging movies on moral, not aesthetic, grounds, arguing that they glorified war, violence, and sexual promiscuity, encouraging children to potentially act out criminal and immoral acts. The W.C.T.U. also claimed that movies were addictive, drawing young people into dark, crowded theaters where they were likely to engage in "illicit lovemaking and iniquity."

The Mystic Theater's founder, Dr. John McNear, Jr., son of prominent Petaluma grain merchant and banker John McNear, sought to defuse any confrontation with the W.C.T.U. at the theater's grand opening by proclaiming the Mystic to be a family-oriented venue, presenting only wholesome, high-quality vaudeville shows

The Mystic Theater, 23 Petaluma Boulevard North, built 1912

and "censored moving pictures."

Censorship was only one of the challenges McNear faced with his new theater. Filmmaking itself was undergoing a massive sea change, emerging from its experimental phase of "shorts"—brief, silent movies that drew content from vaudeville, Wild West shows, melodramas, and comic strips—to longer feature films. Petaluma's first shorts had premiered in 1904 at the Unique Theater on the corner of 4th and C streets. Built in 1875 as an gymnastic auditorium for the German-American Turn Verein Association, the Unique interspersed shorts between live vaudeville acts. The year 1904 also saw the opening of the opulent Hill Opera House at the corner of Keller and Washington streets. Built by Josie Hill, the wealthy widow of banker William Hill, the Hill Opera House quickly established itself as one of the premiere playhouses in the Bay Area. Within months of opening, it was also offering shorts between vaudeville acts.

With the introduction of the nickelodeon in 1905, shorts became the main feature. Many of them were laced with anti-authority themes, poking fun at bumbling cops, corrupt politicians, and intrusive upper-class reformers, as well as providing vivid glimpses of how the other half lived in, featuring urban tenements and ethnic ghettoes, gangsters, loan sharks, and drug addicts. There was also a fair amount of salacious sexual imagery and risqué humor drawn from burlesque halls and vaudeville theaters. Pornographic films were also available, often viewed through the peephole of a small, hand-cranked Kinetoscope.

Commonly set up in a small storefront with wooden seats and a piano to provide musical accompaniment, nickelodeons ran a series of shorts, broken up by live vaudeville acts. By 1907, Petaluma had two nickelodeons, the Star Theater at 138 Kentucky Street (adjacent to the present-day Golden Concourse) and the American Theater, housed inside the American Hotel at 135 Main Street (site of present-day Putnam Plaza). Inexpensive entertainment, the nickelodeons were heavily patronized by immigrant working-class audiences, and so denounced by anti-immigrant groups like the W.C.T.U. as disreputable and dangerous.

In 1909, Josie Hill, owner of the Hill Opera House and a prominent member of the local W.C.T.U., sought to distance the opera house from the nickelodeon craze by featuring only longer, quality films to complement its program of plays and vaudeville acts. By the early 1910s, the growing popularity of longer films gave rise to larger and more comfortable theaters than the tiny storefront nickelodeons. In the summer of 1911, Taylor Squires, owner of the American Nickelodeon, opened a 350-seat theater called the Gem on the first floor of the Wickersham Building at 170 Petaluma Boulevard North. Within a month, both nickelodeons in town closed down. Six months later, Dr. McNear premiered the 750-seat Mystic Theater on the ground floor of his father's newly constructed McNear Building at 23 Petaluma Boulevard North.

McNear was new to the entertainment business, having briefly practiced medicine in San Francisco and then worked as a pharmacist before returning to Petaluma to serve as a property manager for his aging father. To run the Mystic he set up a management company with his sister-in-law, Lulu Egan, a local artist and the daughter of a prominent grocer in town. A year after opening the Mystic, McNear and Egan also assumed management of the 900-seat Hill Opera House. They ran the Hill primarily as a live performance theater with limited film showings, and the Mystic as a cinema with occasional vaudeville acts.

In 1915, the U.S. Supreme Court excluded films from protection under the First Amendment, deeming them commercial, not artistic, enterprises. The ruling set off new demands for censorship from reform groups like the W.C.T.U. In response, the movie industry created the Motion Picture Producers and Distributors of America (later renamed the Motion Picture Association of America) to more rigorously censor films on a voluntary basis. That proved a moving target during the Roaring Twenties, as Victorian standards of decency were swept aside and moviegoing attendance soared. Large theater chains began building lavish movie palaces equipped with the latest in film and sound technology.

In 1924, Josie Hill's family sold the Hill Opera House to a chain called T&D Jr. Enterprises. The new owners demolished everything in the opulent playhouse except its original four walls, investing $100,000 ($1.4 million in early-21st-century currency) to create a 1,078-seat movie house they called the California. Two years later, McNear and Egan also called it quits, turning the Mystic over to T&D Jr. Enterprises.

In 1929, the "talkies" arrived, setting off another round of the seemingly never-ending innovations in

The Phoenix Theater (originally the Hill Opera House), 201 Washington Street, built 1904

sound and film technology and seating comfort. As the country descended into the Great Depression of the 1930s, movie attendance declined. To lure audiences back into theaters, movie studios resorted to films with adult themes touching on sex, violence, and other less-than-wholesome topics, setting off a threat of film boycotts by religious groups. In response, the movie industry adopted a new set of decency standards called the Hays Code, banning from films profanity, sex perversion, white slavery, scenes of passion, explicit adultery, sympathetic treatment of crime or criminals, and dancing with "indecent" moves.

In Petaluma, the California Theater remained in the hands of the T&D Jr. Enterprises chain (eventually known as United Artists Theaters) until 1968, when it was sold to Dan Tocchini, who changed the theater's name to the Showcase. The Mystic, however, went through a number of ownership changes, one of which resulted in a name change in 1938 to the State Theater. In 1959, the State was purchased by Tocchini, who operated it in accordance with the standard formula of the times, changing featured movies three times a week, with Sunday, Monday, and Tuesday usually featuring musicals; Wednesday and Thursday running B-movies; and Friday and Saturday showing westerns.

By the time Alan Finlay purchased the State from Tocchini in 1967, that classic formula was beginning to unravel. A generation of young filmmakers were experimenting with new storytelling techniques and sensibilities influenced by European films. The innovations seeded an artistic renewal in Hollywood, but also made ticket sales more a game of chance than in the old formula days. The steady attraction of R-rated and X-rated films proved the exception, encouraging Finlay to convert the State into a porn theater.

Finlay's trial over exhibiting *Deep Throat* and *Behind the Green Door* was one of the first in the wake of the U.S. Supreme Court's 1973 ruling on obscenity, bringing national attention to Petaluma. After hearing arguments from both sides, local circuit judge Alexander McMahon dismissed the jury, ruling that, in line with the new Supreme Court decision, the prosecution had failed to present evidence of a community standard regarding obscenity. Following the trial, Finlay returned to showing *Deep Throat* at the State. It ran on almost a continuous basis until he sold the theater in 1977.

In the late 20th century, cable television, video rentals, and streaming services further eroded theater attendance. To help stem the tide, Hollywood turned to summer blockbusters and large multiplex theaters, like Petaluma's Boulevard 14 Cinemas, built in 2005.

In Petaluma, X-rated movies continued to draw crowds to the Sonomarin Drive-in along Highway 101 south of town. Operated initially by Finlay and later Tocchini, the drive-in closed in the mid-1980s after pornography movies migrated to home video. Petaluma's two historic theaters, the State, which returned to being called the Mystic in 1992, and the original Hill Opera House, renamed the Phoenix in 1979, both converted to live music halls in the early 1990s.

It was Alan Finlay, however, who would have the last word on cinema's impact in Petaluma. "*Deep Throat*," he said, "put this city on the map."

The Boulevard 14 Cinemas, 200 C Street, built 2005

Hotel Petaluma

The swanky Lanai Lounge opened in the Hotel Petaluma on August 16, 1938. Taking up the hotel's entire front corner, it was adorned with South Seas murals, bananas hanging from the ceiling, a koi fishpond, and a horseshoe-shaped bar that served exotic rum cocktails, transporting its customers to a romantic and languorous tropical paradise of rattan furniture, flower leis, and live Hawaiian music.

To the delight of hotel operator Vernon Peck, the lounge was an overnight sensation. The Golden Gate Bridge had opened the year before, and waves of tourists were passing through town on the Redwood Highway, headed for resorts along the Russian River, where they danced the night away to the big bands of Harry James, Buddy Rogers, and Glenn Miller. Meanwhile, tiki culture was sweeping the Bay Area, having made a big splash in 1937 with the opening of Trader Vic's Restaurant in Oakland. As word spread of Peck's exotic tiki roadside attraction, members of the Bohemian Grove, an exclusive Monte Rio men's club, made ritual stopovers at the lounge on their way from San Francisco to their annual summer gathering on the Russian River, their chauffeured limousines lined up outside the hotel causing a sensation in town.

That cachet helped draw in Peck's other target clientele, Petaluma's "smart set." While a number of bars and grocery taverns had sprung up around town following Prohibition's repeal in 1933, there was a crowd of young men and women more attracted to the lure of night clubs. Mike Gilardi, owner of a cigar store across the street from the hotel, had converted his store into a popular cocktail lounge in 1937, offering jazz, dancing, and an exciting mixology of new slings and fizzes. Piggybacking on Gilardi's success, the Lanai Lounge quickly became the second anchor of Petaluma's "night club row."

Peck needed the business. The Great Depression had sent many hotel properties into receivership, or else turned them entirely into single-room-occupancy hotels, or SROs. Traveling businessmen and salesmen were starting to take rooms in the inexpensive new motels springing up along the highways, which, in addition to convenient parking, also relieved them from running a gauntlet of hotel staff with their hands out for tips.

Still, the financial return from Peck's upgrades were a far cry from the hopes and dreams that had marked Hotel Petaluma's opening in 1924. With the city's egg boom at its peak, the Petaluma Chamber of Commerce had contracted with the Hockenbury System, a community hotel enterprise, to help raise enough local money to build a modern, first-class hotel. Hockenbury's 10-day funding drive netted $258,000 ($3.5 million in early-21st-century currency) from 855 local investors, whose ownership of the hotel was placed in the Petaluma Hotel Company Trust. The remaining $325,000 needed to build the hotel was financed by debt.

Rising five stories above the street, the new Hotel Petaluma featured 96 guest rooms, with an additional 12 rooms for staff lodging. San Francisco architect Frederic Whitton designed the steel and concrete building with a pebbledash cement exterior popularized by the Arts and Crafts movement. The ground floor featured an inviting courtyard entrance, a spacious lobby with an imposing, wood-manteled fireplace, a state-of-the-art kitchen, an ornate dining room that seated 200, and Petaluma's first passenger elevator. On the roof, a golf net provided guests with a chance to practice their swing. To serve as a community hub, a banquet room on the mezzanine level was available for luncheons and conventions of local service clubs and civic organizations.

California Governor Friend Richardson served as guest of honor at the hotel's opening on August 22, 1924. Also on hand was George R. Williams, uncle of prominent Petaluma businessman George P. McNear, the hotel's largest stockholder. Williams recalled assisting his father, early Petaluma settler George P. Williams, in hauling redwood lumber from the Russian River to town by ox team in 1852 to build one of the town's first hotels, the American. Among a handful of hotels built during Petaluma's heyday as a river port, the American Hotel, along with the Continental, the Brooklyn, the Washington, and the Yosemite, were still in operation when the Hotel Petaluma opened in 1924. In their early years the hotels had been financially reliant upon passengers riding the river steamboat lines, their schedules set according to tides on the Petaluma River, which rose and fell as much as four feet twice a day, limiting boat access on the silt-filled slough during low tide. "Up county" people traveling to and from San Francisco often complained that the schedules were rigged so as to force travelers to stay overnight in Petaluma, creating the need for a number of hotels.

The site chosen for the Hotel Petaluma at the northwest corner of Washington and Kentucky streets had once housed the town's first hotel. Erected in 1851 by a

Hotel Petaluma, 205 Kentucky Street, built 1924

Maine seaman named Robert Douglass, it was rebuilt in 1857 after being damaged by fire—a common occurrence for 19th-century hotels given their reliance upon oil and kerosene lamps. It was operating as the Sullivan Hotel in 1869 when Dr. Kelly Tighe, a local Irish undertaker and later county coroner, bought it and renamed it the Brooklyn Hotel. In 1883, Tighe opened a new hotel a block away on the southeast corner of Keller and Washington streets, also naming it the Brooklyn Hotel. He converted the original Brooklyn Hotel into shops and a warehouse. A fire consumed the building in 1900, after which the vacant site was used for street carnivals, merry-go-rounds, and farmers markets before being purchased for construction of the Hotel Petaluma.

In 1940, after successfully guiding the Petaluma Hotel through the Great Depression, Vernon Peck departed to run a hotel in Los Angeles, selling his lease to Harold Eckart, a hotelier from Olympia, Washington. Eckart undertook a major renovation of the hotel in 1945, including a complete makeover of the Lanai Lounge, which he rechristened the Redwood Room. Decorated then with large photo murals of the redwoods, the cocktail lounge quickly became a favorite hangout of Petaluma's postwar café society, known as "the 400." They were serenaded most evenings by Earle Bond, a locally renowned organ player. Eckart also created a studio in the hotel for the Santa Rosa radio station KSRO, and on the roof a Civil Air Patrol spotting station that continued to operate during the Cold War.

The opening of Highway 101 to the east of town in 1956 put an end to travelers passing through the downtown on the Redwood Highway. As inexpensive motels sprung up along the freeway, the Hotel Petaluma converted to being primarily an SRO. In 1959, the local Elks Club, seeking more space for their club gatherings, purchased the hotel from the original Petaluma Hotel Company trust for $91,160, far short of the $285,000 local citizens had invested in 1924. The Elks closed off the Redwood Room, carving it up into retail shops, blocked out the lobby for meeting spaces, and roofed over the open courtyard entrance, turning it into an exclusive barroom for Elks members.

Petaluma's other hotels quickly went by the wayside, leaving the Hotel Petaluma the only remaining hotel in town for three decades. The Brooklyn Hotel, at the southeast corner of Keller and Washington streets, was replaced in 1953 with a complex of medical offices and retail stores. The American, at 129 Petaluma Boulevard North, was torn down in 1966 and replaced by Putnam Plaza Park. The Continental Hotel, at the southwest corner of Kentucky Street and Western Avenue, burned down in 1968, and was replaced by a bank. The eastside Yosemite and Tivoli hotels across from the railroad yard were both torn down in 1972 to widen Washington Street to four lanes.

In 1994, the Elks sold the Hotel Petaluma, and built a new lodge on the east side of town. In 2015, after passing through a couple of ownership changes, the Hotel Petaluma was purchased by hoteliers Satish Patel and Dipak Patel, who undertook a full-scale renovation, returning it to a traditional hotel for overnight guests. In a nod to the 855 citizens who had originally funded the hotel in 1924, they named the new bar inside the lobby "855."

Courtyard entrance to Hotel Petaluma

B'nai Israel Synagogue

In the summer of 1935, apple pickers in Sebastopol went on strike. Anticipating riots in the orchards and fruit packing sheds, Sonoma County Sheriff Harry Patterson deputized 500 citizens as an "Army of Peace." On the evening of August 1st, 250 strikers and labor activists gathered at Santa Rosa's Germania Hall, calling for a wage increase from 25 cents to 40 cents per hour, a nine-hour workday, and time and a half for overtime. Sheriff Patterson sent his Army of Peace to break up the gathering with clubs and sticks. Among those beaten at the event was Sol Nitzberg.

Nitzberg had grown up in a Polish village under the pogroms waged against Jewish residents by Czarist Russia. Instead of becoming a rabbi like his father, Nitzberg became a Socialist, signing up with the Russian Social Revolution Party to fight in the 1905 revolution against Russian Czar Nicholas II. Captured by the Czarist police, he was transported by dogsled on a 300-mile trek to a labor camp in northern Siberia, and interned for three years.

After his release, Nitzberg made his way to Hamburg, Germany, where he boarded a ship for New York City. Enrolling at Cooper Union under a full scholarship, he received a bachelor's degree in engineering in 1917. After graduation, he enlisted in the U.S. Army and was sent back to Europe to fight in World War I. For his service, he was granted American citizenship, and took a job at General Electric in New York. Overcome with wanderlust, he quit his job and set off with a friend on a 2,500-mile walking trek across America. Upon reaching Los Angeles, he heard about a community of Jewish chicken ranchers in Petaluma.

The community had begun in 1904 with Sam Melnick, a Lithuanian immigrant, who established a seven-acre poultry farm near Cotati. A handful of Jewish settlers followed, many of them escaping the pogroms raging across Eastern Europe and Russia or the sweatshops of New York City's Lower East Side. The majority of them arrived in Petaluma with hopes of creating an idealistic community rooted in hard work, Socialist politics, and fresh country air. Similar agricultural communities had been launched in upstate New York, New Jersey, Argentina, and Palestine, all influenced by the Utopian experiments of the 19th century and backed by Jewish philanthropists. Petaluma's main benefactor was the Abraham Haas Memorial Fund, established by heirs of the Levi Strauss fortune.

For roughly $3,500 in seed money ($90,000 in early-21st-century currency), immigrants could settle on five acres with a ranch house, 10 chicken coops, and 1,000 white leghorn hens. By the early 1920s, there were more than 100 Jewish families raising chickens in the Petaluma River Watershed. While the majority of them came from orthodox religious backgrounds, many had rebelled against religion upon immigrating to America, embracing Judaism more as a culture. In 1925, they decided to build a Jewish Community Center on Western Avenue. They had no intention of making it a synagogue until they learned that doing so would provide them with a tax write-off.

Once established, the synagogue hosted nightly events, including concerts, lectures, drama groups, and a Yiddish culture club. It also provided a meeting place for different political groups, ranging from Socialists and Communists on the linke, or left, to Zionists on the rekhte, or right, and anarchists. The factions within the community were united in part by the prejudice they experienced in Petaluma, including being banned from the local country club, subjected to frequent name calling, and greeted in the local newspaper by want ads that read "no Jews need apply." In 1925, the local klavern of the Ku Klux Klan staged a large, nighttime cross-burning at the Petaluma Old Adobe, making it clear that Jews did not belong in their vision of "100 percent Americanism."

Sol Nitzberg quickly made a home for himself upon arriving in Petaluma, marrying a local Jewish widow with two children and settling down on a chicken ranch on Middle Two Rock Road. He also became involved in labor organizing.

Inexpensive labor had been critical to local farming and ranching since the Spanish and Mexicans had enslaved the native Coast Miwoks. Successive generations found cheap new sources of workers among Irish, Chinese, Japanese, Filipino, and Mexican immigrants. But during the Great Depression in the 1930s, immigrant laborers were displaced by refugees from the Dust Bowl. White, English-speaking, and American-born, they expected a fair deal. At first, California farmers appeared to agree. But as more refugees poured into the state, their numbers drove wages down, giving rise to unrest among those laborers trying to support families.

In the spring of 1933, worker strikes erupted throughout California as each seasonal crop ripened for picking. Those actions were followed in 1934 by the

B'nai Israel Synagogue, 740 Western Avenue, built 1925

legendary West Coast longshoremen strike. Lasting 83 days, it completely crippled West Coast shipping of agricultural goods. In response, large business interests and corporate farms formed their own statewide militant group, the Associated Farmers of California. Pushing a platform to "save America," they lobbied for anti-union laws and legislation against picketing and strikes. They also organized vigilante groups known as "Citizens Armies" to end labor protests by any means necessary.

Three weeks after Sheriff Harry Patterson's Army of Peace broke up the gathering at Germania Hall, Sol Nitzberg and other labor activists started organizing a strike of the hops harvest in Healdsburg. On the eve of harvest, a group of 300 vigilantes rounded up five of the labor activists, including Sol Nitzberg, in the middle of the night.

The nightriders were led to Nitzberg's ranch by activist Jack Green, a sign painter seized by vigilantes as he was closing up his Santa Rosa studio. They instructed Green to knock on Nitzberg's front door and lure him outside, away from his wife and two children. Instead, as Nitzberg opened the door, Green darted inside. With the house surrounded by armed vigilantes, Nitzberg grabbed his shotgun and fired off two shots in the air to hold them at bay. Calls to the sheriff's office by Nitzberg's wife went unheeded. After a standoff lasting two hours, the vigilantes started lobbing tear gas canisters into the house. Nitzberg kissed his wife goodbye and, along with Green, surrendered to the mob.

The two men were bound with rope, thrown in the back seat of a sedan, and driven at gunpoint to a warehouse near the train station in Santa Rosa. Along with three other abducted men, they were beaten by a group of angry, masked men, and ordered to kneel down and kiss the American flag. Three of the men acquiesced, leaving bloodstains on the flag. Nitzberg and Green, who had both fought for the United States in World War I, refused.

Howling "Hang the Jew," the vigilantes stripped the two men of their shirts, sheared off their hair, and beat them bloody. Covering them in crank case oil, they showered the men with feathers from a pillow sack, and then marched them through downtown Santa Rosa in the early morning hours, surrounded by a parade of people in cars who circled Courthouse Square, yelling, honking their horns, and firing guns in the air. Led to the city limits, Nitzberg and Green were given 12 hours to leave the county with their families.

Following the so-called "tar party," the Sonoma District Attorney refused to try the vigilantes, citing insufficient evidence. Instead, at the prompting of the American Civil Liberties Union, the State Attorney General's Office took up the case, charging 23 men—including Santa Rosa's mayor, city attorney, a member of the city council, and the president of the Healdsburg Chamber of Commerce—with various crimes against Nitzberg, Green, and the state. The 12 members of the jury—eight of whom were either growers or wives of growers—deliberated just 16 minutes before returning with a "not guilty" verdict for all of the accused.

After the trial, Nitzberg and his family were stalked by vigilantes and their credit was cut off at local feed mills. Nitzberg sold his chickens and moved his family to New York City with plans to continue on to the Soviet Union, but the Soviets refused his immigration request. Instead, he and his family returned to Penngrove, where they rented a chicken ranch.

In the 1950s, Joseph McCarthy's national witch hunt of Communists led to a political split at the Jewish Community Center, with those on the right expelling those on the left. The center proceeded to evolve into more of a traditional synagogue, B'nai Israel, no longer a center of political activism.

The ranch house at 1096-1098 Middle Two Rock Road from which Sol Nitzberg was abducted the evening of August 21, 1935

Bars & Taverns

CIGAR-STORE OWNER Mike Gilardi set out in 1937 to create the swankiest cocktail lounge in the North Bay. Born in Hicks Valley to Swiss-Italian dairy ranchers, Gilardi, well known about town as a "Dapper Dan," had operated his cigar store at the corner of Washington and Kentucky streets since the early 1930s. He gutted the store along with the barbershop next door, and created "Gilardi's Corner," a modern night club the likes of which Petaluma had never seen, outfitting it with large mirrors, indirect mood lighting, cream-colored banquettes, and a curved bar 30 feet long. To attract women to the club, he installed a baby-blue powder room and a large dance floor with a bandstand, and hired the top two mixologists in town, "Happy" Merango and "Red" Cockrill. Within months of opening, Gilardi's Corner became *the* smart spot in town.

Gilardi wasn't the only proprietor intent on wetting the whistles of Petalumans following the 13-year dry spell of Prohibition. New saloons and taverns were springing up all over town. The first to obtain a legal license was Andresen's Tavern, which opened in 1934 immediately after Prohibition's repeal, just half a block from a water fountain erected on Western Avenue in 1891 by the Women's Christian Temperance Union. Engraved with the message "Total Abstinence is the Way to Handle the Alcohol Problem," the fountain had failed to put much of a dent in a town of 3,000 people with 50 saloons, nor did it stop residents from drinking once Prohibition was imposed in 1920. Petalumans simply adapted by making booze at home, imbibing it in speakeasies, or obtaining a doctor's prescription for alcohol-based "tonsil syrup" to treat an epidemic of sore throats.

Another type of popular drinking establishment after Prohibition was the corner grocery tavern, many of which had continued to operate surreptitiously during Prohibition, including Volpi's Grocery, Mario & John's Tavern, Ray's Tavern, and Fairwest Grocery.

But "Diamond" Mike Gilardi wasn't looking for a return to the saloons that had catered primarily to men. He dreamt of a ritzy joint where both men and women came to enjoy highballs, dance, play bar dice, or place a discreet bet on a horse race or a boxing match. The atmosphere would be relaxed, playful, and open to possibilities, the main activities being conversation, drink, and food. Nothing expressed that milieu better at Gilardi's Corner than the birth of one of Petaluma's most illustrious claims to fame—wristwrestling.

An avid sportsman, Gilardi helped each year to organize the Sports Show, a tournament of boxing and wrestling matches that raised money for the March of Dimes's battle against polio. Assisting Gilardi with the show was a young newspaper columnist named Bill Soberanes. A descendant of Mexican comandante Mariano Vallejo, the native-born Soberanes had tried his hand at amateur boxing, followed by a stint in the merchant marine, before settling in as daily columnist for the *Petaluma Argus-Courier*. Fast-talking and nervously energetic, Soberanes plied the streets day and night with his reporter's notebook in hand, a large camera bag slung over his shoulder, and a briar pipe clenched between his teeth. His newspaper column, "So They Tell Me," was classic three-dot journalism, blending news and gossip with homespun tales of social clubs, old-timers, colorful visitors, and local trivia.

In his spare time, Soberanes served as a sports commentator for the local radio station, KAFP. That brought him in contact with Jack Homel, a trainer for the Detroit Tigers baseball team who was living in Boyes Hot Springs during the off-season. A frequent guest at Gilardi's Corner, Homel liked to boast that he had never lost a wristwrestling match in his life, despite having faced hundreds of opponents, including football players, boxers, strong men, steel workers, and longshoremen. In the fall of 1954, Soberanes and Gilardi came up with the idea of hosting a wristwrestling match between Homel and strongest man in the area, Oliver Kullberg, a 200-plus-pound rancher from Lakeville who, like Homel, boasted of being an undefeated wristwrestler.

Gilardi, who regularly hosted victory parties at his bar for Petaluma's semipro football team, the Petaluma Leghorns, convinced the team's coach, Petaluma Creamery manager Gene Benedetti, to add the wristwrestling match to the annual March of Dimes Sports Show benefit. Benedetti, who was also the local March of Dimes chairman, agreed. On the evening of January 27, 1955, Jack Homel and Oliver Kullberg sat down for the match at a round table in the backroom of Gilardi's Corner and clasped hands. For almost three minutes the two men struggled to best each other before the table collapsed beneath them. The referee declared the match a draw.

In the days following the contest, wristwrestling became the most talked about sporting event in town. Recognizing an opportunity, Gilardi, Soberanes, and

Andresen's Tavern, 19 Western Avenue, established 1934

Homel formed a three-man committee to create an annual wristwrestling tournament. A second match was held a year later for the Sports Show, once again at Gilardi's Corner. With Jack Homel serving as the referee, his co-champion, local strong man Oliver Kullberg, locked wrists with Cliff Parlee, a San Anselmo policeman and former weightlifter. Parlee won the match, but because he was technically from Marin County, Kullberg was able to retain his title as "Champion Wristwrestler of Sonoma County."

Setting their sights higher, in 1958 Soberanes and Gilardi announced that the contest would add weight classes and go statewide, meaning that winners would be crowned as state champions. Competitors from all around the state showed up at the event, some accompanied by their managers. For entertainment between wristwrestling bouts a number of variety acts were trotted out, including a magic show, an accordionist, and duck-call demonstration. Thanks to Soberanes's relentless promotions in his column, the bar was packed to capacity, and news of the first statewide competition spread nationally.

Over the next three years, spectator and competitor interest continued to grow, as big men kept coming from farther and farther away to compete. Largely at Soberanes's urging, a variety of actors, public officials, glamorous women, and celebrity athletes also began showing up. In 1961, it became clear the event had outgrown Gilardi's Corner. Teaming up with local promoter Dave Devoto, Gilardi and Soberanes formed the World's Wristwrestling Championship, Inc., with Gilardi serving as chairman and Soberanes as secretary-treasurer. In 1962, they moved the tournament to Hermann Sons Hall on Western Avenue, drawing 1,000 cheering fans, with opening ceremonies kicked off by California's lieutenant governor, Glenn Anderson.

In 1968, "Peanuts" cartoonist Charles Schulz brought the event worldwide exposure when he penned 11 comic strips in which his canine character, Snoopy, came to Petaluma to compete in the championship, only to be disqualified for lacking a thumb. In 1969, the event began to be covered by ABC's Wide World of Sports, where it became one of the show's most popular events, running continuously until 1984. In 1972, Soberanes wristwrestled then-Governor Ronald Reagan for a photo op. Reagan quickly pinned Soberanes's arm to the table, breaking one of his ribs, a feat Soberanes later attributed to cheating.

In 1967, Gilardi's Corner fell to the wrecking ball when Washington Street was widened into four lanes. A parking lot for the corner bank was put in its place. Ten years later, Diamond Mike Gilardi passed away. Bill Soberanes would go on to champion other events that became annual traditions in Petaluma, including the ugly dog contest, the whiskerino contest, and séances summoning the spirit of Harry Houdini on Halloween, but none would ever top Petaluma's notoriety as the "Wristwrestling Capital of the World."

A self-described "peopleologist," Soberanes instead set out to become the most photographed non-celebrity in the world, collecting more than 45,000 photos of himself with a galaxy of Hollywood stars, presidents, sports figures, politicians, gangsters, celebrities, and ordinary people. Priding himself on never missing a deadline, he filed his column in every edition of the *Petaluma Argus-Courier* from June 2, 1954, until his death on June 2, 2003. After he died, the World's Wristwrestling Contest, born in Gilardi's Corner, was relocated to the gambling town of Reno, Nevada.

A sample of local drinking establishments that have withstood the test of time:

FIRST ROW (LEFT TO RIGHT)
McNear's Saloon & Dining Hall, 21 Petaluma Boulevard North, established 1976

Mario & John's, 428 East D Street, established 1947

Buckhorn Tavern, 615 Petaluma Boulevard South, established 1938

SECOND ROW (LEFT TO RIGHT)
The 8 Ball Tavern, 8 Charles Street, Cotati, established 1937

Andresen's Tavern, 19 Western Avenue, established 1934

Ray's Tavern, 900 Western Avenue, established 1947

THIRD ROW (LEFT TO RIGHT)
Twin Oaks Roadhouse, 5745 Old Redwood Highway, Penngrove, established 1924

The Hideaway, 128 Kentucky Street, established 1958

Ernie's Tin Bar, 5100 Lakeville Highway, established 1923

The Turning Basin

The summer of 1976, Helen Putnam found herself back in her characteristic "full speed ahead" mode. In her third term as Petaluma's first woman mayor, Putnam was riding high after the city's recent victory at the U.S. Supreme Court. The high court had chosen not to review a lower appellate court ruling allowing Petaluma to "preserve its small-town character, open spaces, and low density of population" by limiting its growth to 500 new houses per year. The decision made Petaluma the darling of slow-growth advocates across the country.

Petaluma's transformation from agricultural small town to sprawling suburban community officially began with the opening of Highway 101 in 1956. Newcomers, in search of inexpensive housing and a reasonable one-hour commute to San Francisco, gave rise to a development boom in the hayfields east of Petaluma that sent the town's population soaring from 10,000 in 1950 to 25,000 by 1970. Between 1970 and 1972 alone the population grew by another 5,000 people.

The rapid growth overwhelmed city services, forcing schools into double session and taxing water and sewage systems. New shopping centers on the east side drew foot traffic away from the downtown, casting small merchants and long-established anchor stores into a financial tailspin. Commercial landlords, no longer able to command premium rents, let their buildings slowly deteriorate. East Washington Street, the sole, two-lane thoroughfare between the east and west sides of town, became chronically congested and increasingly lined with fast food restaurants. Wendy's Hamburgers was the latest arrival, having purchased the Farrell-Burns house, a once-stately Victorian on the corner of East Washington and Wilson streets, with plans to demolish it for a new Wendy's.

Mayor Putnam saw an opportunity in Wendy's purchase of the Farrell-Burns house to help revive the historic downtown. That hadn't always been her priority. A teacher-principal of Two Rock Union School, Putnam was the first woman to become a major political force in Sonoma County. Born in Bakersfield and raised in Alameda, she had graduated from the University of California, Berkeley with a degree in French, before moving to Petaluma in 1931 to teacher grammar school and then junior high. Elected to the Petaluma School Board in 1947, she got into public speaking through fashion commentary at local gatherings and on her own local radio talk show before being elected mayor in 1965.

Tall and stylishly regal, Putnam was a dynamo of energy, well known for her mass of silver bracelets—as many as 25 on each arm—and her optimism. When necessary, she had the ability to gracefully reduce a political peer to a schoolboy. But it was Putnam's pragmatic ability to compromise when faced with controversial issues that made her an effective politician.

That particular talent was in evidence following a major defeat during her first term as mayor, when she championed a federally sponsored urban renewal plan to convert downtown Petaluma into a shopping mall. The plan called for rerouting Petaluma Boulevard into a six-lane highway running along the west bank of the Petaluma River from D Street to Oak Street. All of the historic buildings on the existing boulevard's east side from Washington to D streets were to be demolished for off-street parking. Kentucky Street between Washington Street and Western Avenue would then be closed off and converted to a mall, with additional off-street parking provided by the demolition of the buildings on the east side of Keller Street.

Voters narrowly rejected the plan in June 1969, concerned about an increase in their property taxes to pay for its development. In the same election, Putnam was reelected by a slim margin to a second term as mayor. During that term, she began to change her stance on downtown development from destruction to restoration. That shift was partly influenced during the fall of 1969 when the Healy Mansion, a grand Queen Anne built in 1902 on the corner of Washington and Keokuk streets for city councilman D.J. Healy, was torn down and replaced with a gas station. Appalled, group of local citizens established Heritage Homes of Petaluma to advocate for the preservation and restoration of significant historical buildings.

In 1971, Putnam and the city council floated a $3.2 million bond to provide services for the runaway development on the east side of town. After voters rejected the bond, Putnam and a majority of the council decided to concede to the demands of many residents and impose limits on Petaluma's growth. It was a risky strategy given that the courts had consistently ruled against such land-use controls, often viewing them as a means of low-income and racial exclusion. Developers sued the city. By the time the U.S. Supreme Court issued their decision on the lawsuit in 1976, Putnam had fully

The historic scow schooner Alma, docked outside Farrell-Burns house built in 1902

embraced historic restoration as a means of preventing the city from becoming just a community of bedrooms.

In 1975, she established an annual Historic Preservation Week to call attention to the town's unique heritage. That same year, working with the chairman of the Bank of Marin, Bill Murray, she lured to town a developer named Skip Sommer who had established an impressive track record converting historic properties in Marin into popular shops and restaurants. With Murray's financial backing, Putnam persuaded Sommer—who had never before set foot in Petaluma—to purchase the abandoned G.P. McNear Hay and Grain Company on the west bank of the Turning Basin, and work his magic on it.

A prominent symbol of Petaluma's days as a vibrant agricultural river port, the company's mill complex at B Street and Petaluma Boulevard had been built by the McNear family in the 1890s. The adjacent warehouse, made of bluestone from a local quarry, was the oldest standing building in Petaluma, having been constructed in 1854 by Tom Baylis for storing wild game meat bound for San Francisco. The mill originally had a twin on the northeast side of the Turning Basin called the Golden Eagle Mill. Built in 1888, that mill had been torn down in 1965 and was in the process of being replaced by the Golden Eagle Shopping Center in 1975.

Before saying yes to the persuasive Putnam, Sommer toured a 100-year-old brick winery in Yountville that had been converted in the late 1960s into a popular destination of shops and eateries called the Vintage 1870. Inspired by Yountville's model, Sommer moved ahead with purchasing the old McNear mill and rebranding it the Great Petaluma Mill. He recycled redwood siding from local abandoned chicken houses to build out a gallery of 30 shops inside of the building, adding touches of 1890s décor and memorabilia from the original mill.

In the winter of 1976, just as Sommer was preparing to open a 10,000-square-foot restaurant inside the mill called Steamer Gold, he received a call from Mayor Putnam. "Have I got a deal for you," she told him. Putnam had brokered a deal with Wendy's Hamburgers to sell the Farrell-Burns House on East Washington Street for $1, on the condition that the new buyer pay for moving it. She had also found the perfect location for the house—a vacant lot on the east bank of the Turning Basin.

Sommer was dubious. The house had been built in 1902 by Ellen Burns and her son Frank, who had inherited his father's grocery business across the street. After Ellen Burns passed away, the house was occupied by Burns's daughter Irene and Irene's husband William Farrell, who operated the local Dodge car dealership and served as Petaluma's mayor from 1929 to 1933. The Farrell-Burns House may have once been a showplace, but by the mid-1970s it had fallen into a dilapidated state.

Unable to say no to Putnam, Sommer bought the Farrell-Burns house and early one morning had it transported to the Turning Basin. After renovating and expanding the house by 2,500 feet, he opened it up as the Farrell House Restaurant. Meanwhile, the Great Petaluma Mill was proving a success. In its first year of operation, city revenues from downtown sales taxes jumped 30 percent, thanks in large part to shoppers being drawn back downtown.

In 1979, Sommer found himself again pressed by Putnam into rescuing another Victorian. The Pometta house, which sat near the northwest corner of Petaluma Boulevard South and D Street, was slated to be razed to accommodate a new 7-Eleven convenience store. Sommer moved the house to the west bank of the Turning Basin, converting it to an office complex called 1 C Street.

Both the Great Petaluma Mill and the Farrell-Burns house were eventually recognized as historic landmarks, and true to Mayor Putnam's vision, became catalysts for the continued revitalization of historic downtown Petaluma, which eventually evolved into a trendy nightlife and shopping district. Over time, Petaluma's limited growth restrictions, although regularly challenged by subsequent city councils, became an accepted part of the city's political and planning process. To further protect the open spaces surrounding the city from urban sprawl, in 1998 voters approved the imposition of a 20-year urban growth boundary on the city.

In 1979, Helen Putnam was elected Sonoma County's first woman supervisor, a position she held until her death in 1984 at the age of 75. Following her passing, West Petaluma Regional Park, a 171-acre park created west of the city in 1979, was renamed in her honor, as was a pocket park in the heart of downtown at 129 Petaluma Boulevard North. Formerly the location of the American Hotel built in 1866, the site had sat abandoned since the hotel was torn down in 1966. Architect Dick Lieb, who designed Helen Putnam Plaza, noted at the park's dedication that Putnam probably would have declared it "lovely."

The Turning Basin at night

Epilogue

A place is made a place only by slow accrual, like a coral reef.

WALLACE STEGNER

Helen Putnam Regional Park

Epilogue

A DEEPLY LIVED-IN PLACE that maintains a strong sense of identity is the more exception than the rule in the West. Many western locales have been overrun by people with a Gold Rush mentality, looking to exploit whatever resources they could get their hands, with little thought of tomorrow. After the boom goes bust or the dream of striking it rich dies, they move on, replaced by others just as hopeful and footloose. While successive waves of new booms have kept some places thriving, it has often come at the expense of the environment and the quality of life for those left behind.

The Petaluma River Watershed has seen its share of booms and busts since the Spanish first made contact with its indigenous people two centuries ago, including the potato boom, the wheat boom, the egg boom, the dairy boom, the bedroom community boom, and the wine boom. Fortunately, over the years true settlers have chosen to put a stake in the ground and advocate for preserving the watershed's unique character and strong sense of place for future generations.

History is the story of individuals responding creatively to the conditions and circumstances in which they find themselves. The 19th-century German statesman Otto von Bismarck described it as a "stream of time," noting that people can neither create nor direct the stream, only navigate it with greater or lesser success.

As the Petaluma River Watershed advances into the 21st century, it faces its share of challenges. The rising cost of living is displacing working families and upcoming generations. The river needs dredging. The potholed streets are clogged with traffic. Big-box malls, once agents of doom for downtown merchants, are now threatened themselves by online merchants. Highway 101, the commuter route so many depend upon for their livelihood, is a daily bottleneck. High land values are making it difficult for young ranchers and farmers to get established. Developers are encroaching upon open fields and hillsides with large estate homes and mini-suburban complexes. Climate change is wreaking havoc with historic droughts, fires, and floods.

At the same time, signs of resilience and renaissance abound in efforts not only to preserve but to leverage the watershed's storied past, agricultural heritage, and eclectic nature, while ensuring its future prosperity. They include such developments as the establishment of Tolay Lake Regional County Park, the restoration of the Sonoma Baylands on San Pablo Bay, and the eventual opening of Lafferty Park atop Sonoma Mountain.

In the working landscape, Petaluma's urban growth boundary, along with community separators and the conservation efforts of the Sonoma Land Trust and the Marin Agricultural Land Trust, have proven instrumental in preserving local family farms and ranches. The watershed is now a leader in the farm-to-table movement, with many small farmers and ranchers employing sustainable and organic techniques to grow fruit and vegetables, raise dairy cows, cattle, sheep, and goats, and produce a wide array of artisanal products including olive oil, farmstead cheese, and wool clothing.

In the city of Petaluma, high-density, infill developments are springing up in former industrial areas along the river. The advocacy of Heritage Homes of Petaluma, along with rising home prices, has led to the restoration of many beautiful homes built during the 19th and early 20th centuries. The historic downtown is thriving as a trendy shopping district and nightlife venue, filled with locally owned shops, restaurants, coffee shops, bars, and music venues. The maker movement has breathed new life into small-scale manufacturing for local craft breweries, distilleries, bakeries, and ice cream factories. The Sonoma-Marin Area Rail Transit (SMART train) has made life more civilized for many commuters. The innovative Ellis Creek Water Recycling Facility has opened up public access to the wetlands. Ambitious plans are under way for the creation of a pedestrian river walk, a community boathouse center at the Turning Basin, the revival of electric train service on the railroad trestle, the incorporation of the Scott Ranch as an extension of Helen Putnam Regional Park, and the expansion of Steamer Landing Park at McNear's Landing.

The future prosperity of the Petaluma River Watershed is reliant upon a stable and rooted community to safeguard, repair, and enrich what has made the watershed such a special and unique place. As developers have sadly demonstrated with their Gold Rush mentality, a place is not instantly made a place. It becomes a place only by the slow, but continual effort of responsible stewards, generation after generation, like a coral reef.

Wetlands walk at Ellis Creek Water Recycling Facility, designed by Patricia Johanson, looking south toward Mount Burdell

Notes & Sources

Prologue

Quote from Arthur Quinn, *Broken Shore: The Marin Peninsula*, (Salt Lake City: Peregrine Smith, 1981), p. 167.

There are a variety of Coast Miwok creation myths. This particular myth is adapted from "How O'-ye the Coyote-man Discovered his Wife," a story told to C. Hart Merriam at Tomales Bay by an aged Hookooeko (Coast Miwok) woman in 1902; from *The Dawn of the World: Tales Told by the Mewan Indians of California*, collected and edited by C. Hart Merriam, (Cleveland: The Arthur H. Clark Company, 1910).

Edward S. Lippitt excerpt from "Annual Address," *Petaluma Argus*, October 8, 1870.

"Letter from Petaluma," excerpt from the *Alta California*, April 16, 1855.

Introduction

Preface

Wendell Berry quote from Wallace Stegner, *Where the Bluebird Sings to the Lemonade Springs*, (New York: The Modern Library, 2002), p. 199.

Wendell Berry, *Recollected Essays 1965-1980*, (San Francisco: North Point Press, 1981).

Tony Hiss, *The Experience of Place*, (New York: Vintage, 1991).

Stegner, *op. cit.*, p. 264.

A Special Place

Quote from Gary Snyder, *The Practice of the Wild*, (Berkeley: North Point Press, 1990), p. 27.

Quote from Eavan Boland, *A Poet's Dublin*, (New York: W.W. Norton & Co., 2016), p. 45.

Southern Sonoma County Resource Conservation District, "Petaluma River Watershed," http://www.sscrcd.org/watershed-petaluma-river.php

Stegner, *op. cit.*

The Photographer

Quote from Dorothea Lange, *Dorothea Lange: A Photographer's Life*, (Syracuse, NY: Syracuse University Press, 2000), p. viii.

The Storyteller

Quote from Max Hastings, "Drawing the Wrong Lesson," *The New York Review of Books*, March 11, 2010.

Part I: The Early Ones

Greg Sarris quote from his interview with Steve Estes and Claudia Luke, February 23, 2016, Osborn Oral History Project, Center for Environmental Inquiry, Sonoma State University.

M. Kat Anderson, *Tending the Wild*, (Berkeley: UC Press, 2005).

"Bihler's Lake Farm," *Petaluma Argus*, June 13, 1873.

Brian Fagan, *Before California*, (Walnut Creek, CA: Alta Mira Press, 2003).

Betty Goerke, *Chief Marin: Leader, Rebel and Legend: A History of Marin County's Namesake and His People*, (Berkeley: Heyday Books, 2007).

Albert Kroeber, *Handbook of the Indians of California*, Bureau of American Ethnology, Bulletin 78, Washington D.C. (New York: Dover Publications, 1976 reprint of 1925 original), pp. 272-278.

George McKale, "Traveling the Old Country Road: Stage Gulch to Tolay Lake," *Sonoma Valley Sun*, August 12, 2014.

C. Hart Merriam, "Distribution and Classification of the Mewan Stock of California," *American Anthropologist*, Volume 9, 1907, pp. 354-357.

E. Breck Parkman: "The Máien" (National Women's Anthropology Newsletter 5(2):16-22. Hayward, California. 1981); "The Máien: A Women's Secret Society on San Francisco Bay," California State Parks, October 10, 2006.

Greg Sarris, "The Charms of Tolay Lake Regional Park," *Bay Nature Magazine*, July – September, 2017.

Charles M. Slaymaker, *Cry for Olompali: An Initial Report on the Geological and Historical Features of Olompali*, private printing of 100 copies, October 1972.

"Tolay Lake Regional Park: Cultural and Natural History," www.sonoma-county.Org/park/pk_history.html, County of Sonoma Regional Parks Department.

Part II: The Working Landscape

Quote from Josiah Royce "The Squatter Riot of '50 in Sacramento," *The Overland Monthly*, Vol. VI, No. 33, September, 1885, p. 234.

Anderson, *op. cit.*

Adair Heig, *History of Petaluma: A California River Town*, (Petaluma, CA: Scottwall Associates, 1982).

Timothy G. Lynch, "Beyond the Golden Gate: A Maritime History of California," National Park Service, May 2012.

Jack Mason, *Early Marin*, (Petaluma: House of Printing, 1971), pp. 70-76.

Josiah Royce, "California," *American Commonwealth Series*, edited by Horace E. Scudder, (Houghlin, Mifflin & Co., 1886), p. 491.

Kevin Starr, *California: A History*, (New York: Modern Library, 2005).

Petaluma Adobe

Harvey J. Hansen, and Jeanne Thurlow Miller, David Wayne Peri, *Wild Oats in Eden*, (Santa Rosa, CA, 1962).

Rodolgo Larlos, *Sonoma, Alta California: 1842-1846, The Crucial Years*, (Rodolgo Larlos, 1984).

Mason, *op. cit.*

Arthur Quinn, *Broken Shore*, (Salt Lake City: Peregrine Smith, 1981).

Alan Rosenus, *General Vallejo and the Advent of the Americas*, (Berkeley: Heyday Press, 1995).

Stephen W. Silliman, *Lost Laborers in Colonial California: Native Americans and the Archaeology of Rancho Petaluma*, (University of Arizona Press, 2004).

Robert S. Smilie, *The Sonoma Mission, San Francisco Solano de Sonoma*, (Fresno: Valley Publishers, 1975).

Rancho Olompali

John Hart, "Rooted in History: The Many Lives of Rancho Olompali," *Bay Nature Magazine*, January 2003.

"Legends and Facts Prove Novato Crossroads in Early Marin History," *Daily Independent Journal*, July 26, 1952.

Dewey Livingston, *Nicasio: The Historic Valley at the Center of Marin*, (Nicasio Historical Society, 2008).

Mason, *op cit.*

Petaluma Argus: Rena Shattuck, "A Bit of Local Indian Lore," November 28, 1901; "James R. Burdell named in $250,000 Suit," July 6, 1925.

Petaluma Argus-Courier: "Burdell Family Roots Span State's History," April 21, 1984.

Joan Reutinger, "Olompali Park Filled With History," *The Coastal Post*, September 1997.

San Francisco Chronicle: "A Legal Document Destroyed," June 28, 1870; "Burdell Estate is Distributed," February 13, 1900.

Dena Seif, *Camilo Ynitia, Coast Miwok (1803-1852), Catholic, Rancho Grant Owner*, (University of California Irvine, 2006).

Two Rock

Jeremy Hay, "Tiny One-Room School South of Petaluma to Stay Open," *Santa Rosa Press Democrat*, February 2, 2016.

Nancy Hoffman, *Woman's 'True' Profession: Voiced from the History of Teaching*, (New York: The Feminist Press at CUNY, 1993).

Interview with Eunice Brooks Collings, conducted by Ron Walters, February 5, 1997. Petaluma Historical Library and Museum.

Petaluma Argus-Courier: "Trustees Visit Boyhood Haunts," March 26, 1955; "Iowa School Built Way Back in 1852," August 17, 1955; Rose Linebaugh, "Spanish Cavaliers Owned Two Rock Long, Long Ago," August 17, 1955; "Old Schools Were Rough," August 17, 1955; "One Room Schools Hold Out Still in the Rural Areas," August 17, 1955; "Schools Keep Growing Within City," August 17, 1955; "Schools Have a Large Niche in Petaluma History," March 26, 2008; Harlan Osborne, "Purvine Road Linked to Pioneer Trails of Old West," August 3, 2017.

"School District Election," *Sonoma County Journal*, December 9, 1859.

Saltwater Highway

Excerpted from Jerry MacMullen, *Paddle-Wheel Days in California*, (CA: Stanford University Press, 1944), pages 120-124.

Haystack Landing

Heig, *op. cit.*

Dutra Haystack Landing Asphalt & Recycling Facility V.D. Cultural Resources, Draft Environmental Impact Report, January 2008.

Gilbert H. Kneiss, *Redwood Railways*, (Berkeley: Howell North, 1956).

MacMullen, *op. cit.*

Nancy Olmsted, "A History of Paving Blocks Along San Francisco's South Beach Waterfront." San Francisco Redevelopment Agency, 1991.

Petaluma Argus-Courier: Ed Mannion, "Ed Mannion's Rear View Mirror" column, September 14, 1963; Ed Mannion, "Historian Recalls Earlier Incident," July 5, 1967.

N.H. Robotham, *The Pony Express*, Volumes 16-18, Pony Express Route & Pioneer Trails Association, 1949.

Robert Thompson, *Historical and Descriptive Sketch of Sonoma County, California*, (Philadelphia: L.H. Everts & Co., 1877).

U.S. Army Corp of Engineers http://www.sam.usace.army.mil/Portals/46/docs/recreation/OPCO/montgomery/pdfs/5thand6th/ahistoryofsteamboats.pdf

Lakeville

"A Brief History of Tolay Lake Regional Park," Sonoma County Parks, http://parks.sonomacounty.ca.gov/uploadedFiles/Parks/Get_Outdoors/Parks/tolay-history-brochure.pdf

An Illustrated History of Sonoma County, California, (Lewis Publishing Company, Chicago, 1889).

"Bihler's Lake Farm," *Petaluma Argus*, June 13, 1873.

Richard Dillon, *Iron Men: Peter, James, and Michael Donahue*, (Candela Press, 1984), pp. 237-242.

James Gerber, "The Gold Rush Origins of California's Wheat Economy," http://www.scielo.org.mx/scielo.php?script=sci_arttext&pid=S1405-22532010000200002

John Hart, *Farming on the Edge: Saving Family Farms in Marin County, California*, (Berkeley: UC Press, 1990).

J.P. Munro-Fraser, *History of Sonoma County*, (San Francisco: Alley, Bowen & Co., 1880).

Nordhoff, Charles, *California: For Health, Pleasure, and Residence, A Book for Travellers and Settlers*, (New York: Harper & Brothers Publishers, 1873), pp. 182-188.

Donald Pisani, *From the Family Farm to Agribusiness*, (Berkeley: UC Press, 1984), pp. 5-10.

Santa Rosa Press Democrat: Gaye LeBaron, "Site of Planned Tolay Park Rich in History," November 7, 2004; Arthur Dawson, "How Tolay Lake Got its Name," December 16, 2014.

"Wetlands in the North Bay Planning Area," San Francisco Bay Conservation and Development Commission, February, 1997.

Sonoma Mountain

"1881 Copeland Creek Easement between Thomas Hopper and M.J. Miller." Courtesy of Michael Healy.

Arthur Dawson and Christina Sloop, "Laguna de Santa Rosa Historical Hydrology Project," Laguna de Santa Rosa Foundation, 2010.

Arthur Dawson: "Magic Mountain," *Kenwood Press*, November 1, 2013; "How Lakeville Got its Name," *Santa Rosa Press Democrat*, December 16, 2014.

History of Sonoma County, (San Francisco: Alley, Bowen & Co., 1880).

Steve Horwick, "The Geology of Sonoma Mountain," *Naturalist Training Guide-Geology*, Sonoma State University, 2007.

Munro-Fraser, *op. cit.*

Petaluma Argus: "Board of City Trustees," June 29, 1877; "Petaluma Water Works," May 21, 1875; "New Reservoir," March 21, 1873; "Sonoma Country and Petaluma Water Company," August 13, 1868; "Water Company," November 16, 1877; "Prospect Ahead for Good Water," May 13, 1871; "Another Water Project," December 9, 1871; "Improvement at the Reservoir," November 21, 1873; "The Water Report," January 12, 1899; "This City Has Abundant Pure Water from Mountain Springs," June 11, 1907; "To Prevent Overflow of Creek," March 19, 1915; "Government Will Survey Copeland Creek to Do Away with Overflows," December 18, 1915; "Lea Secures Petaluma Project by Amended Senate Bill," July 11, 1917; "Cotati Objects to Copeland Creek Diverting Dam," July 1, 1918; "Cotati Land Co. Sues City of Petaluma Over Copeland Creek Work," September 24, 1918.

Petaluma Argus-Courier: "Copeland Creek Dam, Built By California Water Service Company, Proves Difficult Undertaking," June 21, 1945; "Petaluma Water Supply is Adequate and Pure, but Costly," September 29, 1948; "1 Per Center of Country Wells are Called 'Poor,'" June 24, 1950; "Folds, Faults and Eruptions Made Sonoma Mountain," August 17, 1955; "Ed Mannion's Rear View Mirror," June 18, 1961; "Flooding Contaminates Wells," February 22, 1986; "Keep Creek Away from Petaluma," August 17, 2017.

Petaluma Morning Courier: "For City Water," July 21, 1898; "Engineer Report," April 23, 1902; "Supervisors Accept Bridge," December 14, 1918; "City Water and Sewers Discussed by Council," July 7, 1920.

Petaluma River, Detailed Project Report for Flood Control, Sonoma County: Environmental Impact Statement, Part 1, U.S. Army Corp of Engineers, November 1994.

Santa Rosa Press Democrat: "Petaluma Aqueduct Contract Signed," May 10, 1960; "Mayors, Councilmen Briefed on County's Water Future," November 15, 1963; "Iva Warner's Views on Warm Springs Dam," April 21, 1974; "Editorials: Warm Springs," February 25, 1976.

The Oak Groves

Burbank quote from Kevin Starr, *Americans and the California Dream, 1850-1915*, (Oxford University Press, USA, 1986), p. 429.

Anderson, *op. cit.*

Arthur Dawson, "Early Agriculture on Sonoma Mountain," *Kenwood Press*, June 15, 2012.

Jared Farmer, *Trees in Paradise: A California History*, (New York: W.W. Norton & Company, 2013).

Gaye LeBaron, "Santa Rosa Ignored Nature's Lesson," *Washington Post*, October 18, 2017.

Scott Mensing, *The History of Oak Woodlands in California, Part II: The Native American and Historic Period*, California Fire Science Consortium, https://www.cafiresci.org/s/Mensing2006HistOfOAkWoodlandsJA.pdf

Petaluma Argus: October 7, 1869; "Fires," October 14, 1869; "Thousands Lost by Brush Fire," September 21, 1900; "Great Raging Fire in Sonoma Valley," September 17, 1923; "Great Fire Raging Below this City on Monday," September 17, 1923; "The Fire Below Town," September 18, 1923.

Petaluma Argus-Courier: "County Was Real Fortunate Destruction Wasn't Worse," October 21, 1964; "Area Fires Still Uncontrolled," September 17, 1965.

"Fires All Around," *Petaluma Morning Courier*, September 22, 1900.

San Francisco Call: "Burning Woods and Fields," September 23, 1900; "One Hundred Square Miles of Territory Devastated by Fire," September 24, 1900.

"S.F. Is Center for Ring of Growing Fires," *San Francisco Chronicle*, September 18, 1923.

Santa Rosa Press Democrat: "Disaster Area Proclaimed," September 22, 1964; "Fighting the Fire," September 27, 1964; "Historic Wildfires' Catastrophic Lessons," July 12, 2014; Arthur Dawson, "The History of Sonoma County's Woodlands," January 26, 2017; "Tubbs Fires Revives Memory of a Blaze that Now Haunts Santa Rosa," October 14, 2017; "Tubbs, Nuns, Pocket Fires Fully Contained in Sonoma and Napa Counties," October 31, 2017; "New PG&E Reports Show Equipment Problems Near Origins of Northern California Fires," November 1, 2017.

Smilie, *op. cit.*

Chinese Rock Walls

"China Camp State Park" video, Marin History Museum, https://www.youtube.com/watch?v=e8tZpz1YAlE

Hannah Clayborn, *Chinese in Healdsburg*, ourhealdsburg.com, June 2003.

"Five Views: An Ethnic Historic Site Survey for California," National Park Service, https://www.nps.gov/parkhistory/online_books/5views/5views3j.htm#42; *The Mariposa Sentinel*, Vol. XXI, No. 4 (Winter 1978).

Heig, *op. cit.*

Gaye LeBaron column, *Santa Rosa Press Democrat*, January 28, 1979.

"The Boycott," *Petaluma Argus*, March 13, 1886.

Gordon C. Phillips, "The Chinese in Sonoma County, California, 1900-1930: The Aftermath of Exclusion," a masters thesis submitted to Sonoma State University, January 30, 2015.

Skip Sommer, "Dark History of Prejudice in California," *Petaluma Post*, February 2009, p. 24.

Sonoma Stories and the Song Wong Bourbeau Collection, http://smatters.users.sonic.net/wordpress/wp-content/uploads/2014/11/sonoma-stories-historical-context-chinese-american-section-i.pdf

Simone Wilson, *Sonoma Country: The River of Time*, (Chatsworth, CA: Windsor Publications, 1990). pp. 43, 47.

Cattle Ranches

"Cowboy Heroes," http://mycowboyheroes.blogspot.com/2015/08/jesse-stahl-first-black-bronc-rider.html

J. Frank Dobie, *The Longhorns*, (Austin, TX: University of Texas Press, 1980).

Hansen, *op. cit.*

Hart, *op. cit.*

John Ludeke, "No-Fence Law of 1874," *California History*, Vol. 59, No. 2, Summer 1980, pp. 98-115.

Myrtle M. McKittrick, *Vallejo, Son of California*, (Portland, OR: Binfords & Mort, 1944).

Petaluma Argus-Courier: Howard Kessler, "Tim Caulfield is Packed with Stories," October 27, 1955; "Livestock Auctioneer Tony Brazil a Link to Region's Agricultural Past," September 21, 2017.

Pisani, *op. cit.*

Silliman, *op. cit.*

Bill Soberanes, *Petaluma Argus-Courier*: December 15, 1954 column; December 8, 1998 column; "The Goat Who Made Baseball History," July 3, 1970; "Butcher Shops Were Popular Places," April 4, 1973.

Skip Sommer, "Harrison Meacham, Petaluma Rancher 1833-1909," *Petaluma Post*, June 2013.

Battle of the Washoe House

Samuel Cassidy, *An Illustrated History of Sonoma County, California*, (Chicago: Lewis Publishing Company, 1889).

Emmett Guard (Emmet Rifles), California State Military Museum, http://www.military-museum.org/EmmetRifles.html

Hansen, *op.cit.*

Heig, *op. cit.*

LeBaron, Gaye, and Dee Blackman, Joann Mitchell, Harvey Hansen, *Santa Rosa: A Nineteenth Century Town*, (Historia, Ltd, 1985).

Chuck Lucas, "The Blue and the Gray in the Land of the Green," *Penngrove Proud*, Spring 2012.

Penngrove Rock Ranches

Gaye LeBaron, "If Those Old Stone Walls Could Talk," *Santa Rosa Press Democrat*, May 17, 2014.

Chuck Lucas, "Rock Ranches of Penngrove," *Penngrove Proud*, Volume 5, Winter 2011.

Jeff Elliott, "The Wickersham Murders," Santa Rosa History blog, May 28, 2017. http://santarosahistory.com/wordpress/2017/05/wickersham-murders/

Olmsted, *op. cit.*

Peggy B. Perazzo, "Stone Quarries and Beyond," http://quarriesandbeyond.org.

J. Charles Whatford, "Historic Stone Quarries as Rural Cultural Landscapes: An Example from Sonoma Country, California," *Society for California Archaeology*, Volume 8, 1995.

Eucalyptus Stands

Thomas A. Brown, "Sonoma County's Landscape and Horticultural History," *Journal of California Garden & Landscape History Society*, Vol. 15, Number 3, Summer 2012.

Arthur Dawson: "The History of Sonoma County's Woodlands," *Santa Rosa Press Democrat*, January 26, 2017; "Early Agriculture on Sonoma Mountains," *Kenwood Press*, June 15, 2012.

Jeff Elliott, "Jack London, Eucalyptus King," Santa Rosa History blog, July 27, 2014. http://santarosahistory.com/wordpress/2014/07/jack-london-eucalyptus-king/

Farmer, *op. cit.*

Tom Gregory, *History of Sonoma County with Biographical Sketches*, (Los Angeles: Historic Record Company, 1911).

"Jack London Orders Many Eucalyptus Trees," *Santa Rosa Republican*, September 23, 1911.

Scott Mensing, *The History of Oak Woodlands in California, Part II: The Native American and Historic Period*, California Fire Science Consortium, https://www.cafiresci.org/s/Mensing2006HistOfOAkWoodlandsJA.pdf

Petaluma Argus: "Tree Planting," March 26, 1875; "The Eucalyptus," November 5, 1880; "Big Order for Trees," November 1, 1909; "W.A.T. Stratton Talks on Eucalyptus," April 19, 1909; "Not Last Vigilante," March 16, 1915; "When Burbank Worked Here," April 15, 1926. "Stratton Homestead and Nursery Sold and Land to Be

Improved," February 29, 1927; "'Tunzi Parkway,' Petaluma's Newest Residence Court; Completed Today," December 16, 1927.

Cow Heaven

Robert Digitale, "It's All About the Cheese," *Santa Rosa Press Democrat*, December 26, 2007.

Guide to the California Dairy Industry History Collection, California State Parks, 2005.

Hart, *op. cit.*

Dewey Livingston, *Ranching on the Point Reyes Peninsula*, (Historic Resource Study Point Reyes National Seashore, July 1994).

Pisani, *op.cit.*

Robert L. Santos, "Dairying in California Through 1910," *Southern California Quarterly* 76, Summer 1994.

Ann Foley Scheuring, editor, *A Guidebook to California Agriculture,* (Berkeley: U.C. Press, 1983).

Skip Sommer, "Petaluma's Dairymen," *Petaluma Post*, June 2008.

Boss Chicken Town

Maxine Kortum Durney, "The Petaluma Chicken House Project: Interviews, Memoirs and Oral Histories," Petaluma Museum Association, 2000.

Thea Lowry, *Petaluma's Poultry Pioneers*, (Ross, CA: Manifold Press, 1993).

Page Smith and Charles Daniel, *The Chicken Book*, (San Francisco: North Point Press, 1982).

Horse Ranches

"California Horse Farms," *The Overland Monthly*, Vol. XVIII, July-December, 1891, p. 491.

Munro-Fraser, *op. cit.*

Petaluma Argus: "The County Fair," September 19, 1867; "County Fair," May 21, 1868; "Opening Address," October 8, 1870; "Norman Stallion Duke de Chartes," May 25, 1877; "Draft Horses," August 26, 1881; "Draft Horses," November 25, 1881; "Agricultural Park," December 23, 1881; "What Others Think," January 6, 1882; "Normandy Horse Conventions," December 8, 1883; "To England and France," August 1, 1885; "Gone to San Joaquin," February 9, 1899.

Petaluma Morning Courier: "No Appropriations," March 28, 1895; "Local Brevities," December 2, 1902; "A Big Deal," April 2, 1903; "Master of Kenilworth is Dead," June 3, 1909; "Biography of Theo. Skillman," January 19, 1910.

Bill Soberanes, "Many Fine Horses Ran at Kenilworth," *Petaluma Argus-Courier*, August 24, 1958.

Wanda Smith, *Horses of the Wine Country,* (Wanda Smith Productions, 2009).

"Straubville Fair Started by Agricultural Society," *Santa Rosa Press Democrat*, August 24, 1958.

"The Famous Norman Stallions," *Town and Country Journal*, February 28, 1880.

Sheep Ranches

"Agitators Blamed for Farm Strikes at LaFolette Quiz," *Oakland Tribune*, January 14, 1940.

Healdsburg Tribune: February 22, 1940, page 1; March 2, 1940, page 1.

Rachel LaFranchi, "Groverman Ranch: Veterinarian Keeps Family Property in Ag for 100 Years," *Sonoma-Marin Farm News*, August 2017.

Linda Musick, "Transitions: A Visual History of the Petaluma Area's Changing Agriculture Industry," Final Thesis Paper, Academy of Art College. Petaluma Historical Museum Collection.

McKittrick, *op. cit.*

Richard L. Neurberger, "Who Are the Associated Farmers," *Survey Graphic*, September, 1939.

Petaluma Argus-Courier: "Two Defendants Freed as Tar-Feather Case Hearing is Started," August 21, 1936; "Sonoma County Farmers Are Preparing to Cope with Labor Disturbances," December 23, 1936; "Associated Farmers Brand Farm Labor Troubles Work of Reds and Racketeers," December 16, 1937; "Sonoma-Marin Wool Growers Defy Bridges' Threats By Ordering Rail Shipments," February 22, 1938; "Convoy Marin County Milk," April 18, 1936; Harlan Osborne, "Beloved Veterinarian Fostered Deep Petaluma Ties," July 26, 2016.

"Midnight Conflagration: Petaluma Woolen Mills Destroyed by Fire Fiend," *Petaluma Morning Courier*, April 20, 1898.

Claire Rithner, "Migrant Farm Workers, Growers, and the Healdsburg Community, 1941-1945," Master of Arts in History thesis, Sonoma State University, 1997.

Santa Rosa Press Democrat: "Associated Farmers Blame 'Red' Agitators for Attempt to Unionize Farm Workers," April 24, 1938; "S.R. Records Missing in Associated Farmer Probe," December 5, 1939.

William C. Weir, Reuben Albaugh, *California Sheep Production, Manual 16*, University of California, College of Agriculture, October, 1954. http://ucanr.edu/sites/UCCE_LR/files/202119.pdf

The Petaluma Gap

Eria Hannickel, *Empire of Vines: Wine Culture in America* (University of Pennsylvania Press, 2013).

William F. Heintz, *Wine and Viticulture in the Lakeville District, Petaluma, Sonoma County, CA,* 1989.

Gaye LeBaron, *Santa Rosa Press Democrat*: "Site of Planned Tolay Ranch Rich in History," November 7, 2004; "Petaluma Gap Becomes New Sonoma County Wine Appellation," December 9, 2017.

Glennda Gene Luhnow, *A Historical Evaluation of the William Bihler Ranch Complex, Petaluma California,* Spring 1995, Sonoma County Library.

Munro-Fraser, *op. cit.*

Nordhoff, Charles, *California: For Health, Pleasure, and Residence, A Book for Travellers and Settlers,* (New York: Harper & Brothers Publishers, 1873), pp. 182-188.

Petaluma Argus: "Bihler's Lake Farm," June 13, 1873; "Fine Grapes," November 25, 1881; "Small Places for Sale," December 2, 1881; "Grapes," November 14, 1883; "Winery," June 12, 1886; "More Petaluma Industries," April 4, 1888.

petalumagap.com/the-petaluma-gap/history/

Smilie, *op. cit.*

Sonoma Democrat: "Home Notes: Petaluma Grapes," October 15, 1881; "Petaluma News," February 2, 1884.

Charles Sullivan, *Companion to California Wine,* (Berkeley: UC Press, 1998), p. 109.

Part III: The River Town

Main Street

Ed Mannion, "Ed Mannion's Rear-View Mirror" column, *Petaluma Argus-Courier*: September 14, 1963; September 21, 1963.

Cedar Grove

"A. J. Bloom Wedded in San Francisco," *Marin Journal*, Volume 45, Number 37, 17 November 1904.

The American Anthropologist, Volume 9, (Lancaster, PA: The American Anthropological Association, 1907), p. 354-355.

Biographies Of Sonoma County, http://www.rootsweb.ancestry.com/~cagha/biographies2/bios2/bloom-james-b.htm

Heig, *op. cit.*

"A Historical Structures Evaluation of Cedar Grove Property, Petaluma, Sonoma County, California," Archaeological Resource Service, October 25, 2006. Sonoma County Library,

History & Genealogy.

Petaluma Argus: "Our First Pioneer," November 28, 1901.

Petaluma Argus-Courier: "Arrest for Huge Fraud," June 17, 1937; "Life Ends for Adolph J. Bloom," September 29, 1937; "Funeral Rite for Adolph Bloom," October 2, 1937; "City Conceived, Born and Incorporated in Eight Years," August 18, 1955; "J.E. Lockwood—City's 1st Settler," August 18, 1955; Allison Jarrell, "Disheveled Home Set to Be Razed," April 10, 2014.

Dan Peterson, *Petaluma's Architectural Heritage*, (Santa Rosa, CA: Architectural Preservation Associates, 1978).

"Retired Banker of Petaluma is Suicide," *Healdsburg Tribune*, Number 294, 30 September 1937.

Katherine J. Rinehart, "Who Were the Becks?" Sonoma County Library Local History and Genealogy Notes, https://sonomalibrary.org/blogs/history/who-were-the-becks.

Rinehart, *Petaluma, op. cit.*

Greg Sarris, "The Last Woman from Petaluma," *Celebrating Petaluma, op. cit.*

The McNear Buildings

James Gerber, "The Gold Rush Origins of California's Wheat Economy," http://www.scielo.org.mx/scielo.php?script=sci_arttext&pid=S1405-22532010000200002

James Gerber, "Gold Rushes and the Trans-Pacific Wheat Trade, California and Australia, 1848-57," *Pacific and Pacific Rim Economic History Since the 16th Century*, edited by Dennis O. Flynn, A.J.H. Lathan, and Lionell Frost, (New Jersey: Routledge, 1999).

Gregory, *op. cit.*

Heig, *op. cit.*

Carol A. Jensen, *Maritime Contra Costa County*, (Arcadia Publishing, 2014).

LeBaron, Blackman, Mitchell, Hansen, *op. cit.*

"The McNear Family: the Second Generation," *Petaluma Argus-Courier*, June 21, 2006.

"McNear Dream of Industries Booming East of San Rafael," *Daily Independent Journal*, May 17, 1974.

Petaluma Argus: "Immense Volume of Business Transacted Annually in Petaluma by the G.P. McNear Co.," Development Edition, 1915.

Petaluma Morning Courier, "Basin and Canal," February 23, 1893; "Canal Notes," March 22, 1893; "What Our Little City Has Accomplished," December 31, 1894; "Condensed Milk Factory," November 23, 1899; "Woolen Mills," January 16, 1900.

Rinehart, *Petaluma, op. cit.*

Skip Sommer, "The Magnificent McNears," *Petaluma Post*, October 2012.

"Biographies: McNear, John Augustus," Sonoma-San Francisco County, CA, Archives, (Alley, Bowen & Co., 1880).

David Vaught, *After the Gold Rush: Tarnished Dreams in the Sacramento Valley*, (Baltimore: John Hopkins University Press, 2009).

The Train Depot

Alta California: "City Items (Anti-Chinese)," February 13, 1867; "City Items (Anti-Chinese)," February 14, 1867.

Coleman, Charles M., *P. G. And E. of California: The Centennial Story of Pacific Gas and Electric Company, 1852-1952*, (McGraw-Hill Book Company Inc., 1952).

A. Bray Dickinson, *Narrow Gauge to the Redwoods*, (Corona del Mar, CA: Trans-Anglo Books, 1970).

Dillon, *op. cit.*

"Ezekial Denman," *An Illustrated History of Sonoma County, California, op. cit.*

Heig, *op. cit.*

"The Iron Horse Comes to Healdsburg," http://www.ourhealdsburg.com/history/ironhorse.htm

Kneiss, *op. cit.*

Gaye LeBaron, "It Was a Long Way to Gettysburg," *Santa Rosa Press Democrat*, September 30, 1990.

Norma Morris, *Donahue Landing*, Sonoma State Library, 1992.

Munro-Fraser, *op. cit.*

Petaluma Argus: "Railroad Bill," February 27, 1868; "Railroad Meeting," March 28, 1867; "The Rival Routes," April 23, 1868; "The Battle Fought and Victory Won," May 14, 1868; "The Railroad," March 21, 1868; "Fourth of July Celebration," July 1, 1868; "The Railroad," July 1, 1869; "Insurance of the Cargo of the Ship 'Moderation,'" December 11, 1869; "The Railroad," January 15, 1870; "The Railroad Contract," May 21, 1870; "Railroad Election," June 4, 1870; "Peter Donahue," October 1, 1870; "Railroad Bonds," October 22, 1879; "A Trip to Donahue as the Railroad Advances," December 3, 1870; "Completion of the Railroad," December 31, 1870.

Petaluma Argus-Courier: "Livery Stables Played Key Role Here," January 27, 2018; A.S. Keenan, "Donahue Landing Flourished, Died," Centennial Edition, August 18, 1955; Ed Mannion, "Reminiscences from a Native Son," August 12, 1961.

Railways, Locomotives, and Cars, Volume 21, (Simmons-Boardman Publishing Corp., 1868).

"Ship Passengers: 1846-1899, Peter Donahue," The Maritime Heritage Project, http://www.maritimeheritage.org/vips/Peter-Donahue.html

Fred A. Stindt and Guy L. Dunscomb, *The Northwestern Pacific Railroad, Redwood Empire Route*, (Redwood City, CA: Stindt and Dunscomb, 1964).

Robert Wilson, "The Great Diamond Hoax," *Smithsonian Magazine*, June, 2004.

The Hatcheries

Gary J. Allen and Ken Albala, *The Business of Good: Encyclopedia of the Food and Drink Industries*, (ABC-CLIO, 2007) pp. 304-305.

Heig, *op. cit.*

Lowry, *op. cit.*

Katherine J. Rinehart, "Inventing the First Commercial Hatchery," *Santa Rosa Press Democrat*, July 17, 2007.

Rinehart, *Petaluma, op. cit.*

Smith and Daniel, *op. cit.*

Simone Wilson, *Images of America: Petaluma, California*, (Chicago: Arcadia Publishing, 2001).

Towers of Grain

Celebrating Petaluma, op. cit.

"Chickens Once Ruled the Roost in Petaluma," *Petaluma Argus-Courier*, April 20, 1985.

Heig, *op. cit.*

Lowry, *op. cit.*

Walter Hogan, *The Call of the Hen*, (Petaluma, CA: The Petaluma Daily Courier), 1913.

Petaluma Argus: "It's Going to Rain Eggs in S.F.," August 17, 1922; "'Cluck Clucks' Invitation to Meet Friday," December 27, 1922.

Petaluma Morning Courier: "Particular Events for Annual Egg Day Fiesta," August 20, 1921; "Sending Out Invitations for Annual Festival," July 8, 1922.

Katherine J. Rinehart, "Dairyman's Feed – A Petaluma Landmark Worthy of Respect," Sonoma County Library, https://sonomalibrary.org/blogs/history/dairymans-feed-a-petaluma-landmark-worthy-of-respect

Rinehart, *Petaluma, op. cit.*

Ferron Salniker, "Petaluma, Land of Eggs & Butter," *Edible, Marin & Wine Country*, March 1, 2014.

The Silk Mill

"Enthusiastic Ladies," *San Francisco Call*, July 17, 1892.

J. Gottschalk, "Competing Images: Silk and Rayon in Popular U.S. Publications of the Nineteen Thirties," Textile Society of America, 2002. http://digitalcommons.unl.edu/tsaconf/390/

Gaye LeBaron, "It's Official: The Old Silk Mill is a Landmark," *Santa Rosa Press Democrat*, April 27, 1986.

Petaluma Morning Courier: "The Silk Mill," December 8, 1891; "Carlson-Currier Company," October 19, 1892; "Silk Reeling," January 24, 1893; "An Early Morning Fire," April 17, 1906; "Petaluma Silk Mills Have Changed Hands," March 31, 1915; "Housing Problem Continues Serious," March 22, 1922.

Petaluma Argus-Courier: "Sunset Line, Twine Co. Buys Silk Mill," February 7, 1940; Skip Sommer: "The Silk Mill Has Deep Roots in Petaluma's History," February 10, 2016.

"Petaluma Silk Mill in a Big $20 Million Merger," *Petaluma Argus*, December 28, 1925.

Skip Sommer, "Hotel Planned for Historic Landmark," *Petaluma Post*, October, 2009.

The Creamery

Articles of Incorporation of the Petaluma Co-operative Creamery, 1913.

"North Coast Farmers Won't Use Cow Hormone," *Ukiah Daily Journal*, February 1, 1994.

Oral History of Gene Benedetti, Founder of Clover Stornetta Farms, The Bancroft Library, University of California, Berkeley, California.

Penny Hastings, "Petaluma Remembers Pioneering Football Team," *SF Gate*, February 27, 2004.

Petaluma Argus-Courier: Kenneth Evans, "Production Record of the Petaluma Cooperative Creamery Places it at the Top of the Milk Marketing List in Region," July 17, 1954; Eric Gneckow, "Larry Peter Honored for Contribution to Local Dairy Industry," April 25, 2015; Yovanna Bieberich, "10 Million Bank Loan Helps Local Cheesemaker Finance, Expand," June 19, 2007.

"Petaluma Creamery," *Daily Independent Journal*, August 20, 1975.

Katherine J. Rinehart, "Clover Fun Facts," Local History and Genealogy Notes, Sonoma County Library, https://sonomalibrary.org/blogs/history/clover-fun-facts.

Santa Rosa Press Democrat: Tim Tesconi, "Ag Business Leader Remembered as WWII Hero, Leghorns Football Coach," January 14, 2006; Tim Tesconi, "Spring Hill Jersey Cheese to Reopen Plant Shuttered in June; Price Not Disclosed," August 17, 2004; Michael Coit, "Spring Hill Jersey Cheese Founder Revives Century-old Petaluma Facility, Brand," June 13, 2008; Robert Digitale, "Clover Stornetta Taps into New Generation," August 30, 2015; Robert Digitale, "North Bay Dairies' Shift to Organic Milk Production Offers Economic Buffer," August 3, 2016.

The Railroad Trestle

Borden, Stanley T., "Petaluma & Santa Rosa Electric Railroad," *The Western Railroader*.

Heig, *op. cit.*

LeBaron, Blackman, Mitchell, Hansen, *op. cit.*

Mendocino Coast Model Railroad & Historical Society, "Northwestern Pacific Railway Owner," http://www.mendorailhistory.org/1_railroads/nwp/owner.htm

Petaluma Argus: "The Request is Refused," December 20, 1904; "Opens Next Thursday," November 24, 1904; "Cross is Allowed," December 10, 1904; "May Allow Crossing," December 7, 1904; "Fares on the New Electric Railway Line," December 2, 1904; "And the Crossing is Laid at Last," March 2, 1905; "Towne Sues A. Bowen," February 8, 1905; "Bought the Old Street Railway," November 11, 1903.

Petaluma Morning Courier: "Plan Ferry Service," August 25, 1918; "Injunction Suit Goes Over Once More," February 3, 1905; "Going to Point Pedro," April 15, 1905. "Electric Road Answers," January 17, 1905; "Railway to Dillon Beach," July 31, 1905; "An Electric Railway," May 26, 1903; "In Working Order; Wheels Whirl and Engines Throb at the New Electric Light Station," June 11, 1897; "Work Commenced; The Site of the Cold Storage and Electric Light Plant Presents a Busy Scene," December 18, 1896; "The Sales Made; The Petaluma Electric Light Power Company's Business Plant Already Sold," December 13, 1895; "Rumored Change; The Electric Light Plant Like to Change Hands," December 12, 1895; "Pierce's New Telephones," March 29, 1894.

"Rails Orders for New Line," *San Francisco Chronicle*, November 14, 1903.

San Francisco Call: "Petaluma Electric and the California Northwestern Men Fight in Santa Rosa," March 2, 1905; "Santa Rosa Electric Line Completes Road," February 1905; "Merchants Wage War on Railroad," December 21, 1904; "Dissolves Railroad Injunction," February 1, 1905.

Schmale, John, and Kristina Schmale, *Petaluma and Santa Rosa Railway*, (Arcadia Publishing, 2009).

Allen Tracy, The Petaluma & Santa Rosa Electric Railway – Electric Railway Pioneer. http://www.petalumatrolley.org/staging/wp-content/uploads/2016/07/history-PSR-tacy.pdf

The Plazas

John Benanti "Cypress Hill Cemetery," *Petaluma Museum Association Newsletter*, Volume 23, Issue 4, Fall 2013.

Jane Cunningham Croly, *The History of the Woman's Club Movement in America*, (New York: H. G. Allen and Co., 1898).

John L. Crompton, "The Role of the Proximate Principle in the Emergence of Urban Parks in the United Kingdom and in the United States," *Leisure Studies*, Vol. 26, No. 2, 213-234, April 2007.

Heig, *op. cit.*

Gregory, *op. cit.*, pp. 720-721.

Marianne Hurley, Katherine J. Rinehart, Lucy Kortum, "Petaluma Landmarks," *Celebrating Petaluma, op. cit.*

Petaluma Argus: "D Street Plaza Deed," December 26, 1873; "Let Us Have a Park," December 4, 1874; "Main Street Plaza Stone Wall," August 9, 1878; "Our Plazas," January 28, 1876; "Walnuts," January 9, 1886; "Improvement Club Historic Meeting," May 23, 1918; "Petaluma Rises to Fresh Fame and Glory," May 1, 1901; "Thanksgiving Argus Edition," November 28, 1901.

Petaluma Argus-Courier: "The City Board," June 10, 1896; "Palm Trees," February 28, 1900; "Obituary of Rena Shattuck," February 26, 1942; "Hill Plaza Parking Opposed by Greenery Lovers," January 19, 1960; Ed Mannion, "Women Championed the Green Spot," January 30, 1960; "Old Building Coming Down," December 9, 1960; "Ed Mannion's Rear View Mirror" column, September 30, 1961, October 7, 1961; "Woman's Club," May 17, 1963. Bill Soberanes, "History of the Petaluma Woman's Club," February 26, 1986; "Once a Sleepy River Town, Petaluma Has Grown Up in 160 Years," September 25, 2015.

Petaluma Morning Courier: "Another Fountain," March 14, 1900; "These Ladies Worked," April 29, 1898; December 29, 1886; March 16, 1900; "D Street Plaza," January 13, 1886; "Reducing Hill Plaza," March 3, 1886; "Once a Public Plaza, Always a Public Plaza," December 1, 1886; "The Work Goes On," September 15, 1886; "The Improvement Club," July 22, 1896; "Grand Marshall Collins," May 27, 1896; "Improvement Club Meeting," September 7, 1896; "The League Meet," July 8, 1896. "Contracts Awarded," March 21, 1899.

Petaluma Woman's Club Year Books, 1903, 1913-1914, 1914-1915, 1915-1916. Petaluma Historical Museum collection.

Sonoma County Journal: "The Plaza Question," November 7, 1859.

Katherine J. Rinehart: "Controversial Plans Rocked Downtown Plaza," *Petaluma Magazine*, Summer 2008; "Hill Plaza History Timeline," Sonoma Country Historical Library Collection.

Janet Gracyk, "Walnut Park, Written Historical and Descriptive Data," Historic Landscapes Survey, National Park Service, May 10, 2009. https://cdn.loc.gov/master/pnp/habshaer/ca/ca3600/ca3639/data/ca3639data.pdf

Jeanette Gibson Jones, "The Petaluma Woman's Club," January 27, 1914. Petaluma Historical Museum collection.

Paige Meltzer, "The Pulse and Conscience of America" The General Federation and Women's Citizenship, 1945-1960," Frontiers: A Journal of Women Studies (2009), Vol. 30 Issue 3, p52-76. http://muse.jhu.edu/article/370523

Minutes of Ladies Improvement Club 1896-1900. Petaluma Historical Museum collection.

Rinehart, *Petaluma, op. cit.*

"Sale of Petalumian," *Ukiah Daily Journal*, January 22, 1897.

"Rena Shattuck," *San Francisco Call*, June 22, 1896.

Robert A. Thompson, "Petaluma, Sonoma County," *Out West: A Magazine of the Old Pacific and the New,* (Lost Angeles: Land of Sunshine Publishing Company, Volume 16, 1902).

"Wheelmen Race at Petaluma," *San Francisco Chronicle*, July 5, 1896.

Places Called Home

A Guide to Historic Architecture in Fresno, California. http://historicfresno.org/bio/mcdougal.htm

Joseph Barkoff, "Saving Time at the Comstock House," *The Oak Leaf*, May 13, 2013.

James Dixon, "When and Why Styles Changed: Victorian and Edwardian," video series, http://jdarchitect.com/Site/Styles__Victorian_%26_Edwardian.html

"McDougall Bros., Architects, Have Worked for Greater City," *San Francisco Call*, Volume 107, Number 82, February 20, 1910.

Shawn Montoya, *Brainerd Jones, 1869-1945*. http://www.sonic.net/~tdn/jones.html

National Register of Historic Places Form For the Ellis-Martin House, 2006, https://npgallery.nps.gov/GetAssett/c356be7e-7bf6-4de2-62b396fa9c52

Peterson, *op. cit.*

Dave Weinstein, "The Man Who Built Petaluma," *San Francisco Chronicle*, February 18, 2006.

Dave Weinstein, *The Signature Architects of the San Francisco Bay Area*, (Layton, UT: Gibbs Smith, 2006).

St. Vincent's Church

Brian Dervin Dillon, Richard H. Dillon, John Dervin Yi An Dillon, "California, the Irish Paradise: 1795-1898," *The California Territorial Quarterly*, No. 108, Winter 2016-17.

Ed Mannion, *St. Vincent de Paul, 1857-1962*, booklet of historical sketch prepared for dedication of new high school, March 17, 1962, Petaluma History Room, Petaluma Library.

"The New St. Vincent's Unsurpassed in California," *Petaluma Argus,* March 31, 1927.

Petaluma Argus-Courier: "Historical Review of St. Vincent's Parish," September 20, 1937; Bill Sobranes, "So They Tell Me" column, May 5, 1955; "Many Faiths Represented in Petaluma Churches," August 17, 1955; "Father Kiely's Golden Anniversary," August 16, 1965; "Noteworthy Petalumans of the 20th Century," December 29, 1999.

Petaluma Morning Courier: "Pentecost Observance," May 25, 1898; "Holy Ghost Sunday," May 12, 1894.

Rejoice 150 Years: St. Vincent de Paul Parish, 1857-2007, Petaluma History Room, Petaluma Library.

The King of Hardware Stores

"John Bauer," California Genealogy and History Archives Biographies of Sonoma County, http://www.rootsweb.ancestry.com/~cagha/biographies2/bios2/bauer-john-w.htm

Lowry, *Petaluma's Poultry Pioneers, op. cit.*, pp. 65-67.

"New Building on Kentucky," *Petaluma Morning Courier*, November 23, 1906.

"Northbay Chief Retires," *Healdsburg Tribune, Enterprise and Scimitar,* Number 81, 4 May 1984.

"Old Tools Archive," http://swingleydev.com/ot/get/138478/thread/

Petaluma Argus-Courier: "A.F. Tomasini Dies on Thanksgiving Eve," November 22, 1940; "George Hobbie is Lieutenant in U.S. Navy," July 11, 1942; "George Hobbie," February 13, 1945; "Tomasini Hardware Co. Celebrates its Birthday," January 14, 1955; "Tomasini Firm Will Move to Keller St.," June 4, 1956; "Schluckebier Store Sold," November 17, 1959; "Tomasini Hardware to Be Closed," October 18, 1961.

Vern Piccinotti, *Celebrating Petaluma, op. cit, p. 127.*

Remembrances of Fred M. Jennings, Sonoma Historical Library archive.

"Rex Mercantile Company Celebrates Twentieth Anniversary," *Petaluma Argus*, September 6, 1927.

Rinehart, *Petaluma, op. cit., p. 22.*

Santa Rosa Press Democrat: "Obituary – George Tomasini," July 14, 2005; "Return of Downtown Business Draws More than 1,000 Visitors, Along with Praise for Owner," August 26, 2007.

The Last Tugboat Company

Matthew Morse Booker, "Oyster Growers and Oyster Pirates in San Francisco Bay," MIT Publishing. Division of Mines and Geology, Volumes 94-98, 1968.

Peter Fimrite, "2 Million Oysters in Bay Begin Restoration Effort," *SF Gate*, November 15, 2013.

Lynn Schnitzer, "Christian Linds' Company, Jerico Products, Thrives on the Petaluma River," *Petaluma Argus-Courier*, November 12, 2009.

Susan Pultz Williams, "Oysters, the Story of the 'O'," *San Francisco Bay Crossings*, April 2005.

The Speakeasy

LeBaron, Mitchell, *op. cit.*

Petaluma Argus: "Selections," July 3, 1899; "Solari Grocery," January 31, 1900; "Local Firms Will Move," April 2, 1909; "Four Liquor Raids Conducted Here Today by Police Officers," September 14, 1922; "Solari Pleads Guilty to Charge," October 9, 1922; "Arrest Two Here in Liquor Ring Expose; Ten Others Involved," April 14, 1937; "Garzoli Held for Huge Fraud," June 17, 1937; "Three in Jail, Seven Free on Bail, Four at Large in Still Case Count," June 18, 1937; "6 Petalumans Get Jail, 3 Fined in Federal Court," October 5, 1937.

Petaluma Morning Courier: "Solari Grocery," July 3, 1899, January 23, 1900, October 31, 1925; "Notice of Intended Sale of Personal Property," February 19, 1925.

Charles Romeo Garzoli, Morelli Family website, http://www.morelli-family.org/ps01/ps01_052.htm

Okrent, Daniel, *Last Call: The Rise and Fall of Prohibition,* (New York: Scribner, 2010).

Santa Rosa Press Democrat: Chris Samson, "Petaluma Old-Timers Share Stories of Smuggling, Stills, Raids and Speakeasies," October 14, 2011; Diann Espinosa, "Volpi's: A Story of Speakeasies, Squeezeboxes and Family," September 2, 2013.

The Brothels

Jeff Elliott, santarosahistory.com: "Tenderloin Crackdown," August 2012; "The Year Santa Rosa Legalized Prostitution," July 2010.

Angela C. Fitzpatrick, *Women of Ill Fame: Discourses of Prostitution and the American Dream in California, 1850-1890*, (Berkeley: University of California Press, 2013).

Marion S. Goldman, *Gold Diggers and Silver Miners: Prostitution and Social Life on the Comstock Lode*, (Ann Arbor: University of Michigan Press, 1981).

Gregory, "William Hill," *op. cit.*

Gaye LeBaron, "Gaye LeBaron's Notebook," *Santa Rosa Press Democrat:* January 11, 1981; April 7, 1991.

Paige Meltzer, "The Pulse and Conscience of America: The General Federation and Women's Citizenship, 1945–1960," *Frontiers: A Journal of Women Studies* (2009), Vol. 30 Issue 3, pp. 52–76.

Petaluma Argus: "Hill Opera House is Finest in the State," October 6, 1904; "Whole House Soon Sold," November 28, 1904; "Harper Company Makes a Hit in Camille," May 2, 1905; "A Disgraceful Affair," May 2, 1905; "Compliment for Local Lady," December 9, 1914; "An Abatement Suit Commenced," February 10, 1915.

Petaluma Morning Courier: "Board of Trustees," October 4, 1897; "She Kept the Coat," October 23, 1899; "Not Guilty," October 25, 1899; "Will of Frances Gaffney," December 11, 1900; "Fire This Afternoon," January 29, 1901; "Death of Samuel Rasmussen," March 31, 1902; "Guilty of Battery," July 16, 1902; "Petty Larceny," August 10, 1903; "Twelfth Night," December 5, 1904; "A Queen of the Drama," April, 28, 1905; "Georgie Herbert Acquitted," May 15, 1907; "Trustees Do Lots of Work," May 21, 1907; "Former Local Woman is Charged with Being a White Slaver," July 10, 1911; "Fannie Brown Convicted and Fined," October 28, 1915; "Women to Be Punished for Contempt of Court," August 6, 1916; "Says Red Light is Violated," February 28, 1916; "Red Light Action in Superior Court," October 8, 1918; "Two Theaters Provide Good Amusement," May 24, 1925.

"Petaluma Dive Closed Over Head Of District Attorney," *Healdsburg Tribune*, June 2, 1925.

Brian Roberts, *American Alchemy: The California Gold Rush and Middle-Class Culture* (Chapel Hill: University of North Carolina Press, 2000).

Ruth Rosen, *The Lost Sisterhood: Prostitution in America, 1900-1918*, (Baltimore: The Johns Hopkins University Press, 1982).

Schubert, John C., with Valerie A. Munthe, *Hidden History of Sonoma County*, (Charleston, SC: The History Press, 2017).

The Theaters

Tim Durham, "Censorship in American Filmmaking," *Saturday Evening Post*, April 17, 2014.

Gregory, "William Hill, *op. cit.*

Alison M. Parker, "Mothering the Movies," *Movies Censorship and American Culture*, Francis G. Couvares, ed. (University of Massachusetts Press, 2006).

Petaluma Argus: "A Disgraceful Affair," May 2, 1905; "Hill Opera House is Finest in the State," October 6, 1904; "Whole House Soon Sold," November 28, 1904; "Harper Company Makes a Hit in Camille," May 2, 1905; "Note to the Public," May 28, 1907; "Attractions at the Nickelodeons," July 16, 1908; "Orpheum Now Nickelodeon," November 24, 1908; "Pictures at the Hill," December 27, 1909; "Tonight the Mystic Theater Will be Formally Thrown Open," January 25, 1912; "The Beautiful New Mystic Theater Opens in a Blaze of Glory," January 26, 1912; "Compliment for Local Lady," December 9, 1914; "An Abatement Suit Commenced," February 10, 1915; "Wickersham Building Gutted in Costly Fire," August 8, 1917; "Dr. John A. McNear to Construct Class-A Theater," December 15, 1920; "Hill Opera House Sold to T&D," July 9, 1924; "New California Theater Formally Opened Tomorrow," January 22, 1925; "T&D Enterprises, Inc. Leases The Mystic Theater for Long Period of Years," July 19, 1926.

Petaluma Argus-Courier: "California Tenth Anniversary," January 25, 1935; "California Theater Sold," September 25, 1968; "X-Rated Movies Charges Filed," June 11, 1973; "Openings Set for New Firms," July 15, 1976; "Drive-in Theaters a Dying Breed," January 25, 1980; "Parkway Closure Ends An Era," January 24, 1986; Harlan Osborne, "Tocchini Family Builds Legacy with Sonoma County Theaters," December 8, 2016.

Petaluma Morning Courier: "Twelfth Night," December 5, 1904; "A Queen of the Drama," April, 28, 1905; "Two Theaters Provide Good Amusement," May 24, 1925.

Santa Rosa Press Democrat: Steve Daly, "The Tale of a Printer's Devil," May 8, 1938; "Theater Owner Questions Letter," February 1, 1971; "Petaluma Row on 'Deep Throat,'" May 8, 1973; "The Judge's Ruling in Porn Case," September 20, 1973.

"Sex in Cinema: Pre-1920s," http://www.filmsite.org/sexinfilms1.html

The Hotel Petaluma

Heig, *op. cit.*

History of Sonoma County, op. cit.

Carole Kelleher, "A Peek Inside Beautiful Restored Hotel Petaluma," *Sonoma Magazine*, March 2017.

Petaluma Argus: "Destructive Fire Yesterday," June 23, 1873; "Argus Scribe Tours Hotel Petaluma," "Second Hotel on This Site," April 10, 1924; "Opening Dinner and Ball of the New Hotel Petaluma," "History Recalled by Hotel Guest," April 23, 1924.

Petaluma Argus-Courier: "Lanai Cocktail Lounge Opens at Hotel," August 17, 1938; "KSRO to Close Local Station," February 16, 1951; "Through the New Hotel Petaluma this City Offers Accommodations to Local People, Travelers-Unexcelled," November 29, 1953; "Historic Brooklyn Hotel Now Being Torn Down," May 11, 1953; "Elks Hotel Project Will Cost $50,000," January 22, 1960; "History Burns in Hotel Fire," May 6, 1968; "Colorful Fifties in Petaluma," January 22, 1969; "Historic Hotel is Sold," July 5, 1994; "Youth Spur Elks Lodge Move," November 15, 1996; "The Streets of Petaluma," August 30, 1996.

Petaluma Morning Courier: "Fire," May 29, 1878; "Historical: Petaluma's Birth and Growth," October 19, 1892; "The Old Brooklyn Hotel At Last Victim of the Fiery Element," April 10, 1900.

Bill Soberanes column, *Petaluma Argus-Courier:* July 3, 1959; August 17, 1971; October 29, 1974; July 7, 1978; October 24, 1980; February 2, 2000.

"$35,000 to be Invested in 'Motels,'" *Santa Rosa Press Democrat*, March 20, 1938.

B'nai Israel Synagogue

Joeseph Brandes, *Immigrants to Freedom: Jewish Agricultural Communities in Rural New Jersey Since 1882*, (University of Pennsylvania Press, 1971).

"Defiant Reds are Driven Out of County in Sporadic Raids," *Sotoyome Scimitar*, August 22, 1935.

"Eye-Witness Gives Vivid Account of Terror Raids, Gun Fight and Beatings," *Oakland Tribune*, August 22, 1935.

Sue Fishkoff, "When Left-Wingers and Chicken Wings Populated Petaluma," *jweekly.com*, May 7, 1999.

Healdsburg Tribune: "Two Reds Tarred and Feathered, Three Others Scared; Shots are Fired Before Tear Gas is Used; Victims Ordered Out Of County Today or Else," August 22, 1935; "Vigilante Quiz by Grand Jury Finished With No Indictments Vote After Hearing Cases," August 13, 1936; "Vigilante Hearing To Resume

Friday In Superior Court," August 27, 1936.

Kenneth L. Kahn, *Comrades and Chicken Ranchers*, (Cornell University Press, 1993).

Kahn, Kenneth, and Joe Rappoport, *The Life of A Jewish Radical*, (Philadelphia: Temple University Press, 1981).

Gaye LeBaron, "Gaye LeBaron's Notebook," *The Press Democrat*: "Remembering ACLU Award's Namesake Jack Green," June 6, 2015; "Jack Green Has An Award Named for Him," January 14, 1990.

LeBaron, Mitchell, *op. cit.*

Carey McWilliams, *Factories in the Field: The Story of Migratory Labor in California*, (Berkeley: University of California Press, 2000).

Petaluma Argus-Courier: "New Vigilante Outbreaks Feared," August 27, 1935; "Mob Kidnaps Asserted "Reds," August 22, 1935; "Civil Liberties League Demands Action Against the Vigilantes," August 23, 1935; "Jurist, Counsel Clash in Tar Case," August 22, 1936.

Jack Withington, "A Night of Tar, Feathers, and Terror," *Sonoma Historian*, 2006.

Bars & Taverns

"The Early Days of Wristwrestling in Petaluma: How a Game Became a Sport," *Armwrestlers Only*, December 5, 2013.

"Marin Cop Wins Sonoma Wristwrestling Crown," *Daily Independent Journal*, February 18, 1956.

Petaluma Argus-Courier: "Gala Opening at Gilardi Tap Room," January 14, 1937; Estelle Bartram, "People You Should Know," October 30, 1937; "Dimes Parade, Sports Show, Kick Off Tonight," February 13, 1954; Bob Lipman, "Wristwrestling Title Up for Grabs," February 2, 1962.

Petaluma Post: "53rd Annual Wristwrestling Championships Stir Memories," October, 2004; Skip Sommer, "Is it Armwrestling or is it Wristwrestling?" October, 2011.

Pamela J. Podger, "Bill Soberanes – Newsman in Petaluma for 50 years," *SF Gate*, June 11, 2003.

Chris Samson, "Petaluma Old-Timers Share Stories of Smuggling, Stills, Raids and Speakeasies," *Santa Rosa Press Democrat*, October 14, 2011.

Bill Soberanes column, *Petaluma Argus-Courier*: October 23, 1954; December 11, 1954; December 15, 1954; January 30, 1962; March 29, 1967; September 28, 1977.

The Turning Basin

Heig, *op. cit.*

"Mrs. E. Burns Passed Away," *Petaluma Argus*, April 11, 1924.

Petaluma Argus-Courier: "Mayor, Three Councilmen, City Attorney Tender Resignations," January 26, 1934; "Downtown Decline Told," March 6, 1968; "The Future of Petaluma Depends on All of Us," March 20, 1968; "Panel Fields Critical Questions of Residents," February 4, 1971; "A Walking Tour of Old Buildings Schedule Sunday," May 8, 1975; Bill Soberanes, "Burns, Not Farrell House," February 24, 1977; "Progress Relocates Historic Home," February 25, 1977; Bill Soberanes, "So They Tell Me" column, November 10, 1978; "Proposed Moratorium on Agenda," December 20, 1976; "Mill Played a Key Role in Downtown Revitalization," January 9, 1980; "Regional Park to Be Dedicated to Helen Putnam," August 9, 1985; "In the 1970s, the Petaluma Plan Became the First in the Nation to Effectively Limit a City's Growth," March 25, 2008.

Skip Sommer, *Petaluma Post:* "The Secrets in the Riverhouse Attic," October, 2001; "Bill Murray and Mayor Putnam," February, 2014.

"Petaluma Dedicates a Park," *Santa Rosa Press Democrat*, December 30, 1987.

Epilogue

Quote from Wallace Stegner, *Where the Bluebird Sings to the Lemonade Springs*, (Modern Library Classics, 2002).

Quote from Otto Pflanze, *Bismarck and the Development of Germany*, (Princeton, NJ: Princeton University Press, 1968).

Index

A
Abraham Haas Memorial Fund 190
Act for the Government and Protection of Indians 38
Act to Settle Private Land Claims 114
Adams Box Factory 140
Adobe Creek 60, 64
Agricultural Lime and Compost Company 168
Agricultural Park 96
Alaguali 28
Alameda 198
Alaska 34
Alcatraz 126
Alexander, Cyrus 72
Alexander Valley 72
Alma scow schooner 198
Alta California 6, 34, 38, 128
Altimira, José 28, 106
Alvarado, Juan 34, 38
American Civil Liberties Union 192
American Federation of Labor 102
American Hotel 110, 182, 186, 188, 200
American Legion 102
American Nickelodeon 182
American River 80
American South 136
American West 174
Anderson, Glenn 196
Andresen's Tavern 194, 196
Angel Island 48, 84
Anti-Chinese League 70, 124, 140
Architecture of Country Houses 158
Argentina 190
Arkansas 94
Armstrong, James 78
Army Corps of Engineers 12
Arts and Crafts movement 158, 160
Associated Farmers of California 102, 104, 192
Atwater, Addie 154, 156
Atwater, Henry 154
Auger, Louis A. 162
Australia 58, 66, 82, 84, 100, 104, 120, 140
Azores 74, 88, 164

B
Bakersfield 198
Balsa de Tomales 44
Baltimore, Maryland 92
Bank of America 102
Bank of California 126, 128, 130
Bank of Marin 200
Bank of Sonoma County 116, 122
Barnes Rock Ranch 80
Battle of Sebastopol Avenue 148
Battle of Shiloh 126
Bauer, Carl 166
Bauer, Florentine 166
Bay Area 80, 82, 158, 162, 168, 182, 186
Baylis, Thomas F. 78, 116, 200
Bear Flaggers 38
Beauregard, P.G.T. 126
Beauty Ranch 82
Belding, Alvah 142
Belding Brothers & Company 140, 142
Bellegrade, Minnesota 92
Bellwether Farms 104
Benedetti, Dan 144
Benedetti, Gene 144
Benedetti, Marcus 144
Berry, Wendell 10
Bianchini, Bill 44
Bihler's Slough 106
Bihler, William 28, 54, 72, 96, 106, 110
Bismarck, Otto von 204
Black, James 26, 40, 146
Black Mountain 40
Black Point 48, 124
Blackwell Builders 72
Bloom, Adolph 118, 172
Bloom, Americo 44, 118, 172
Bloom Company 118
Bloom, Eva 118
Bloomfield 78
Bloom-Tunstall House 118
Blucher 44
B'nai Israel Synagogue 190, 192
Bodega 78
Bodega Bay 44
Boggs, Lilburn 78
Bohemian Grove 186
Boitano, Louie 172
Boland, Eavan 12
Bolinas 162
Bond, Earle 188
Boulevard 14 Cinemas 184
Bourke, Alphonse 134
Bowen, Alfred 146
Bowen, William 148, 150
Bowles, J.M. 78
Boyes Hot Springs 68, 180, 194
Bradley, A.M. 54
Brewster, J.E. 114
British Columbia 140
British Isles 66
Brooklyn Hotel 186, 188
Brown Bag Farms 74
Brown, Fannie 174, 176, 178
Brown, William 176
Brush, Frank 146, 150
Buckhorn Tavern 196
Budd, James 98
Buena Vista Winery 70, 106
Bundesen, Herbert 92, 94
Burbank, Luther 66
Burdell Building 42, 146
Burdell Creamery 42
Burdell Island 42
Burdell, Galen 26, 40, 42, 116
Burdell, James 42
Burdell, Mary 42, 146, 156
Burdell Ranch 156
Burns, Ellen 200
Burns, Frank 200
Burton, Frank 60
Butte, Montana 92
Byce, Lyman 90, 94, 124, 132, 134

C
Cagnazzo, Angelo 170
California 4, 12, 22, 32, 34, 36, 38, 40, 52, 54, 58, 70, 72, 76, 80, 82, 84, 86, 88, 94, 96, 98, 100, 102, 106, 110, 114, 120, 122, 124, 126, 128, 140, 146, 152, 158, 162, 164, 166, 168, 174, 178
California Cooperative Creamery 144
California Northwestern Railroad 150
California Northwest Railway 148
California Pacific Railroad 128, 130
California Packing Corporation 102
California Savings Bank of Petaluma 118
California's Irish Brigade 78
California State Law Enforcement League 178
California Theater 184
California Water Service Company 64
Calistoga 68
Call of the Hen 136
Cal Poly 88
Calvary Cemetery 162, 164
Camozzi, A.J. 80
Cañada de la Jonive 40
Canepa Building 170
Canton of Ticino 74, 88, 162
Cape Horn 46, 52, 54, 58, 74, 82, 96, 106, 120, 132
Carlson-Currier Silk Mill 140, 142
Carlson, Edward 140
Carlson, Heimer 94
Carnegie Public Library 158
Carneros 110
Carquinez Strait 124
Casa Grande Road 36
Casey, Catherine 54
Casey, Jeremiah 54, 58
Casey, John 54, 58
Casey, Juila 58
Casey, Mary 54
Cassiday, Samuel 78
Cassiday, Sarah 154, 156
Cassidy, J.W. 110
Caulfield Brothers 74
Caulfield, James 74
Caulfield Jr., Tom 72, 74
Caulfield's Meat Market 74, 76
Caulfield Sr., Thomas 72, 74
Caulfield Stockyards 72, 76
Caulfield, Will 74, 76
Cavanagh, John 78
Cazadero 68
Cedar Grove 24, 118
Centennial Livery Stables 176
Central America 140
Central California 104

Central Pacific Railroad 126
Central Park 156
Central Valley 32, 76, 88, 114, 136, 144, 166
Chamber of Commerce 102
Cherry Valley 110
Chicago 96, 128, 158
Chief Olompali 40
Chief Solano 36, 72
Chile 122
Chileno Valley 1, 9, 42, 44, 94, 102, 118
China 140, 142
Chinese Exclusion Act 70, 140
Cholequibit 28
Chosen Family 42
Cinnabar junction 148
Cinnabar railroad trestle 130
Ciran, Fannie 176
Civil War 58, 78, 120, 126
Cleary, James 162
Cleveland, Ohio 92
Cloudy Bend 48, 50
Clover 144, 162
Cloverdale 68, 70, 74, 128, 148
Clover-Stornetta Farms 144
Coast Miwok 2, 22, 24, 26, 28, 32, 36, 40, 44, 60, 66, 68, 72, 86, 100, 114, 118, 168, 190
Cockrill, "Red" 194
Cold War 188
Collings, Francis 44, 46
Colorado 102
Comstock Lode 96, 110, 126
Congress of Industrial Organizations 102
Connecticut 142
Continental Hotel 176, 186, 188
Cooper Union 190
Copeland Creek 60, 64
Corona junction 148
Corticelli Company 142
Cotati 14, 36, 60, 74, 90, 144, 190
Cotati Land Company 64
Cottage Residences 158
County Antrim, Ireland 92
County Kerry, Ireland 54
Courthouse Square 102, 192
Cows and Chickens Line 148
Coxhead, Ernest 160

Coyote Dam 64
Craig, Ellen 6
Crane Canyon 68
Crimean War 120
Crocker, Charles 126, 128
Cypress Hill Cemetery 64, 122, 162

D
Dairy Farmers of America 144
Dairyman's Feed and Supply Co-Operative 136
Daly, James 162
Danish Sisterhood and Danish Brotherhood 170
Dannenbaum, Sol 100
Daughters of Charity of St. Vincent de Paul 162
Davis, Jefferson 78, 126
Del Maestro, Melvin 178
Denman, Ezekiel 152
Denman junction 148
Denman Ranch 144
Denmark 132, 136
DeTurck, Isaac 110
Devoto, Dave 196
Dias, Isaac 90, 124, 132, 134
Dickinson, Ables Bray 44
Dillon Beach 150
Dolcini Ranch 4
Donohue, James 128
Donahue, Peter 52, 58, 122, 126, 128, 130
Donahue, township of 122, 130, 162
Don Bartolomeo Bojorques 44
Dondero, George 144
Donohue, Mervyn 130
Donohue, Michael 128
Donovan, Lavelle Marie Roderick 92
Dos Piedras 44
Douglass, Robert 188
Downing, Andrew Jackson 158
Drakes Bay 34, 168
Draper, Prue King 92
Druids 170
D Street drawbridge 51
D Street Plaza 152, 154, 156
Duck, Ang Tai 70
Duke de Chartres 96

Dumas, Alexander 174
Durney, Maxine Kortum 90, 92, 94
Dust Bowl 102, 190
Duval, Frankie 178

E
Eades, George 54
East Bay 52
East Coast 74, 86, 168
Eastern Europe 190
East Petaluma 72, 76, 122, 140, 172
Eatherton, Ruby Scott 92
Eckart, Harold 188
E. Corning steamer 6
Eel River 128
Egan, Lulu 182
Egasus Ranch 98
Egg Basket of the World 12, 48, 134, 136, 158, 168
Egg City 136
Egg Day Queen 170
18th Amendment to the Constitution 170
Electric Light & Power Company of Petaluma 42
Elim Lutheran Church 164
Eliot's Candyland 172
Elks Club 102, 170, 188
Elliott, Jeff 160
Ellis, John 158
Ellis Creek Water Recycling Facility 82, 204
Elphic Spring 60
Embarcadero 82
Emmett Rifles 78
England 100, 104, 122, 128, 154, 178
Ernie's Tin Bar 196
Estero Gap 12
Eureka 48
Europe 36, 52, 58, 110, 120, 166
Evans, Georgina Volkerts 90
Exchange Saloon 170

F
Factory District 140, 142, 146
Fair, James G. 110
Fairbanks, Hiram 116, 152
Fairbanks, William 42
Fairbanks, Zoe 154

Fairwest Grocery 194
Fair Winery 110
Farr, Albert 160
Farrell-Burns house 198, 200
Farrell House Restaurant 200
Federated Indians of Graton Rancheria 22
Figueroa, José 34, 36, 40
Finlay, Alan 180, 184
First Bay Area Tradition 158, 160
Flogdell, Dave 116
Follis, Fred 42
Foreign Miner's Tax Law 70
Forestville 148
Fort Gunnybags 82
Fort Ross 34, 36, 38, 40, 44
Foster, Arthur W. 110, 148, 150
France 96, 98, 100, 106
Frisbie, John 128

G
Gaffney, Frances 178
Garzoli, Charlie 172
Geary, Thomas 70
Gem Theater 182
General Electric 190
Georgia 94
Gericke, Adolph 116
German-American Turn Verein Association 182
Germania Hall 102, 190, 192
Germany 106, 136
Geyserville 64
Gilardi, James 58
Gilardi, Mike 186, 194, 196
Gilardi's Corner 194, 196
Gilardi's Lakeville Marina 54, 58
Glasgow, Scotland 128
Glen Ellen 68, 82
Golden Concourse 182
Golden Eagle Mill 116, 200
Golden Eagle Shopping Center 200
Golden Gate 128
Golden Gate Bridge 150, 186
Golden Gate Nursery 82
Gold Rush 12, 24, 32, 40, 44, 52, 54, 72, 80, 82, 86, 96, 116, 120, 126, 128, 158, 168, 174, 204

Gold steamer 146, 150
Gossage, Dr. Harry S. 160
Gossage, Mary 160
G.P. McNear Company 124, 200
Grace Brothers Brewery 148
Grant, Edwin C. 178
Grass Valley 96
Grateful Dead 42
Great Basin 66
Great Britain 58
Great Depression 32, 94, 100, 136, 142, 144, 166, 170, 184, 186, 188, 190
Great Diamond Hoax 130
Great Petaluma Mill 124, 150, 200
Great Plains 124
Green House 178
Green, Jack 102, 192
Gregory, John 54
Groverman, Bernard 100, 102, 104
Groverman, Fred 104
Groverman Ranch 104
Guangdong Province 70
Guerneville 150
Gwin, William McKendree 114
Gwinn, J.E. 154
Gwinn, J.H. 160
Gwinn, Josephine 160

H
Haberer, Jack 90
Hamburg, Germany 190
Hanly Fire 68
Hantzche, Paul 90
Haraszthy, Agoston 70, 106
Hardin, Henry 60
Harpending, Ashbury 126, 128, 130
Harper, Georgia 174
Harringan, Anna Hansen 90, 94
Harte, Bret 174
Havens, Charles I. 140
Haverton Hill Creamery 104
Havilah 126
Hawaiian Islands 140
Hays Code 180
Haystacks, the 48, 116
Haystack Landing 51, 52, 80

Healdsburg 48, 68, 78, 126, 128, 130, 148, 150, 192
Healdsburg Chamber of Commerce 192
Healy, D.J. 198
Healy Mansion 198
Hein Quarry 80
Helen Putnam Plaza 200
Helen Putnam Regional Park 203, 204
Helgason, "Icy" 90
Heminway Silk 142
Herbert, Georgie 174, 176, 178
Heritage Homes of Petaluma 198, 204
Hermann Sons Hall 196
Heyermann, Johann Frederick August 116, 118
Hicks Valley 4, 194
Hideaway bar 196
Highway 101 32, 68, 114, 188, 198
Hill, Josie 174, 176, 182
Hill Opera House 174, 176, 182, 184
Hill Plaza Park 94, 134, 156
Hill, William 60, 152, 174, 182
Hintzelman, Henry 52
H&N Hatchery 94
Hobbie, Ernest 166
Hobbie, George 166
Hockenbury System 186
Hogan, Walter 136
hoipu 26
Holland 140
Hollywood 184
Homel, Jack 194, 196
Hong Kong 70
Hopkins, Gertrude 154
Hopkins, Mark 126, 128
Hopper, Thomas 60
Horick Ranch 96
Hotel Petaluma 186, 188
Hueñux (Camilio Ynitia) 26, 40
Hueston Guards 78
Humboldt County 128
Hunt and Behrens Feed Mill 94
Huntington, Collins P. 126, 128

I
Idaho 172
Illinois 96
Iowa 96

Iowa School 44
Iowa School District 46
Ireland 54, 80, 92
Isle of Fohr 74, 88
Isthmus of Panama 86
Italy 80, 106, 162

J
James, Harry 186
Japan 136, 142, 168
Jewell, Sallie 154
Jewish Community Center 190, 192
Johanson, Patricia 204
Johnson, Ella 154
Jones, Brainerd 18, 46, 118, 124, 134, 142, 158, 160
Josie McNear steamer 122

K
KAFP radio station 194
Kansas 102, 142, 166
Kate Hayes steamer 52
Keats, John 156
Keehn, Hilda Tiemann 90
Keller, Garrett 114, 152
Kelsey, Emily Light 94
Kenilworth Park 98, 152
Kentucky 78, 126
Kentucky Street 18
Kenwood 68
Keokuk, Iowa 116
Kern County 126
Kerrigan, Bert 134, 136
Kessler, Jack 68
Keyes, John 162
Kiley, James 162, 164
Kohler, Johanna 176, 178
Kortum, Lucy 142
Kortum, Max 90
Ko-to-lah, the frog-woman 2
KSRO radio station 188
Ku Klux Klan 190
Kullberg, Oliver 194, 196

L
Ladies Improvement Club 154, 156
Lafferty Park 204

Lafferty Ranch 64, 68
LaFollete Civil Liberties Committee 104
Laguna de San Antonio 44
Laguna de Santa Rosa 60
Laguna Lake 42
Lake Mendocino 64
Lakeville 18, 52, 54, 58, 96, 106, 110, 122, 148, 162, 178, 194
Lakeville Bridge 24
Lanai Lounge 186, 188
Land Mart Building 174
Lange, Dorothea 16
Lan Mart Building 176
Larkin, Polly 152
Latham, Milton 128, 130
Lawler Ranch 60
Lawler Reservoir 64
Lea, Clarence 64, 178
Lekituit 24, 106, 118
Lemus, John 116
Levitt, Joe 52
Lewis, M.G. 52
Liberty District 90
Liberty junction 148
Lieb, Dick 200
Lincoln, Abraham 78, 126
Linda Del Mar subdivision 118
Lind Marine 168
Lippitt, Edward S. 4, 154
Lippitt, Frank 152
Live Oak junction 148
Liverpool 120
Lockwood, Tom 114, 116, 118
Lodi 170
Lohrman, Hanna 166
London, Jack 74, 82, 84
Los Angeles 188, 190
Lucky Stores 76
Lynch Creek 64

M
MacMullen, Jerry 48
Madeira 74, 164
Maggia River 74, 88
Magnolia Farm 96, 98
máiens 26

Maine 120
Main Street Plaza 152, 156
Mardorf, Fannie 176
Mardorf, William 176
Marin County 12, 40, 80, 96, 146, 150, 168, 180, 196
Marin Sun Farms 76
Mario & John's Tavern 194, 196
Marsh, Alman 50
Martin, Claude 44, 46
Martin, Silas 44
Masonic Building 10
Masons of California 162
Maybeck, Bernard 158
McCarthy, Joseph 192
McClain, Robert 102, 104
McClellan, George 78
McCrellish, Fred 128
McCune Building 152
McDougall Brothers 158
McDougall, C.C. 158
McMahon, Alexander 184
McNear & Brother 120
McNear Buildings 70, 120, 182
McNear Canal 100, 122, 124, 140, 146
McNear, Clara 120, 122
McNear, Ezekiel Denman 160
McNear, George 58, 120, 122, 124
McNear, George P. 46, 124, 140, 146, 150, 186
McNear, Ida Belle 140, 142
McNear, John 52, 58, 70, 100, 116, 120, 122, 124, 126, 128, 130, 140, 142, 146, 150, 152, 154, 156, 180
McNear, Jr., John 124, 180, 182, 184
McNear Park 118, 124
McNear's Landing 204
McNear's Point 150
McNear's Saloon & Dining Hall 196
McNeil Island Penitentiary 172
Meacham, Harrison 72, 82, 96
Melnick, Sam 190
Meltzer, Paige 152
Mendocino 96
Mendocino County 180
Merango, "Happy" 194
Methodist Church 154
Mexican-American War 44, 114, 162

Mexican Sierras 126
Mexico 28, 34, 36, 38, 72, 86, 104, 126, 164
Micheltorena, Manuel 38
Michigan 140
Mickelsen, George 44
Mickelson, Martin 92
Middletown 74
Midwest 58, 74, 120
Miller, Glenn 186
Miller, Hattie 122
Mill Valley 74, 92
Minneapolis, Minnesota 92, 94
Minturn, Charles 52, 54, 122
Mira Monte Gun Club 42
Miramontes, Ignacio 38
Mission Dolores 106
Mission San Francisco de Asis 106
Mission San Francisco de Solano 28, 34, 36, 72, 100, 106
Mission San Rafael 34, 36, 40
Mississippi 94, 120
Mississippi River 96
Missouri 74, 78
Monterey 36
Monte Rio 186
Morgan, John Stillwell 168
Morgan, Julia 158, 160
Morgan Oyster Company 168
Moriarty, Julia 54
Morris, William 158
Mount Burdell 12, 26, 28, 40, 54, 68, 146, 204
Mount Diablo 28
Mount Olompais 26, 40
Mount St. Helena 9, 28, 68
Mount Tamalpais 28
Mulberry craze 140
Murch, Bill 92, 94
Murphy, Timothy 100
Murray, Bill 200
Must Hatch Incubator Company 94, 134
Mystic Theater 18, 124, 180, 182, 184

N
Napa 80, 96
Napa County 106, 128, 180
NASA 142

National Association of Importers and Breeders of Norman Horses 98
National Egg Day 136
National Register of Historic Places 158
Nation magazine 102
Native Americans 72
Native Sons of the Golden West 102
Nevada 96, 110
Newberg, Estelle 154
New England 36, 120, 140
New Jersey 96, 128, 190
New Mexico 102
New Orleans 120
Newtown 52
New York 100, 190
New York City 86, 156, 168, 190, 192
New Zealand 58, 104, 120, 140
Nicaragua 126
Nicasio 34, 36, 38, 68, 166
Nicasio Reservoir 40
Nielsen, Anna Keyes 92
Nimitz, Chester W. 166
Nisson, Christopher 90, 132, 134
Nitzberg, Sol 102, 190, 192
"No-Fence" law 74
Nolan-Earl Shoe Factory 140
North Bay 34, 36, 80, 124, 146, 166
Northbay Savings and Loan 166
North Coast 76
Northern California 34, 38, 116, 144, 164
North Pacific Coast Railroad 42
Northwestern Pacific Railroad 48, 80, 110, 150
Novak, John 72
Nuns Fire 68

O
Oak Hill Cemetery 64, 156
Oak Hill Improvement Club 156
Oak Hill Park 64
Oakland 66, 82, 96, 122, 140, 146, 162, 164, 170, 186
Oberto, Mary 170
Odd Fellows 162
Odd Fellows Hall 116
O'Farrell, Jasper 40
Ohio 78, 86, 100

Ohlone tribe 168
Oklahoma 102
Olema 162
Olmsted, Frederick Law 156
Olompali 16, 26, 40
Olompali Ranch 42
Olompali State Historic Park 26
Olympia, Washington 168, 188
Omaha Beach 144
Oona-pa'is 2, 60
Open Field Farm 32, 92, 102
Order of the Cluck Clucks 136
Order of the Moose 102
Oregon 172
Ortman, George 116
Ortman, William T. 113, 116
O-ye the Coyote-man 2

P
Pacheco, Maria Loreto 40
Pacheco, Ygnacio 42
Pacific Coast 90, 96, 152
Pacific Gas & Electric Company 102, 146
Pacific Northwest 66
Pacific Rim 140
Paddle-Wheel Days in California 48
Padre Ventura 106
Palestine 190
Palmer, Emma 154, 156
Panama 86
Panic of 1873 130
Parkway Drive-in Theater 180, 184
Patel, B.B. 142
Patel, Dipak 188
Patel, Satish 188
Patterson, Harry 190, 192
Payran, Stephen 98
Peck, Vernon 186, 188
Pendleton 116, 118
Penngrove 12, 60, 64, 78, 80, 90, 144, 172, 192
Penn Grove Hotel 176, 178
Pennsylvania 100
Penry Park 94, 98, 124, 134, 152, 156
Penry, Richard 156
Perry, James 96
Petaluma Adobe 34, 36, 66, 100

Petaluma Argus 60, 78, 150, 152, 154, 156, 158, 160, 174
Petaluma Argus-Courier 180, 194, 196
Petaluma Board of Education 154
Petaluma Chamber of Commerce 124, 134, 136, 186
Petaluma City Council 64
Petaluma, city of 6, 18, 24, 32, 44, 46, 48, 52, 54, 58, 60, 64, 66, 68, 70, 72, 74, 78, 80, 82, 88, 90, 92, 94, 96, 98, 100, 102, 110, 113, 114, 116, 118, 120, 122, 126, 128, 130, 134, 136, 140, 142, 146, 148, 152, 154, 158, 160, 162, 164, 166, 168, 172, 174, 176, 178, 180, 182, 184, 188, 190, 194, 196, 198, 204
Petaluma & Cloverdale Railroad 122
Petaluma Cooperative Creamery 144, 162
Petaluma Courier 140, 152, 156
Petaluma Creamery 144, 194
Petaluma Creek 48, 114
Petaluma Electric Light and Power Company 146
Petaluma Gap 106, 110
Petaluma & Haystack Railroad 52
Petaluma & Healdsburg Railroad 122, 126
Petaluma High School 96, 124
Petaluma Historical Library and Museum 18
Petaluma Hotel 6
Petaluma Hotel Company Trust 186
Petaluma Incubator Company 90, 132
Petaluma Ladies Improvement Club 152, 154
Petaluma Leghorns 144, 194
Petaluma Livestock Auction Yard 76
Petaluma Minstrels 170
Petaluma Mountain Water Company 60
Petaluma National Bank 166
Petaluma Old Adobe 190
Petaluma Opera House 118, 156
Petaluma Post Office 154
Petaluma Poultry Journal 142, 168
Petaluma River 6, 12, 24, 26, 28, 32, 40, 42, 48, 51, 52, 54, 58, 60, 64, 68, 70, 106, 110, 114, 118, 120, 124, 126, 132, 140, 146, 152, 166, 168, 186
Petaluma River Watershed 10, 12, 16, 22, 32, 54, 66, 68, 72, 74, 78, 86, 88, 90, 100, 104, 106, 118, 132, 134, 136, 144, 190, 204
Petaluma & Santa Rosa Railway 44, 48, 124, 146, 150
Petaluma Savings Bank 116
Petaluma School Board 198
Petaluma Militia 78
Petaluma Stables 98
Petaluma steamer 48, 146, 150
Petaluma Train Depot 126
Petaluma Trolley Living History Railway Museum 150
Petaluma Valley 26, 36, 60
Petaluma Water Company 60, 64
Petaluma Wheelmen 152, 156
Petaluma Women's Club 152, 156, 160
Petaluma Women's Silk Association 140, 142
Petaluma Woolen Mills 100
Petalumian newspaper 152, 156
Peter Donahue Building 130
Peter, Larry 144
Phoenix Theater 182, 184
Picoult, Jodi 18
Pierce, Abram 146
Pierce Ranch 146
Pierce Telephone Company 146
Pierce, Will 146
Pioneer Hatchery 90, 132, 134
Point Reyes Peninsula 88, 146
Point Reyes Station 42, 146
Polk, Willis 158
Pollock 96
Pometta house 200
Port Costa 124
Portland Cement Company 168
Portugal 162
Poultry Producers of Central California 90, 102, 104, 136
Praetzel, Bertha 92
Progressive Era 152, 154, 174
Progressive Moment 176
Prohibition 110, 170, 186, 194
Proximate principle 156
Puget Sound 168
Purvine, Charles 44, 46
Purvine, Ella 46
Putnam, Helen 198, 200
Putnam Plaza Park 146, 182, 188
Pyburn, Levi 116, 118

R
Railway Express 92
Ralston, William "Billy" 126, 128, 130
Rancho Arroyo de San Antonio 114
Rancho Nicasio 40
Rancho Olompali 40
Rancho Petaluma 36, 38, 72, 106
Ray's Tavern 194, 196
Reagan, Ronald 196
Red Cross 156
Red Jacket steamboat 52
Red Light Abatement Act 178
Redwood Room 188
Reed, Daisy 154
Reif & Brody 144
Rex Hardware Merchandise 166
Richardson, Friend 186
Richmond, Virginia 146
Rincon Valley 66
River View Stock Farm 96
Roaring Twenties 182
Robinson & Farrell 154
Robinson, William 154
Roblar de la Miseria 44
Rockin' H Ranch 110
Rocky Dog Park 52
Rocky Mountains 66
Rogers, Buddy 186
Rohnert Park 60
Royal Tallow and Soap Company 76
Ruskin, John 158
Russia 58, 136, 190
Russian River 64, 68, 128, 130, 148, 186
Russian River Valley 78, 122
Russian River Watershed 60
Russian Social Revolution Party 190

S
Sacramento River 52
Sacred Expedition 12, 34
Saez, Justo 40
Saez, Maria Augustina 40
Salt Lake City 98
San Antonio Creek 26, 40, 42
San Francisco 6, 32, 34, 40, 46, 48, 52, 54, 58, 64, 66, 70, 72, 78, 80, 82, 86, 90, 94, 96, 100, 102, 104, 106, 114, 116, 118, 122, 124, 126, 128, 130, 132, 134, 136, 140, 142, 144, 146, 148, 150, 158, 162, 168, 172, 180, 182, 186, 198, 200
San Francisco Bay 66, 82, 84, 168
San Francisco Bulletin 54
San Francisco Committee of Vigilance 82, 84
San Francisco Embarcadero 48
San Francisco & Humboldt Bay Railroad 128
San Francisco & North Pacific Railroad 32, 52, 58, 114, 118, 120, 122, 128, 130, 140, 146, 148, 162
San Francisco Presidio 36, 106
San Francisco & San Jose Railroad 130
San Joaquin Valley 98
San Jose 40
San Leandro 172
San Pablo Bay 12, 28, 32, 36, 42, 48, 52, 54, 60, 106, 110, 114, 148, 204
San Rafael 38, 52, 122, 130, 148, 162
Santa Clara 100
Santa Rosa 32, 48, 66, 68, 78, 102, 122, 128, 130, 146, 148, 150, 180, 192
Santa Rosa City Council 176, 178
Santa Rosa Junior College 144
Santa Rosa Plain 60
Santa Rosa Press Democrat 178
Santa Rosa Valley 78
Sarris, Greg 21
Sausalito 128
Schellville 144
Schluckebier Hardware Company 166
Schluckebier, Henry 166
Schluckebier, Ludwig 166
Schulz, Charles 196
Scotland 80, 96
Scott Ranch 204
Sebastopol 48, 68, 102, 148, 190
Senator steamer 52
Serra, Junipero 34
Settlers' League 78
Shattuck, Frank 152
Shattuck, Rena 152, 154, 156
Shimizu, Hideo 94
Shollenberger Park 50
Showcase Theater 180, 184
Sibalowsky, Morris 172
Siberia 190

Sierra foothills 168
Silva, George 172
Skillman, Theodore 96, 98
Smith, Hanna Stewart 160
Snoopy 196
Snow, Frank 142
Snow, L.J. 156
Snyder, Gary 9
Sobel, Marjorie Forster 92
Soberanes, Bill 194, 196
Solano 80
Solari, Emilia 170
Solari, Louis 170
Sommer, Skip 200
Sonoma 28, 38, 52, 54, 72, 74, 80, 96, 100, 106, 118
Sonoma and Marin Agricultural Society 98
Sonoma Baylands 204
Sonoma County 28, 32, 44, 66, 68, 70, 72, 74, 76, 78, 80, 98, 102, 104, 106, 110, 114, 116, 120, 122, 126, 128, 144, 146, 150, 152, 162, 170, 176, 180, 190, 198, 200
Sonoma County Farm Bureau 102
Sonoma County National Bank 124
Sonoma County Railroad Company 122, 126
Sonoma County Water Company 64
Sonoma County Water Works 122
Sonoma Democrat 78, 110
Sonoma Estero 106
Sonoma Land Trust 204
Sonoma-Marin Area Rail Transit 42
Sonoma-Marin District Fair 96, 98
Sonoma & Marin Railroad 122
Sonoma-Marin Wool Growers Association 104
Sonoma Mountain 1, 2, 12, 16, 18, 60, 66, 70, 80, 82, 162, 204
Sonoma Valley 26, 68, 106, 122, 180
Sons of Italy 170
Soren, Dave 136
Sorensen, Walter 94
South Bay 142
Southern California 84, 118, 144
Southern Pacific Company 150
Southern Patwin 24, 36
Southern Pomo 22, 24, 28, 36

South San Francisco Bay 168
Soviet Union 192
Spain 34, 100, 106
Sperry Flour Company 90
Spreckels, Rudolph 146
Spring Hill Jersey Cheese 144
Squires, Taylor 182
Staedler, J.G. 110
Stanford, Leland 78, 126, 128
Starke, Frederick 118
Starke's Park 118
Star Nickelodeon 182
State Theater 180, 184
Steamer Landing Park 204
Steamer Gold restaurant 200
Steele Brothers Cheddar 86
Steele, Clara 86
Steele, George 86
Steele, Rensselaer 86
Stegner, Wallace 203
Steinbeck, John 104
St. Helena 68
St. James Church 164
St. Louis 128
St. Vincent de Paul 162
St. Vincent's Academy 164
St. Vincent's Church 162
Stony Point junction 148
Stornetta Dairy 144
Stover, Harry 98
Stratton, William 82, 84, 156
Suisun tribe 72
Sullivan Hotel 188
Sullivan, New York 82
Sunset Line and Twine 142
Sutter, John 38
Sweden 80, 136
Switzerland 162

T
Talamentes, Tim 94
T&D Jr. Enterprises 182, 184
Temple & Bauer Hardware 166
Temple, Conrad 166
Temple Rock 22
Tennessee 78

Terra Firma Farm 90
Texas 72, 86, 102
The Octagon House: A Home for All, or a New, Cheap, Convenient, and Superior Mode of Building 44
Thompson, Jan Day 92
Thompson, Thomas L. 78
Tibbets, Angie 154
Tiburon 58, 122, 130, 148
Tiemann, Amalie 90
Tiemann, John 90
Tighe, Kelly 188
Tillman, Clyde 164
Tivoli Hotel 188
Tocchini, Dan 180, 184
Tola 28
Tolay Lake 28, 54, 106, 110
Tolay Lake Regional County Park 28, 204
Tomales 44, 150
Tomales Bay 40, 42, 168
Tomasini, Americo 160, 166
Tomasini, Esther 160
Tomasini, George 166
Tomasini, Henry 166
Tomasini, Jeff 166
Tomasini's Rex Ace Hardware and Country Store 166
Towne, Charles 146
Trader Vic's Restaurant 186
Transcontinental Railroad 168
Treaty of Guadalupe Hidalgo 114
Tubbs Fire 68
Tunstall, Elizabeth 118
Tunzi, M.F. 84
Tunzi Parkway 84
Turning Basin 6, 51, 198, 200
Tuscany 80
Twin House 48
Twin Oaks Roadhouse 172, 196
Two Rock 14, 44, 72, 82, 86, 88, 90, 92, 104, 132, 134, 144, 148, 172
Two Rock School 44, 46
Two Rock School District 44, 46
Two Rock Union School 44, 198
Two Rock Valley 44

U
Union Army 78
Union Iron Works 122, 128
Union Pacific 126
Unique Theater 182
United Artists Theaters 184
United States Land Commission 40
University of California, Berkeley 198
University of California, Davis 88, 90, 104
University of San Francisco 144
U.S. Army 190
U.S. Army Corps of Engineers 64
U.S. Congress 178
U.S. Forest Service 84
U.S. Mint 126
U.S. Navy 166
U.S. Supreme Court 78, 180, 182, 184, 198

V
Valentine's Day Storm of 1986 64
Vallejo, city of 126, 128
Vallejo, Mariano G. 34, 36, 38, 40, 44, 66, 72, 86, 100, 106, 110, 126, 194
Vallejo & Sonoma Valley Railroad 122
Valley Ford 68
Valley of the Moon 74
Valparaiso, Chile 128
Vermont 100
Vintage 1870 200
Virginia 78
Vogle, Verna Hogberg 94
Volpi, Giovanna 170
Volpi, John 172
Volpi, Mary 172
Volpi, Mary Lee 172
Volpi's Grocery 170, 172, 194
Volpi, Silvio 170, 172
Volpi's Ristorante & Bar 170, 172
Volstead Act 110

W
Waipahu, Hawaii 94
Wales 80
wál·ipoh 26
Walker, Helen 178
Walker School 44, 46

Walker, William 82
Walnut Park 122, 152, 154, 156
Wappo tribe 24, 36
Warhol, Andy 180
Warm Springs Dam 64
Washington 28, 172
Washington Hotel 186
Washington Territory 168
Washoe House 78, 82, 176
Watson, John 102, 104
Wek-wek 2
West Coast 96, 98, 102, 104, 192
Western Refrigerating Company 42
West Marin 72, 88, 104
Weston, Henry L. 152, 154
Weston, Kittie 154, 156
West Petaluma Regional Park 200
West Petaluma Spur and Trestle 146, 150
White leghorn chickens 134
Whitton, Frederic 186
W.H. Pepper's Liberty Nurseries 82
Wiatt, Lemarcus 116
Wickersham Banking Company 154
Wickersham Building 176, 178
Wickersham, Isaac 70, 116, 122, 126, 128, 130, 152, 154, 156, 160
Wickersham, Jesse C. 70, 154, 160
Wickersham, Lizzie 154
Wickersham, Sarah 70, 154, 160
Williams, George 120
Williams, George P. 186
Williams, George R. 186
Willits 148
Wilson Hill Grade 12
Windsor 74
Women's Christian Temperance Union 156, 170, 176, 178, 180, 182, 194
Woodson, Jasper 142
World War I 100, 102, 136, 156, 170, 178, 190, 192
World War II 18, 32, 72, 94, 104, 136, 142, 144, 150, 166
Wright, Frank Lloyd 160
Wristwrestling Capital of the World 196

Y
Ynitia, Camilo 26, 40, 42
Yokohama, Japan 70
Yosemite Hotel 186, 188
Young England's Glory 96, 106
Yountville 200

Biographies

SCOTT HESS is a commercial and arts photographer based in Petaluma. His subjects extend from people to architecture and landscapes. His work has been widely exhibited in galleries and public venues, as well as featured in numerous publications, including *The Sun, Shift, VIA, Shots, Smithsonian, San Francisco Chronicle, Miami, Bay Nature, Cultural Survival,* and *Terrain.*

JOHN SHEEHY was born and reared in Petaluma. A graduate of Reed College, he has worked as an editor and publisher for a number of media companies, including Time Inc., Bertelsmann, *Dwell, Afar, Parabola, Utne Reader,* and *Mindful.* He is the author of the award-winning book *Comrades of the Quest,* recipient of the Elizabeth B. Mason Award from the Oral History Association. He and his wife live on Sonoma Mountain.

LAURIE SZUJEWSKA (shoe yév skä) is a printmaker, typographer, and graphic designer. She once worked in the printing trades and lived and played in New York City with the band *The Chairs,* while creating graphics for the performing arts venue *Roulette* during its early years, and studying at the Center for Book Arts. After receiving her MFA from the Yale School of Art, she moved west to California and worked as a designer and art director at Adobe Systems, where she created many award-winning graphics and the popular typeface Giddyup. Her prints and graphic work have been exhibited in various venues in Europe and the United States, and are included in many Artist Book Collections at universities, libraries, and private collections. Her home and studio are in Penngrove.

Acknowledgments

ASSEMBLING a historical and pictorial rendering of a place is a community affair that relies upon the knowledge, advice, and experience of a network of generous, cooperative, and trusting people. We are especially grateful to the owners of ranches, farms, homes, and establishments who provided us with access for taking photographs. As well as to Jesse Kaltenbach, who collaborated on the aerial photographs, and to Suzanne Biaggi, who provided support in so many ways.

The manuscript portion of the book was built upon hundreds of journal entries, manuscripts, government documents, newspapers, books, and other sources buried in libraries, museums, and archives. We are greatly indebted to the archivists whose patience and guidance have been paramount in directing us in our research, specifically Katherine Rinehart and her staff at the Sonoma County Library Annex; Lucy Kortum, John Benanti, John FitzGerald, Solange Russek, and Angela Ryan at the Petaluma Historical Library and Museum; and the librarians at the Petaluma History Room.

We have benefited enormously from the local historians who have provided us with advice and references, shared their personal collections and writings, read early versions of the manuscript, and offered encouragement and stimulating discussion about the Petaluma River Watershed. They include the members of the Volpi's Historian Society—Dan Brown, Lisle Brown, Tom Corbett, John FitzGerald, Will Gorenfeld, Jim Johnson, Chuck Lucas, Terry Park, Don Siemens, Skip Sommer, and Jack Withington—as well as Paula Freund, Chris Samson, Lee Torliatt, Arthur Dawson, Frances Rivetti, Matt Maguire, Fred Codoni, Breck Parkman, Tom Gaffey, and the members of the Petaluma Sages of Yesteryear: Susan Coolidge, Marshall West, Sherri Ortegren, and the late Bill Hammerman. We are also indebted to the work of Ed Mannion and Ed Fratini, two Petaluma historians who left us with a legacy of invaluable historical research and writings.

This book wouldn't have come together without the help and expertise of Susan West, our editor, who thoughtfully edited every page and helped to shape the stories in the book. We are also grateful to Mark Rhynsburger for his proofreading and to Lorna Johnson for her production skills and inspiration.

Finally, we would like to acknowledge our appreciation for the organizations that have sought to preserve and enhance the quality of life in the watershed, including Heritage Homes of Petaluma, the Open Space District, Greenbelt Alliance, Sonoma Land Trust, Marin Agricultural Land Trust, Sonoma County Agricultural Preservation and Open Space District, Friends of the Petaluma River, Petaluma Wetlands Alliance, Petaluma Sunrise Rotary Club, and Rotary Club of Petaluma. Thank you and others for your stewardship.

Scott Hess would like to thank his sons, Evan and Lukas, for anchoring him to Petaluma. John Sheehy would like to thank his wife, Laurie, for helping him find his way back home.

Colophon

On a River Winding Home has been designed by Laurie Szujewska. The typeface is Adobe Caslon, designed by Carol Twombly. All photographs are by Scott Hess, with the exceptions of the photographs of on pages 15, 20, 62-63, 112, 123, and the cover, which are collaborations by Scott Hess and Jesse Kaltenbach of SkylandPhotography.com, and the photograph on page 17 taken by Suzanne Biaggi. Printed in China by Lorna Johnson Print.

Photographs copyright © 2018 Scott Hess
Editorial content copyright © 2018 John Sheehy

All photos by Scott Hess unless so noted.

All rights reserved. No part of this publication may be reproduced or transmitted in any form or by any means, electronic or mechanical, including photocopying, recording, or any information or retrieval system, without permission in writing from Ensatina Press.

Excerpt from *Paddle-Wheel Days in California*, by Jerry MacMullen © 1944 is reprinted by permission of Stanford University Press.

FIRST EDITION

First published in 2018 by Ensatina Press
Designed by Laurie Szujewska
Map created by Arthur Dawson
Photo on page 17 by Suzanne Biaggi
Photos on pages 15, 20, 62-63, 112, 123, and the cover by
Scott Hess in collaboration with Jesse Kaltenbach
Printed and bound in China through
Lorna Johnson Print

Publisher's Cataloging-in-Publication data
Hess, Scott.
On a River Winding Home:
Stories and Visions of the Petaluma River Watershed /
Scott Hess and John Sheehy.
p. cm.
ISBN 978-0-692-13715-4.

1. Petaluma, California—in history.
2. Petaluma, California—in art.
3. Sonoma County, California—in history.
I. Sheehy, John. II. Title.

F868.S7S54 2018
979.418
2018947525

Orders, inquiries & correspondence should be addressed to:

ENSATINA PRESS
P.O. Box 521
Penngrove, CA 94951
www.ensatinapressbooks.com

For ordering photographic prints contact
Scott Hess at Scott@ScottHess.com

OVERLEAF: *Petaluma Turning Basin*